P9-BJR-800

FINDING AND USING EDUCATIONAL VIDEOS

A How-To-Do-It Manual

Barbara Stein
Gary Treadway
Lauralee Ingram

*HOW-TO-DO-IT MANUALS
FOR LIBRARIANS*

NUMBER 84

NEAL-SCHUMAN PUBLISHERS, INC.
New York, London

Published by Neal-Schuman Publishers, Inc.
100 Varick Street
New York, NY 10013

Printed and bound in the United States of America.

Library of Congress Cataloging-in-Publication Data

Stein, Barbara L.
    Finding and using educational videos : a how-to-do-it manual / by
Barbara Stein, Gary Treadway, Lauralee Ingram.
      p. cm. — (How-to-do-it manuals for libraries : # 84)
    Includes bibliographical references and index.
    ISBN 1-55570-278-3
    1. Video tapes in education—Handbooks, manuals, etc.
I. Treadway, Gary. II. Ingram, Lauralee. III. Title. IV. Series:
How-to-do-it manuals for libraries ; no. 84.
LB1044.75.S84   1998
371.33'523—dc21   98-22516
                                     CIP

DEDICATION

Dedicated to:

Barry Stein, for introducing me to media
—Barbara Stein

Colette and Frances
—Gary Treadway

Jim and Beverly Ingram, Glynn D., and Sybil Harrell for my education
—Lauralee Ingram

CONTENTS

PREFACE

Finding and Using Educational Videos: A How-To-Do-It Manual is intended to serve as a "one stop" resource for elementary and middle school educators who want to select and use videos in instruction. Used effectively, video can bring learning alive for students, allowing them to actually see and hear history, science, and story. In the classroom, videos give new meaning to the old adage "a picture is worth a thousand words" because it allows for different learning styles and brings change to the pace of instruction.

Section One, "Using Video in the Classroom," is designed to help educators maximize the instructional value of the videos they select. Lesson-planning strategies, actual lesson plans, teaching techniques, and sources for recording your own educational videos are all included in this "how-to-do-it" section. The National Teacher Training Institute developed by New York's WNET Public Broadcasting Station served as a rich source of ideas for the strategies in this section.

Section Two, the "Annotated List of Recommended Videos Arranged by Title," provides an alphabetical listing of videos covering a generous array of curricular areas. Although the authors could have included literally thousands of videos in this videography, they chose to be very selective. Every video included in Section Two meets the following selection criteria:

1. Its content is relevant to most elementary or middle schools' curriculum.
2. It received a favorable review in a professional journal. Most of the videos were reviewed in one or more of the following sources: *Booklist, The Book Report, Children's Video Review Newsletter, Landers Film Review, School Library Journal,* or *Video Rating Guide for Libraries.*
3. It was produced between 1989 and 1997.
4. The authors consider both the content and the presentation appropriate for instructional use.
5. As a final check, several librarians reviewed and reacted to early drafts of our videography. The authors are most appreciative of their time and input.

Each entry includes the following eleven elements:

1. The video's title
2. Producer
3. Series name (if there is one)
4. Year of production
5. Call number
6. Length
7. List price
8. Sources of reviews
9. Grade levels suggested by the producers
10. Key descriptive words
11. Brief annotation

Section Three, "Recommended Videos Arranged by Subject," provides an in-depth index to the videos selected for inclusion in the videography. Since the topics used correspond to the key descriptive words listed in each entry, you can use the key descriptive words listed to find related videos.

Appendix A contains an alphabetical list of distributors and producers with contact information. Almost all the videos can be ordered directly from their producers, although most librarians find it more convenient to purchase videos from their book distributors. In the event that a video must be ordered from a specific distributor, that name is listed immediately following the producer's name in the entry. Appendix B lists the titles of videos from three popular television series, Reading Rainbow, Wishbone, and GhostWriter, so that educators who want to dovetail lessons with those series have a convenient source of information. Appendix C lists Cable in the Classroom programmers. Appendix D provides a form for evaluating instructional videos.

The authors hope that *Finding and Using Educational Videos: A How-To-Do-It Manual* will be a convenient tool that helps you enhance instruction with high-quality video programs.

SECTION I
USING VIDEO IN THE CLASSROOM

PREPARE STUDENTS FOR A DIFFERENT KIND OF VIEWING

Outside of the classroom, most students and teachers seldom use the television as a tool for learning. At best, newscasts and occasional documentaries share the viewing landscape with sitcoms, soap operas, talk shows, and music videos. Even then, the blurring pace of newscasts and the overwhelming depth of documentaries combined with their lack of contextual background make them a fleeting learning experience. Television is most often viewed as an entertainment medium.

Students need to know, however, that when television is used in the classroom it is intended as an aid in learning the concepts being taught. Though sometimes the programs viewed will be entertaining, entertainment is not the goal, nor does a lack of entertainment value lessen the students' responsibility for the subject matter presented. The message is the focus, not the medium.

Too often teachers are reluctant to use videos that do not match the entertainment value of commercial television. When students are made aware that the goal is learning, not entertainment, they will be less likely to dismiss the content of a program that does not meet the same entertainment value they have come to expect from the commercial television programs they watch at home. For this reason, when television is used in the classroom it is important that the programs are directly tied to the instructional concepts. Using television as a passive entertainment medium in a school setting subverts efforts to transform student attitudes about television as a learning tool. The misuse of the medium can lead to administrative restrictions on any use of television for fear that it is being used as a baby sitter or a time killer rather than as an instructional tool. The first teaching technique, then, is to explore with your students how television used in class is different from television as used at home. Here is an activity to show how this can be done.

First, ask students to:

1. write the name of one of the television programs they watched recently
2. summarize what the program was about
3. list things that they learned from that program. Although students will probably remember the name of the program, most will have difficulty summarizing it and listing anything they learned.

Next, give the students a homework assignment to watch a television program, summarize it, and make a list of anything they learned from the program. Then in class:

- Compare these summaries with the first ones done from memory. Ask students why the summaries they did for homework were more complete and accurate than the ones they did from memory.
- Ask students what they were doing during the homework program (taking notes, listening carefully, etc.) compared to what they usually do while watching television (eating, talking, etc.).
- Discuss the role of purposeful viewing in the comprehension and retention of program content.

Finally, explain to the students the stated purpose or goal for watching television in class:

- Tell them that they will be just as responsible for the information presented in the video programs as they are for their textbook information.
- Describe how television viewing in the classroom will differ from television viewing at home.
- Tell them that the programs will relate directly to the concepts that are currently being studied, that you will cue them for specific points to look for and think about, and that you will frequently stop the program to discuss what has just been viewed and how it relates to the concepts being studied.
- Reinforce that their active participation will be required.
- When viewing the video, leave the lights on. This not only makes it easier for the students to take notes on key concepts but also reinforces their responsibility for information presented and assists in the transition from passive to active viewing.
- End up by discussing the advantages of learning via television.

Covering these ground rules for television viewing in the classroom sets the stage for students to be actively engaged in the learning process. You will save the time and frustration of having students learning the hard way that television viewed at home for entertainment and television viewed at school are two very different activities. While it may seem obvious to teachers that students are responsible for information presented in class, whatever the format, the fact that information was presented via a medium used mainly for entertainment may cause some students to treat it lightly.

Once the students understand how the television viewing they do in class will be different from what they do at home, it is up to the teacher consistently to use the television as a teaching tool. Any use of television not directly associated with the concepts being taught will undermine the significance the students place on television as a medium for learning.

An additional benefit to preparing students for classroom television is that they will be able to communicate the difference to their parents. The importance of educating parents regarding the purposeful nature of television viewing cannot be overemphasized. The medium of television has been targeted as a negative influence on children's learning by the general press. This negative press, whether deserved or not, makes television use in school a controversial topic. Parents need to understand the difference between classroom television viewing and television viewing done at home. Ensuring that their child understands the difference goes a long way to accomplishing this goal.

There are some school administrators as well who are skeptical of television as an instructional tool—especially since television has been misused in many classrooms as entertainment and reward and "something to do" on a rainy Friday. To counteract this, incorporate these techniques:

- Carefully prepare and document the direct curricular correlations of the television programs to the concepts being taught.
- Use active teaching to help convey that you are using television as a teaching technology that can do what no other teaching tool can.
- To alleviate any concerns, invite parents and administrators to observe your class on a day you are using video. They will then see, firsthand, how television viewing can be a positive force for student learning.

Active television viewing habits do not develop automatically. Active viewing requires concentration, anticipation, and critical thinking. The teacher must assist students in their role as viewers by providing a context for applying the content of the video. This context is the concrete learning that must take place in order for the students to be able to learn from the examples, applications, and models presented in the video.

EFFECTIVE LESSON PLANNING

A good lesson plan that clearly defines learning objectives and teaching strategies is just as essential with video as without. Likewise, you should have a thorough knowledge of available teaching resources that enable a teacher to use a variety of teaching strategies to accomplish the stated learning objectives. Just as a teacher must plan how library resources or a textbook will be used to teach a lesson, so too does adding video as a teaching tool require advance planning.

When planning to use video in a lesson, three factors should be considered: (1) What video will be used? (2) When will the video be used? (3) What purpose will the video serve?

The first step is to know what videos are available. Most schools either have their own video library or have video available from some centralized location off-campus. In order to plan effectively, a teacher must research what video is immediately accessible on-campus and what video will take time to order from an off-campus resource.

Teachers who regularly use video as a teaching resource add to the on-campus and off-campus video resources by creating their own video libraries as they come across video programs that cover their specific subject. By keeping abreast of programs being broadcast on public television and cable, teachers can build an extensive video library that is always at their disposal. Within copyright guidelines, teachers have access to a wide range of video programming (see "Fair Use Copyright Guidelines," later in this section).

Being familiar with which video programs have printed support material is also important. Some teachers' guides that accompany video programs provide background material that can be used not only when you are using the video but throughout the lesson. In fact, some support materials are so extensive that they can be used as a primary teaching resource.

PREVIEWING

The next step is to preview the video, which is the most important, and most time-consuming, part of lesson planning.

When previewing, look for a good, short, broad overview of the general topic you are teaching. For example, if you are teaching a unit on Life Cycles, you may find video segments that illustrate the concept of cycles by showing the water cycle, the food chain, and evolution. If you are lucky, these examples and their relationship to the concept of cycles will be explained. If not, you will need to use these visual examples to lead students to an understanding of the broad concept.

You can also use short segments from several different videos to illustrate specific concepts that you are teaching. In the Life Cycles example, you may find one video of a caterpillar becoming a butterfly, another of a tadpole becoming a frog, one of a seed becoming a flower, and one of a baby becoming an adult.

Pausing the video allows you to make the viewing interactive and enables students to get the most benefit from the video content. When looking for where to pause in the video, note the location of the segments on the video either by the approximate time they appear (e.g., five minutes into the program) or another visual marker (e.g., after the host introduces the second segment). Since tape counters are not standard on all VCRs, noting the counter numbers at the pause points will only be effective if you use the same VCR in your classroom. Noting visual and/or verbal cues that indicate pause points eliminates this problem.

You may need to troubleshoot points of confusion. When you preview, locate possible concerns, such as the narrative on the video using different terminology from what you use in class, or the video's diagrams and graphics being different from those in a textbook. Noting these possible confusion points and planning for their remedy puts you in a position to proactively avoid such problems by either clarifying the differences in advance or pausing the video to have students provide the clarification.

Give priority to videos that have a multicultural cast. We live in a multicultural society and it is important that the video we use in the classroom reflect this diversity. Students from every ethnicity should be able to see representatives from their cultures in all teaching materials, including video. The same consideration needs to be given to adequacy of representation of males and females and people who are physically challenged.

When will the video be used? Placement of video in the teaching sequence will largely be determined by the video's content.

- Video segments giving an overview of concepts to be covered in a unit are best suited for use at the beginning of a unit as an introduction or at the end as a review.
- Video segments showing specific examples should be used to illustrate those distinct points.
- Careful selection and strategic placement of short video segments will enhance the effectiveness of your lesson by heightening students' attention, providing visual examples, and acting as a springboard to discussion.

What purpose will the video serve? The key to effective use of video as a teaching tool lies in your ability to use it selectively and purposefully. A video can be effective if it:

- brings resource people into the classroom to show how concepts being learned are applied in real-life situations
- uses close-ups, time-lapse photography, and computer-generated graphics to offer concrete visual examples that illustrate abstract concepts
- uses documentary footage to present a historical perspective on concepts being taught
- takes a different approach than that used in other instructional activities to teaching a concept.

Lesson planning that integrates video requires the same skills as for all lesson planning: determining specific learning objectives, setting up the sequence of instruction, locating teaching resources, and developing teaching activities. Taking the time to preview, select segments, and plan for their placement in the teaching sequence beforehand will add to the students' learning experience and increase the effectiveness of the lesson.

PRIOR TO VIEWING THE VIDEO

One way to ensure that optimum learning takes place is to do an introductory activity that creates an anticipatory learning set for students that is directly tied to the video content. For example, if students are studying metamorphosis and the video uses time-lapse photography to show a tadpole becoming a frog, an introductory activity might be showing pictures of various baby animals and adult animal pairs and discussing their similarity. The teacher could then show students a caterpillar and ask what they think the adult caterpillar would look like. After discussing how some animals change appearance or metamorphose as they age, the teacher would then tell the class that they are about to watch a video that shows another example of metamorphosis. This activity and clue about the content of the video heightens student interest in what is going to happen next.

A FOCUS FOR VIEWING

The teacher then tells the students what to look for as they watch the video. "Watch for the stages this animal experiences as it goes through metamorphosis. You will be drawing the animal at different stages, so pay close attention to what it looks like at each one." Students then know what to look for, what they will be held accountable for, and what they will be doing when the video ends.

INTERACTIVE VIEWING

The power of video technology in the classroom lies in your ability to control the images on the screen. Using the pause button either on the VCR or the remote control:

- allows the teacher to stop the tape to spotlight important points and expand on them
- ensures that students are actively engaged in the content being presented in the video
- allows the teacher to ask students questions that will allow them to apply and synthesize the concepts being studied.

In the lesson on metamorphosis, the teacher could pause the video at the point that the tadpole grows hind legs and then ask the students what change had taken place. This type of question checks for comprehension. The teacher could also ask the students what they think the next change will be. Predicting what will happen next is a higher-level thinking skill than mere comprehension and one that is particularly well suited to interactive viewing. Vocabulary development can also be supplemented by using the pause technique. If the video talks about adaptation, for example, the teacher can pause the tape to discuss what adaptation means and how it applies to metamorphosis.

REWIND AND REVIEW

Another technique that takes advantage of video technology is the use of the rewind or review function. After pausing the tape and asking comprehension questions, if it is discovered that there is uncertainty over what the video has just covered, the teacher can rewind the tape and play it back. This technique is the same one we use when we reread a passage in a difficult book to get a clearer understanding of what the author said. After students become familiar with the interactive use of video, they will begin asking the teacher to rewind the tape to review parts they do not understand or to confirm that their understanding is correct.

FAST FORWARD

Fast forwarding to skip extraneous material is an essential active-viewing technique. There are two factors that make fast forwarding necessary: copyright law, and the lack of editing equipment. Copyright law prohibits teachers from creating video anthologies or "clip tapes" without the permission of the copyright holder. In any event, most teachers do not have access to the editing equipment necessary to make such anthologies. Therefore, fast forward to get from one segment of a video to another segment on the same tape.

OTHER VCR FEATURES

Depending on the sophistication of the VCR, there may be other interactive techniques that can be used. One convenient feature is the use of a "real time" counter, that is, the counter that measures the videotape in minutes and seconds. This feature provides a measure of tape counter standardization from one VCR to another. Some VCRs also have slow-motion capabilities that allow the teacher to show students, frame by frame, a tadpole growing hind legs or losing its tail. Others allow indexed searches, wherein the teacher marks the videotape at certain points to which the tape will later automatically stop when fast forwarded. As VCRs continue to improve, there may be more features added to make interactive viewing easier and more convenient. But even the most rudimentary VCR can be a powerful tool in the hands of a skilled educator.

AFTER VIEWING THE VIDEO

An anticipatory learning set was created with the introductory activity, and a focus for viewing provided an interactive, purposeful viewing of the video to increase students' comprehension of key concepts. After viewing the video, engaging in another activity allows students to apply what they have learned in a meaningful way. It is this application of knowledge that enables students to make the learning their own. This concluding activity reinforces the video, which in itself is a reinforcement of the overall lesson.

Successful concluding activities are interactive and experiential. One way to facilitate interactivity is to have students form cooperative learning groups to engage in activities that apply the concepts being studied. An advantage of such grouping is that students with different levels of understanding can be put in the same group to learn from each other. It is important, however, that each student in a cooperative group have specific responsibilities and be held accountable both for participating in group activities and learning concepts discovered in the concluding activities.

A wide variety of experiential activities is possible. Science, for example, lends itself particularly well to this type of hands-on activity. Science teachers have traditionally used labs as a teaching method to allow students to apply scientific concepts being studied. Interactive viewing of a video is simply an extension of this experience and can be reinforced with further lab work. Social studies and language arts teachers may choose to follow up on a historical documentary with classroom projects such as mock reporting of news events, trials, or other experiences.

Fine arts teachers are an excellent example of using experiential learning as part of the learning process since the best way to learn art, music, and dance is by practicing it. Video provides an extension to these experiences as well. An art teacher, for example, can use video to provide rich visual images that can be the inspiration to students who could not experience those images any other way. Students miles from the ocean can be shown video of waves breaking on a coastline to provide a visualization for a painting that enforces the lesson. Dance teachers can follow videos of world famous dance troupes with further practice. More important, teachers who do not have fine arts backgrounds can use video to provide students with experiences that would otherwise be unavailable to them and follow up with the experiences already planned.

EXTENDING THE LESSON

To synthesize their learning, students must do something with the knowledge they have obtained. It does require some creativity on your part to find ways to extend the lesson to provide students opportunities to follow through on what they have learned and experienced. But taking the time to develop projects that allow students to apply the concepts they have learned to real-life pays off by showing students the relevance of what they are learning to their lives. Extension activities answer the age-old student question, "Why are we learning this?"

INTERDISCIPLINARY CORRELATIONS

Connecting concepts taught in one discipline to applications in other disciplines helps students synthesize learning and apply higher-level thinking skills. These interdisciplinary correlations can be made clear by using video and activities that help students make this leap. Too often, particularly at the upper-grade levels, students go from one subject to the next and never see any connections in what they are learning. This is less true at the primary level, where the teaching of thematic units is more prevalent. Since video exists on so many topics and concepts, it is a readily available source of examples of application of concepts in many subjects.

A single video can be used in several subjects. Historical documentaries and newsreels can depict the events that were concurrent with the writing of a literary work. These same videos can be used by fine arts teachers to give students a historical perspective to use as a backdrop when studying art or music history. With video, students achieve a new depth of understanding in an enriched context to apply to their current learning.

No matter the discipline, teaching techniques that enhance student learning need to be applied consistently. Segmenting the video; providing a focus for viewing and introductory activities; making the viewing interactive by using the pause, rewind, and fast forward techniques; and providing experiential-learning concluding activities are all part of effective use of video.

SAMPLE LESSON PLAN

GOALS/OBJECTIVES

At the end of this lesson, students will understand the concept of electrical circuits. They will apply this understanding by building a model of the electrical circuit that starts at the electrical power plant and ends at their homes.

VIDEO

Electricity and Electrical Safety

MATERIALS

Introductory Activity (per small group)

Flashlight bulb
Two size D batteries
Two 3" Pieces of wire

Concluding Activity (per small group)

One 12" x 12" piece of cardboard
Glue
Objects to represent the following:
     —power plant (e.g., picture of a battery)
     —step-up transformer (e.g., a cut-out of a "plus" sign)
     —transmission lines (e.g., straightened paper clips)
     —insulators (e.g., rubber erasers)
     —substation (e.g., a cut-out of a "minus" sign)
     —pole step-down transformer (e.g., a toothpick)
     —home (e.g., a cut-out of a house)

VOCABULARY

power lines
return wires
circuit
power plant
step-up and step-down transformers
voltage
insulators (glass, rubber, plastic, paper)
substation
pole transformers
fuse
circuit breaker

INTRODUCTORY ACTIVITY

Divide students into small cooperative groups. Tell the students that you are going to give them a flashlight bulb, two size D batteries, and two pieces of wire. Their goal is to experiment with these materials until they can make the flashlight bulb light. Then they are to come up with an explanation of how this works.

When groups have successfully completed the experiment, have them give their explanation of how the electrical circuit they built works. Using the materials in the experiment, explain the concept of an electrical circuit.

Tell the students they are going to watch a video that shows how this simple concept of an electrical circuit is used in getting electricity from the power plant to their homes. Tell them to raise their hand whenever they hear one of the vocabulary words listed on the board or handout.

INTERACTIVE VIEWING

- Start the videotape where the narrator says, "When the electric current leaves the power plant . . . " (approximately 0:3:30 into tape).
- Pause the video when the narrator refers to the power plant (students should have raised their hands at this point). Ask the students what is the same as the power plant in the circuit they built (answer: batteries).
- Pause when the narrator mentions power lines. Ask the students what is the same as power lines in their circuits (answer: wire).
- Continue to pause when the narrator mentions a vocabulary word. Have students explain the function of each of the items in the vocabulary list. At points where students show confusion or are unable to explain the function of a particular item, rewind the tape and let them view the explanation again.
- Stop the videotape when the narrator says, "The voltage must be lowered so that the electricity can be safely used in your home" (approximately 0:5:45 into tape). Ask the students what is the same as the home in the circuit they built (answer: the flashlight bulb).

CONCLUDING ACTIVITY

Tell the students that they are going to build a model of the electrical circuit that they just saw. Hand out the materials to each group. Circulate among the groups to be sure that the students understand the concept of electrical circuits and the function of each of the items on the vocabulary list. When the groups have completed their models, choose one spokesperson per group to show the group's model to the class and explain how the circuit works and the name and functions of each of the items represented on the model.

EXTENSIONS

View the same segment of the tape again to look for other information. Pause the tape when the narrator says, "The pressure of the electric current leaving the transformer may be as high as 765,000 volts." Have them write this number down. Stop the tape when the narrator says, "They reduce the voltage to either 120 or 240 volts." Have students calculate the number of times greater the voltage is leaving the step-up transformer than the voltage that comes into their homes (765,000 volts = 6,375 times 120 volts; 765,000 volts = 3,187.5 times 240 volts).

Tell the students that their homework tonight is to write down examples of household appliances that require 120 volts and appliances that require 240 volts to operate.

INTERDISCIPLINARY CORRELATIONS

Have students research Thomas Edison and compare his laboratory experiments with electricity to the simple circuit that they built and to the complex circuit that brings electrical power to their homes.

EVALUATION

What concepts and vocabulary did the students find easiest to understand? What concepts and vocabulary were the most difficult? How else could these concepts be explained and/or demonstrated? What other experiments would help teach this concept? What other videos or teaching resources are available to help teach this concept?

ADAPTING VIDEOS TO THE STUDENT

Videos, like textbooks, are intended by their creators to be used by students at specific grade levels. However, there are ways to adapt videos that make it possible to use successfully a video intended for one level on a completely different level of student. Teachers need not eliminate a high quality video simply because it was not produced specifically for the level of students they teach.

Often a video intended for an upper-level audience has much more depth and background information than is suitable for primary students. To adapt an upper-level video to primary students:

- Use only selected segments of a video to tailor the amount of content.
- Focus student viewing on the broad concepts that you are teaching so that students can filter out extraneous information that is beyond their comprehension.

Since the learning is primarily visual and aural, students are not impeded by a lack of reading skill. The vocabulary they are exposed to is accompanied by visuals that provide context clues to help unlock meaning. Teachers can adapt a video to a wider audience range by:

- selecting only certain segments for viewing
- making the viewing interactive by pausing at key points in the video to highlight key concepts
- probing for student understanding
- rewinding to review, reinforce, and clarify any points of confusion.

USE OF SOUND

A good way to adapt video to various instructional levels is to turn the sound off and supply your own narration. In this way the teacher can use the visual images on the screen to focus student attention by highlighting relevant images. Using this technique allows the teacher to control both the amount of content delivered and the vocabulary used to deliver it. For example, primary teachers using segments of a video that would otherwise be too sophisticated for students at that level can customize the video to fit the students. Similarly, an upper-level science teacher could use a segment of a program from the *Reading Rainbow* series that goes on location to an active volcano in Hawaii. The visual images are stunning, and when the teacher uses just that segment along with vocabulary suitable to an older audience, student learning is enhanced and the intended audience level of the video is no longer an issue.

Conversely, teachers can also use just the audio portion of a video. Eliminating the video images by covering the screen or turning down the brightness adjustment on the television set allows students to develop their listening skills and to use their imaginations. Students can be asked to draw or describe what they think the images were in a segment that they just heard. They must be able to justify what they think with specific quotes from the video. The video can then be replayed with the picture on to confirm the students' predictions.

USING CLOSED-CAPTIONED VIDEO

Closed-captioned video provides a means to use television to increase student reading skills. Although primarily used by hearing-impaired audiences, closed-captioned television has also proven effective with remedial readers, limited English proficient students, adult basic literacy students, and students in the regular classroom. And since July 1, 1993, all television sets manufactured that are 13 inches or larger must be able to display closed captioning. No longer are expensive decoding devices needed to take advantage of this capability, and closed-captioned videos, often denoted by the CC label, are widely available.

In using closed-captioned video, be sure that the content is appropriate for classroom use. Combining content-rich video with the closed-captioned capability enhances student reading skills while teaching key concepts in several disciplines.

Closed-captioned video also allows the medium of television to be analyzed from a writer's perspective. In language arts instruction, captions can be used to teach parts of speech, similes and metaphors, and different styles of writing. Students can observe how to write dialogue in drama and examples of persuasive writing in captions from documentaries. Instructional videos also provide excellent examples of expository writing.

In reading instruction, closed-captioned video can be used to teach vocabulary, comprehension, and oral reading fluency. Leaving the sound on while captions appear on the screen lets students combine the audio and visual context to discover word meaning. To increase oral reading fluency, watch the video with the sound on once, then replay the segment without sound and have the students read orally. Hearing the segment, reading the words, and seeing the video build student confidence and improve oral reading fluency.

The drama and visualization in closed-captioned video allows students to read captions above their reading level. Captions are presented at a rate of 100–120 words per minute. Most captions are verbatim (word-for-word), although some real-time broadcasts, such as news programs, paraphrase captions because the rate of speech is too rapid for verbatim captioning.

There are some additional considerations when using closed-captioned video:

- Due to the size of the captions, closed captioning needs to be used with small groups (six to eight students).
- A semicircular seating arrangement allows all students to see the captions without obstruction.

- If the captions are illegible, the "tracking" control on the VCR probably needs to be adjusted.

The primary advantage of using closed-captioned video is that it increases student motivation. The desire to understand what is happening on the screen increases the desire to focus on the printed word. This is an important advantage when teaching students who dislike reading. Television has been accused of decreasing students' reading abilities and motivation; using closed-captioned video allows television to do the exact opposite.

RECORDING VIDEO PROGRAMS

Another way to build your video library is to record programs from broadcast or cable television. The main advantage to this type of video programming is that it is economical. The disadvantages are that you have to locate the programming you want from an assortment of guides, then record and label the programs yourself. Where purchasing specific titles from video distributors is like ordering fish at a restaurant, recording your own programming is like buying your own tackle, researching where the fish are biting, then catching and cleaning the fish before you can enjoy your meal. You are limited to the fish biting at the time, but those fish may not be on the restaurant menu at all!

Programs recorded from broadcast or cable television are also frequently time sensitive due to copyright restrictions. Some programs created for classroom use carry liberal copyright clearance, the most liberal of which is the right to use the program "in perpetuity." Other programs might have copyright clearance for "life of tape," meaning until the tape the program is recorded on breaks or can no longer be used. *Reading Rainbow* programs broadcast on public television have a three-year copyright clearance. Most education-oriented programs on PBS have copyright clearance for one year from the original broadcast. Some have copyright clearance for a year from each broadcast, so if a program is repeated six months after its original broadcast, the copyright clearance is also extended by six months.

As you can see, programs recorded from broadcast or cable television have a variety of copyright restrictions. If you are unsure of the copyright clearance, you can assume that you have only "fair use" rights for the program.

FAIR USE COPYRIGHT GUIDELINES

1. These guidelines were developed to apply only to recordings made by nonprofit educational institutions.
2. A program may be recorded and retained by a nonprofit educational institution for a period not to exceed forty-five calendar days after the date of the recording. Upon conclusion of such retention period, all recordings must be erased or destroyed.
3. Recordings may be used once by individual teachers in the course of relevant teaching activities, and repeated once only when instructional reinforcement is necessary, in classrooms and in similar places devoted to instruction within a single building. The program must be used during the first ten consecutive school days in the forty-five-calendar-day retention period. "School days" are school session days and do not include weekends, vacations, or holidays.
4. Recordings may be made only at the request of and used by individual teachers, and may not be regularly recorded in anticipation of a request.
5. A limited number of copies may be reproduced from the recording to meet the legitimate needs of teachers under these guidelines. Each additional copy is subject to all provisions covering the original recording.
6. After the first ten consecutive school days, recordings may be used up to the end of the forty-five-calendar-day retention period only for teacher-evaluation purposes.
7. Recordings need not be used in their entirety, but may not be altered from their original content or combined into compilations or anthologies.
8. All copies of programs must include the copyright notice on the program as recorded.
9. Educational institutions are expected to establish appropriate control procedures to maintain the integrity of these guidelines.

The bottom line is that you are responsible for keeping track of when the programs were recorded, what the copyright restrictions are, and when, if ever, the programs must be erased.

With that caveat, let's look at several different sources of video programming.

BROADCAST TELEVISION

Public Broadcasting Service

One source of educational programming that is available through open broadcast to virtually everyone in the United States is the Public Broadcasting Service (PBS). PBS broadcasts many programs that, although educational, are produced for a general audience. Often the programs are part of a larger series such as *Eyes on the Prize*, *The Civil War*, and *Baseball* and must be segmented to be used effectively in the classroom. Other series such as *Bill Nye the Science Guy*, *GhostWriter*, and *Reading Rainbow* offer half-hour-length programs that are suitable for classroom use as well as home viewing.

Using PBS Prime-Time "Edutainment" Programming

Most PBS documentaries are suitable, when segmented, to secondary school students. Often series—such as *Nova*, *National Geographic*, and *Scientific American Frontiers*—have guides that assist teachers in integrating the programs into the curriculum by giving background information and suggestions for discussion. PBS series that are more appropriate for elementary level classrooms such as *Reading Rainbow*, *Bill Nye the Science Guy*, *GhostWriter*, and *Where in the World Is Carmen Sandiego?* also have teachers' guides available.

Most, but not all, programs broadcast on PBS that are suitable for classroom use have copyright clearances that permit teachers to use the program for one year from its original broadcast. Many programs are also available for purchase from PBS Video or other producers and distributors (see Appendix A.)

Each public television station is independently operated, which means that, the times and dates programs are broadcast may vary from location to location. Independent operation and scheduling is why you see the phrase "Check local listings" on national promotions of PBS programming. In addition to listing program schedules in newspapers and TV guides, most PBS stations send members a local programming guide—a valuable commodity that lists the monthly schedule of upcoming programming as well as program descriptions.

Instructional Television (ITV)

Some public television stations also offer an instructional television service in addition to their general audience programming. Instructional television (ITV) programming is curriculum based and is designed to be used in the classroom to augment the instruction being delivered by teachers in the academic disciplines.

ITV programs are often shorter in length (fifteen to twenty minutes) than most traditional television programming and can be used during a single class period. Often ITV programs are designed as a series of programs that cover specific content in a given subject—such as *Many Voices*, a series of fifteen-minute programs dealing with sensitivity to multicultural diversity.

Most ITV programs have a teacher's guide that details objectives for each program and gives activities to do with students to introduce the programs and to extend the concepts covered. These series guides are essentially lesson plans for the teacher. Teacher's guides for elementary-level programs often have reproducible activity sheets to reinforce program content, and upper-level teacher's guides may have historical background information and sources for further reading on a given topic.

Public television stations offering an instructional television service purchase copyright privileges from program producers and distributors on an annual basis. The stations then pass on these rights to schools in their viewing area. The fees stations pay for copyrights are either paid for by the state educational authority or by the individual school systems. In either case, the savings realized by purchasing copyright privileges to a number of ITV series enables schools to have access to a library of video programs that would otherwise be unaffordable.

Commercial Network Television

Commercial networks such as ABC, NBC, and CBS are also sources of educational video. News-magazine-format programs such as *60 Minutes* can be excellent tools for bringing current events into the classroom. The main drawback to using programming recorded from commercial network television is that there are rarely copyright privileges available beyond "fair use."

CABLE TELEVISION

Cable television is not as generally accessible as open broadcast because it requires special wiring and a connection to a local cable television provider. An increasing number of schools are being provided such connections, however, through Cable in the Classroom—a partnership of local cable television service providers and national cable program producers that gives schools free basic cable service and hundreds of hours of commercial-free programs.

One of the greatest assets of the Cable in the Classroom project is *Cable in the Classroom Magazine*. This monthly publication breaks programs down by discipline and level, gives program descriptions and schedules, and lists copyright clearances for each program. Feature articles highlighting successful utilization strategies, contest announcements, and information about how to obtain printed resource materials are also provided. Some cable companies provide *Cable in the Classroom Magazine* free to local schools, other schools pay for it.

Not all cable television services carry all Cable in the Classroom programmers. Here is a list and description of some of the most popular programmers:

- Arts & Entertainment Network. Under the banner "A&E Classroom," this cable programmer airs commercial-free programming suitable for classroom use. Specific days of the week are devoted to a particular academic discipline (e.g., Mondays, history). Twice a year, teacher materials are distributed with five months advance scheduling information and program descriptions. A&E Classroom programs can be used for one year after their air date.

- C-SPAN (Cable-Satellite Public Affairs Network) The C-SPAN in the Classroom educational service makes available teachers' guides and lesson plans for its commercial-free coverage of congressional floor activity and press conferences. C-SPAN programs can be used in the classroom in perpetuity.

- Cable News Network. CNN Newsroom is a special, commercial-free, fifteen-minute news program designed for classroom use. Teachers' guides are available daily on-line and can be downloaded and printed. CNN Newsroom programs can be used in the classroom in perpetuity.

- The Discovery Channel. "Assignment Discovery" is an hour-long block of two curriculum-oriented documentaries geared for classroom use. Like A&E Classroom, Assignment Discovery devotes particular days during the week to specific curriculum areas (e.g., Monday, science and technology). A *Discovery Network's Educator Guide* is free to teachers and includes schedules and program descriptions. Assignment Discovery programs can be used for one year from their broadcast date.

- The History Channel. The History Channel is a programming service of the Arts & Entertainment Network and features commercial-free, historical documentaries, movies, and miniseries. Support materials such as study guides and program calendars are available.

- The Learning Channel. Both "TLC Elementary School" and "Teacher TV" are part of the Cable in the Classroom project. TLC Elementary School is an hour-long block of several short, commercial-free programs that are curriculum based and geared for the K–6 classroom. Teacher TV, coproduced by the National

Education Association, highlights educators involved in innovative projects throughout the nation. Learning Channel programs can be retained for two years from their broadcast date.

- Nickelodeon. Aimed at children aged five to fifteen, *Nick News* and *Launch Box* are half-hour programs suitable for use in the classroom. The current-events program *Nick News* airs Monday through Thursday, and *Launch Box* airs on Fridays and has a six-minute video teacher's guide in each program. These two programs can be used for six months from their air dates.
- The Weather Channel. *The Weather Classroom* is a ten-minute program that airs weekdays and covers a specific weather-related topic each day. A student workbook accompanying *The Weather Classroom* is also available. This ten-minute program can be used in perpetuity.

SECTION II:

ANNOTATED LIST OF RECOMMENDED VIDEOS ARRANGED BY TITLE

This section lists the videos we recommend. It is arranged alphabetically by title. Each entry includes keywords. You can use these keywords to locate videos on closely related topics when you use Part III, Recommended Videos Arranged by Subject.

Use the margins in this section to record such handy information as: local call number, names of libraries in your district or area that own the video, or classes or dates when you used the video (as well as your own—or students' or other teachers'—reactions to it).

Title: *Abuelita's Paradise*
Producer: Reading Adventures
Series: Friends and Neighbors Multicultural Story Videos
Year Released: 1993
Call Number: Easy Fiction
Length: 9 minutes
Price: $45.00
Reviewed in: *Video Rating Guide for Libraries*
Grade Level: K–4
Keywords: Literature; Multicultural; Puerto Ricans

Book by Carmen Nodar, illustrated by Diane Paterson. Marita sits in Abuelita's rocking chair, holding the blanket with the faded letters that spell PARAISO and remembers the wonderful stories her Abuelita—her grandmother—told her about her Puerto Rican childhood.

Title: *Aesop's Fables*
Producer: Churchill Media
Series: Not Applicable
Year Released: 1991
Call Number: 398.2
Length: 15 minutes
Price: $60.00
Reviewed in: *School Library Journal, Video Rating Guide for Libraries*
Grade Level: K–6
Keywords: Fables; Literature

Five traditional Aesop's fables are presented with drawings and songs. Stories included are: "The Grasshopper and the Ant," "The Sun and the Wind," "The Fox and the Grapes," "The Animals and the Children," and "Donkey Trip." Includes teacher's guide.

Title: *AIDS: A Different Kind of Germ*
Producer: Dary Mitchell Film Company/Coronet/MTI Film & Video
Series: Not Applicable
Year Released: 1990
Call Number: 616.97
Length: 16 minutes
Price: $295.00
Reviewed in: *Video Rating Guide for Libraries*

Grade Level: K–3
Keywords: AIDS; Health

With the help of a young girl named Tracy, and her cartoon friend Microscopic Mike, youngsters learn why HIV, the virus that causes AIDS, is different from other kinds of infections, and how adults and children are most commonly exposed. The program also reassures children by emphasizing that the virus is difficult to catch, outlining precautions to follow, and explaining that it cannot be spread through crying, spitting, sneezing, or kissing. Includes teacher's guide.

Title: *Alexander and the Terrible, Horrible, No Good, Very Bad Day*
Producer: AIMS Media
Series: Not Applicable
Year Released: 1989
Call Number: Easy Fiction
Length: 14 minutes
Price: $70.00
Reviewed in: *Video Rating Guide for Libraries*
Grade Level: K–6
Keywords: Humor; Literature

An adaptation of Judith Viorst's book. Alexander knew the minute he woke up with gum in his hair that it was going to be a very bad day, and it was. A series of mishaps befall poor Alexander on a day that just happens to go not quite as planned.

Title: *Alexander, Who Used to Be Rich Last Sunday*
Producer: Bernard Wilets Productions/AIMS Media
Series: Not Applicable
Year Released: 1989
Call Number: Easy Fiction
Length: 14 minutes
Price: $70.00
Reviewed in: *Video Rating Guide for Libraries*
Grade Level: K–6
Keywords: Literature; Money

Based on the book by Judith Viorst. When Alexander's grandparents give him five dollars, he is rich! With his new fortune, Alexander embarks on a whimsical spending spree that ultimately teaches the value of saving and spending money carefully.

Title: *Alice Walker*
Producer: Schlessinger Video Productions
Series: Black Americans of Achievement Video Series 2
Year Released: 1994
Call Number: Biography
Length: 30 minutes
Price: $40.00
Reviewed in: *School Librarian Journal*, *Video Librarian*, *Video Rating Guide for Libraries*
Grade Level: 4–6
Keywords: African Americans; Biographies; Walker, Alice

This video biography contains interviews with authorities on the subject's life accompanied by archival footage, photographs, and period music. Topics include basic biographical information, the inspirational and motivational factors in her life, her message, and the significance of Alice Walker in society today.

Title: *All about Angles*
Producer: Allied Video
Series: Assistant Professor
Year Released: 1992
Call Number: 516
Length: 20 minutes
Price: $30.00
Reviewed in: *Video Rating Guide for Libraries*
Grade Level: 4–6
Keywords: Geometry; Mathematics

Explains what angles are, how angles are measured, and why angles are useful and important in our daily lives.

Title: *All about Boats*
Producer: Pint Size Productions
Series: Not Applicable
Year Released: 1994
Call Number: 623.82
Length: 30 minutes

Price: $20.00
Reviewed in: *Booklist, Video Librarian*
Grade Level: K–3
Keywords: Boats; Transportation

Each boat in this live-action program uses its own personality and musical style to teach about the function of boats, boating safety, and nautical lore. Captain Buck tours harbors from coast to coast, exploring ships and boats alike while meeting friends and singing along with on-screen lyrics.

Title: *All about Neighborhoods*
Producer: Colman Communications/United Learning
Series: Not Applicable
Year Released: 1997
Call Number: 307
Length: 12 minutes
Price: $79.95
Reviewed in: *School Library Journal*
Grade Level: K–3
Keywords: Community; Social Studies; Stereotypes

This program defines neighborhoods, shows that neighborhoods may look different depending on geographic factors or the country where they are located, and explains that neighborhoods may be made up of people with similar or different backgrounds. Includes teacher's guide.

Title: *All about Shapes*
Producer: Crystalroe Productions/DK Publishing
Series: Hullaballoo
Year Released: 1995
Call Number: 516
Length: 30 minutes
Price: $10.00
Reviewed in: *Booklist, School Library Journal*
Grade Level: PreK–1
Keywords: Early Childhood; Shapes

This program combines animation, puppetry, games, and songs to teach children about shapes.

Title: *All the Colors of the Earth*
Producer: Weston Woods
Series: Not Applicable
Year Released: 1997
Call Number: Easy Fiction
Length: 8 minutes
Price: $60.00
Reviewed in: *Booklist*
Grade Level: PreK–3
Keywords: Literature; Prejudice; Stories in Rhyme

Based on the book. Celebrates the diversity of children everywhere. Through the use of images of children and families and simple text, the story helps children discover cultural diversity.

Title: *Amazing Grace*
Producer: Paul R. Gagne/Weston Woods Studios
Series: Not Applicable
Year Released: 1994
Call Number: Easy Fiction
Length: 10 minutes
Price: $90.00
Reviewed in: *Booklist, School Library Journal*
Grade Level: K–3
Keywords: Literature; Self-esteem; Theater

Even though her classmates discourage Grace from trying out for Peter Pan in the school play because she is black and a girl, Grace wins the part and proves that she can be anything she wants to be. Narrated by Alfre Woodard. Based on the book by Mary Hoffman.

Title: *Amazing North America*
Producer: National Geographic Society Educational Services
Series: Really Wild Animals
Year Released: 1994
Call Number: 591.93
Length: 45 minutes
Price: $24.20
Reviewed in: *Booklist*

Grade Level: K–4
Keywords: Animals; Zoos

Narrated by Dudley Moore. Meet a variety of animals such as polar bears, snakes, and alligators as you zip around with Spin, an animated globe. Includes teacher's guide.

Title: *America's State Capitals*, Vols. 1–4
Producer: City Productions, Inc.
Series: America's State Capitals
Year Released: 1994
Call Number: 973
Length: 60 minutes
Price: $119.80
Reviewed in: *Booklist*
Grade Level: K–6
Keywords: Social Studies; State Capitals

This four-video set takes a tour of each state capital as it entered the Union. The video takes viewers through the times and events that shaped the states. Students discover state flags, mottoes, nicknames, flowers, and much more.

Title: *American Independence*
Producer: Schlessinger Video Productions/Library Video Company
Series: American History for Children
Year Released: 1996
Call Number: 973
Length: 25 minutes
Price: $30.00
Reviewed in: *Booklist*
Grade Level: 1–5
Keywords: American History; Social Studies

Covers the story of the Declaration of Independence, Thomas Jefferson, the Liberty Bell and Independence Hall, and life for a child under British rule.

Title: *Amistad Revolt, The: All We Want Is Make Us Free*
Producer: Amistad Committee/Shoe String Press
Series: Not Applicable
Year Released: 1996
Call Number: 306.3
Length: 33 minutes
Price: $39.95
Reviewed in: *School Library Journal*
Grade Level: 6 and up
Keywords: African Americans, Social Studies.

Recounts the causes, events, and aftermath of the mutiny of African slaves aboard the schooner *Amistad* en route to the Americas in 1839.

Title: *Amphibian*
Producer: BBC Wildvision, BBC Lionheart TV, Dorling Kindersley Vision in association with Oregon Public Broadcasting/Dorling Kindersley/Houghton Mifflin
Series: Eyewitness Video
Year Released: 1995
Call Number: 597.6
Length: 35 minutes
Price: $13.00
Reviewed in: *Booklist, School Library Journal*
Grade Level: PreK–6
Keywords: Amphibians; Animals

Viewers will journey into a three-dimensional "virtual museum" where live-action wildlife photography creates the sensation of being there. This program presents a completely different view of the marvels and mysteries of the natural world as they have never been seen before. Also included is behind-the-scenes, "making of the series" footage. Narrated by Martin Sheen.

Title: *Anansi and the Moss-Covered Rock*
Producer: Live Oak Media
Series: Not Applicable
Year Released: 1990
Call Number: 398.2
Length: 11 minutes
Price: $38.00

Reviewed in: *Booklist, School Library Journal, Video Rating Guide for Libraries*
Grade Level: K–3
Keywords: African Folklore; Folk Tales; Literature; Spiders

This video is based on the book by Eric A. Kimmel, with illustrations by Janet Stevens. Anansi the spider, the master trickster of them all, uses the powers of a magical rock to dupe his neighbors out of their food hoards until Little Bush Deer beats him at his own game and sets things right. Includes teacher's guide.

Title: *Anatole*
Producer: Rembrandt Films/Churchill Media
Series: Not Applicable
Year Released: 1995
Call Number: Easy Fiction
Length: 9 minutes
Price: $60.00
Reviewed in: *School Library Journal*
Grade Level: K–6
Keywords: Literature; Mice

Based on the Caldecott Honor book by Eve Titus, this is the classic story of a mouse who spends his evenings at the Duval Cheese Factory. The owner is at first appalled that a mouse has been running through his factory, but he soon begins to appreciate Anatole's remarkable cheese-tasting ability. In the end, Anatole is given a permanent job tasting cheese. All voices by Carl Reiner. Includes guide.

Title: *Angry John*
Producer: Pyramid Film and Video-Education Division
Series: Not Applicable
Year Released: 1993
Call Number: 152.47
Length: 23 minutes
Price: $295.00
Reviewed in: *School Library Journal, Video Rating Guide for Libraries*
Grade Level: 1–6
Keywords: Anger; Behavior

In this film on anger management, an eleven-year-old boy named Cliff becomes caught up in fighting and petty vandalism at the urging of an animated television bully named Angry John and soon finds himself in a lot of trouble. Cliff's anger and behavior seem out of control until a school counselor helps him learn how to manage his anger.

Title: *Animal Life in a Tidepool*
Producer: AIMS Media
Series: Not Applicable
Year Released: 1992
Call Number: 574.9
Length: 12 minutes
Price: $100.00
Reviewed in: *Video Rating Guide for Libraries*
Grade Level: 4–6
Keywords: Oceans; Science—Life; Tidepools

The wonder of life in a tidepool is vividly depicted in this nature program, which features exceptional underwater photography. A segment on ocean tides and tidepool formation is also introduced. Includes teacher's guide.

Title: *Animals of the Amazon River Basin*
Producer: ABC/Kane Productions/AIMS Media
Series: World of Discovery
Year Released: 1994
Call Number: 574.5
Length: 25 minutes
Price: $100.00
Reviewed in: *Booklist, School Library Journal*
Grade Level: 4–6
Keywords: Animals; Rain Forest; South America

This program explores the dazzling world of Brazil's rain forest in the Amazon River basin as it focuses on the extraordinary wildlife in the area. During the rainy season when the river can rise more than twenty feet, the river's fresh-water dolphins move with the flood waters into the forest and dart around the treetops. An array of animal life comes into view as the program moves from day into night.

Title: *Animals of the Rainforest*
Producer: Schlessinger Video Productions/Library Video Company
Series: Rainforest for Children
Year Released: 1996
Call Number: 574
Length: 25 minutes
Price: $29.95
Reviewed in: *School Library Journal*
Grade Level: 3–6
Keywords: Rain Forests; Science—Life

Filmed in the rain forest of Costa Rica, this video offers information on the animals of the rain forest. The four layers of the rain forest are defined along with the interdependent relationships of the ecosystem.

Title: *Animated Almanac, The*
Producer: Society for Visual Education
Series: Animated Reference Library
Year Released: 1991
Call Number: 025.5
Length: 18 minutes
Price: $79.00
Reviewed in: *School Library Journal, Video Rating Guide for Libraries*
Grade Level: 3–6
Keywords: Almanacs; Library Skills

Students suffering from "fact attacks" get help from a variety of animated, talking almanacs. Students learn about the purpose and content of general almanacs and discover how they can use an index to find information, how to read and use tables, and how to use headings and captions to locate information. In addition to these skills, viewers learn how almanacs are put together. Includes teacher's guide.

Title: *Animated Atlas, The*
Producer: Society for Visual Education
Series: Animated Reference Library
Year Released: 1991
Call Number: 025.5
Length: 18 minutes
Price: $79.00
Reviewed in: *School Library Journal, Video Rating Guide for Libraries*
Grade Level: 3–6
Keywords: Atlases; Library Skills

Animated talking atlases take amazed kids on a tour of this reference tool's many uses. Skills covered include how to locate and decode the symbols used in an atlas, how to identify and read special maps, how to identify coordinates and page numbers in an atlas index, how to use coordinates to locate a specific place, and how to distinguish between general and special atlases. Includes teacher's guide.

Title: *Animated Dictionary, The*
Producer: Society for Visual Education
Series: Animated Reference Library
Year Released: 1991
Call Number: 025.5
Length: 18 minutes
Price: $79.00
Reviewed in: *School Library Journal, Video Rating Guide for Libraries*
Grade Level: 3–6
Keywords: Dictionaries; Library Skills

Students will learn usage skills from alphabetizing and using guide words to reading pronunciations and other components of dictionary definitions. Also includes an overview of the thesaurus and a look at other specialized dictionaries. Includes teacher's guide.

Title: *Animated Encyclopedia, The*
Producer: Society for Visual Education
Series: Animated Reference Library
Year Released: 1991

Call Number: 025.5
Length: 18 minutes
Price: $79.00
Reviewed in: *School Library Journal, Video Rating Guide for Libraries*
Grade Level: 3–6
Keywords: Encyclopedias; Library Skills

Encyclopedia volumes bicker among themselves as students discover how to use this all-important reference tool. This video takes students step-by-step through the research process: using guide words and the index; locating and interpreting entry words in the index; using pictures, maps, graphs, and charts; using headings and subheadings; using cross-references; and using the study aids at the end of the articles. Includes teacher's guide.

Title: *Antarctic Adventure*
Producer: Bennett Marine Video/Children's Television International
Series: Blue Frontier
Year Released: 1990
Call Number: 919.89
Length: 15 minutes
Price: $40.00
Reviewed in: *Video Rating Guide for Libraries*
Grade Level: 1–6
Keywords: Animals; Antarctic; Penguins

A group of scientists from the Hubbs Marine Research Institute brave the rigors of the Antarctic weather to obtain penguin eggs to be hatched in an incubator. It turns out to be a successful experiment. Teacher's guide available for purchase.

Title: *Apache, The*
Producer: InVision Communication
Series: Indians of North America Video Collection 1
Year Released: 1993
Call Number: 305.897
Length: 30 minutes
Price: $40.00
Reviewed in: *Booklist, School Library Journal*
Grade Level: 4–6

Keywords: Apache Indians; Indians of North America; Multicultural; Native Americans

Leading Native American scholars discuss the specific history of the Apache, including myths and stereotypes. There are interviews, combined with archival photographs and film footage, tribal music, crafts, and ceremonies to help students examine the spiritual relationship with nature, the role of women in Indian society, and the role of the U.S. government in Indian affairs.

Title: *Aquaspace Adventure*
Producer: Bennett Marine Video/Children's Television International
Series: Blue Frontier
Year Released: 1990
Call Number: 599.5
Length: 15 minutes
Price: $40.00
Reviewed in: *Video Rating Guide for Libraries*
Grade Level: 1–6
Keywords: Oceans; Science—Life; Submarines

Take a look at undersea exploration from the early days of hard-hat diving to the present-day submersibles like the *Alvin* that are enabling scientists to learn much about the mysteries of ocean floors. Teacher's guide available for purchase.

Title: *Are You Afraid of the Dark? Ghostly Tales*
Producer: Ronald A. Weinberg for YTV, Cinar Productions, and Nickelodeon/Baker & Taylor
Series: Nickelodeon Collection,
Year Released: 1994
Call Number: 808.83
Length: 50 minutes
Price: $13.00
Reviewed in: *Booklist*
Grade Level: 4–6
Keywords: Ghosts; Literature; Horror

Two spooky episodes from Nickelodeon's anthology series that use creativity and imagination. Titles: "Tale of the Frozen Ghost" and "Tale of the Shiny Red Bicycle."

Title: *Argentina*
Producer: Centre Communications
Series: Not Applicable
Year Released: 1990
Call Number: 982
Length: 18 minutes
Price: $100.00
Reviewed in: *Landers Film Review, School Library Journal, Video Rating Guide for Libraries*
Grade Level: 4–6
Keywords: Argentina; Social Studies; South America

Launch an expedition to one of the most intriguing countries of South America with this program. Students journey from a steaming, equatorial jungle to an Arctic rain forest and visit the majestic Andes mountains. Along the way, students gain a rich knowledge of Argentina's people, culture, wildlife, history, and agricultural industry. Used as an introduction or as an overview, this program shows the tremendous diversity of Argentina. Includes teacher's guide.

Title: *Arkelope*
Producer: National Film Board of Canada/Bullfrog Films
Series: Not Applicable
Year Released: 1995
Call Number: 574.529
Length: 6 minutes
Price: $95.00
Reviewed in: *School Library Journal*
Grade Level: 5–6
Keywords: Endangered Species; Extinction; Science—Life

In this video, a middle-aged couple watching television tune into a nature documentary. For sport, fashion, food, and financial gain, humans have tracked the Arkelope until now it teeters on the brink of extinction! This short film challenges us to face up to our careless treatment of the other species on the planet before we ourselves meet a similar fate. Includes teacher's guide.

Title: *Arthur Writes a Story*
Producer: Random House Home Video/Sony Wonder
Series: Arthur Series
Year Released: 1997
Call Number: Easy Fiction
Length: 30 minutes
Price: $12.98
Reviewed in: *School Library Journal*
Grade Level: PreK–3
Keywords: Imagination, Literature

Struggling with a school assignment, Arthur decides that all he needs is a little imagination to make his life sound more interesting than it really is.

Title: *Ashok by Any Other Name*
Producer: Pied Piper/AIMS Media
Series: Not Applicable
Year Released: 1994
Call Number: 305.8
Length: 14 minutes
Price: $70.00
Reviewed in: *Booklist, School Library Journal*
Grade Level: K–6
Keywords: Literature; Multicultural; Names

In this video based on the book by Sandra S. Yamate, Ashok doesn't care if he was named after a famous Indian king, he wants to change his ethnic sounding name to something more American—something easier to pronounce! Viewers will follow Ashok's misadventures in trying to find an "ordinary American name" and will see why he ultimately realizes that his given name is the best fit after all. An interview with the author is included at the end of the program.

Title: *Astronomy 101: A Family Adventure and Beginner's Guide to the Night Sky*
Producer: Mazon Production
Series: Not Applicable
Year Released: 1995
Call Number: 523
Length: 25 minutes
Price: $20.00

Reviewed in: *Booklist, USA Today*
Grade Level: 1–6
Keywords: Astronomy; Science—Space; Telescopes

This video introduces the night sky and how it works. Join Michelle and her mother as they show students how they explore the night sky together. Animation shows how telescopes work and how and why constellations seem to move across the night sky. Includes bibliography.

Title: *At the Zoo*
Producer: Goldsholl: Learning Videos/Alphabet Factory Home Video
Series: Picture This Sing-A-Long
Year Released: 1993
Call Number: 590.74
Length: 23 minutes
Price: $13.00
Reviewed in: *Video Rating Guide for Libraries*
Grade Level: PreK–3
Keywords: Animals; Music; Zoos

This video explores the zoo, with its many inhabitants. It also shows children the proper care needed for the animals and their environment.

Title: *Australia*
Producer: Lucerne Media
Series: Changing Face of Asia
Year Released: 1994
Call Number: 994
Length: 15 minutes
Price: $195.00
Reviewed in: *School Library Journal*
Grade Level: 5–6
Keywords: Asia; Australia

Once known mostly for its kangaroos and koalas, Australia today is seen by some as a last western outpost in the Pacific, and by others as a key element in the new, emerging Asia. This video provides information on the history, geography, and industry of Australia as well as the culture of the people.

Title: *Away We Go: All about Transportation*
Producer: Rainbow Educational Media
Series: Not Applicable
Year Released: 1990
Call Number: 388
Length: 20 minutes
Price: $89.00
Reviewed in: *Booklist, School Library Journal*
Grade Level: 1–4
Keywords: Community; Transportation

Whether we are traveling to some faraway place or simply going to school, transportation is an important part of our lives. Transportation brings food from farms and factories to our homes. Visiting grandparents, friends, or taking a vacation requires the use of transportation. This video compares transportation in the past to the present and shows how the development of more advanced forms of transportation have brought people closer together and made travel and trade easier. Includes teacher's guide.

Title: *Aztec, The*
Producer: Schlessinger Video Productions
Series: Indians of North America Video Collection 1
Year Released: 1993
Call Number: 970.3
Length: 30 minutes
Price: $40.00
Reviewed in: *Booklist, School Library Journal*
Grade Level: 4–6
Keywords: Aztec Indians; Indians of North America; Multicultural; Native Americans

Leading Native American scholars discuss the specific history of the Aztec, including myths and stereotypes. There are interviews, combined with archival photographs and film footage, tribal music, crafts, and ceremonies to help students examine the spiritual relationship with nature, the role of women in Indian society, and the role of the U.S. government in Indian affairs.

Title: *Babies and Their Parents*
Producer: Partridge Films, Ltd./Coronet/MTI Films and Video
Series: Animal Behavior
Year Released: 1991
Call Number: 306.85
Length: 12 minutes
Price: $215.00
Reviewed in: *Video Rating Guide for Libraries*
Grade Level: K–6
Keywords: Animals; Families; Science—Life

There is great range in the kind and duration of parental care in the animal world. Moving in a sequence from amphibians to reptiles to birds and mammals, this program reveals and compares parental care of animal babies of several different species. Viewers discover that the amount of care depends on the time it takes for each kind of baby to grow up and on what survival skills each needs to acquire. Includes teacher's guide.

Title: *Baby Animals*
Producer: Vermont Story Works
Series: Not Applicable
Year Released: 1995
Call Number: 630
Length: 30 minutes
Price: $15.00
Reviewed in: *Booklist*
Grade Level: PreK–2
Keywords: Animals; Babies; Farms

This video lets children learn about all of the different kinds of baby animals that can be found on a farm.

Title: *Backyard Wilderness*
Producer: California Academy of Sciences/Video Project
Series: Kids From CAOS
Year Released: 1995
Call Number: 363.72
Length: 30 minutes
Price: $60.00

Reviewed in: *Booklist, School Library Journal*
Grade Level: 6
Keywords: Ecology; Environmental Concerns

This video presents a three-part look at the wilderness and animal life that are right in our own backyards. "The Presidio" looks at how park rangers and young people are working to restore native plant species in our newest national park, right in San Francisco. "The Big Guy" profiles renowned entomologist Vernard Lewis and his daughter, who are studying the habits of the wily termite and other bugs. "Witness" portrays wildlife photographers who spent three years capturing threatened life forms on film. Includes teacher's guide.

Title: *Baltic States, The: Facing Independence*
Producer: Interfilm, Sweden
Series: Not Applicable
Year Released: 1991
Call Number: 947
Length: 21 minutes
Price: $90.00
Reviewed in: *Landers Film Review, School Library Journal, Video Rating Guide for Libraries*
Grade Level: 4–6
Keywords: Baltic States; Russia; Social Studies; Soviet Union

This program provides a detailed view of the history, culture, problems, dreams of newly independent Estonia, Latvia, and Lithuania. Students follow an Estonian family on a summer tour of the Baltic states. Along the way, they learn about the unique heritage of the region. Students discover that each country has its own language, culture, myths, and history. The problems and dreams of the people from each country are also chronicled.

Title: *Barry's Scrapbook: A Window into Art*
Producer: ALA Video/Library Video Network
Series: Not Applicable
Year Released: 1994
Call Number: 701.1
Length: 40 minutes
Price: $20.00
Reviewed in: *Children's Video Review Newsletter, Video Librarian*

Grade Level: 1–6
Keywords: Art; Museums; Music

Explore art with nationally acclaimed singer, songwriter, and author Barry Louis Polisar. Barry's favorite things—the library, music, and art—are combined into a fun- and fact-filled video journey. Includes a trip to the art museum, making recyclable art projects, visits with working artists, and sing-alongs.

Title: *Bear Cubs, Baby Ducks, and Kooky Kookaburras*
Producer: National Geographic Society Educational Services
Series: GeoKids
Year Released: 1994
Call Number: 599
Length: 33 minutes
Price: $15.00
Reviewed in: *Booklist*
Grade Level: PreK–1
Keywords: Animals; Babies

After Sunny Hone-Possum and Bobby Bushbaby see a mother monkey caring for her baby, Balzac de Chameleon tells them about all different kinds of animal babies and how they grow up.

Title: *Bears!*
Producer: Bullfrog Films
Series: Not Applicable
Year Released: 1990
Call Number: 599.74
Length: 13 minutes
Price: $195.00
Reviewed in: *Video Rating Guide for Libraries*
Grade Level: K–3
Keywords: Animals; Bears

With narration by a six-year-old boy, and music by Carolyn Saso, this video shows young people what being a bear is about. Survival needs of bears are shown, from food to open space; their seasons of sleeping, eating, and raising their young; and some myths about these creatures are explored. Includes study guide.

Title: *Being a Friend: What Does It Mean?*
Producer: Sunburst Communications
Series: Not Applicable
Year Released: 1995
Call Number: 177
Length: 21 minutes
Price: $149.00
Reviewed in: *Booklist, School Library Journal*
Grade Level: 5–6
Keywords: Behavior; Friendship; Self-esteem

Involved with their peers again, young adolescents find problems of acceptance and rejection loom large in their lives. This program raises thought-provoking issues connected to building healthy friendships, working out typical conflicts, and recognizing the difference between constructive and destructive friendships. Questions designed to encourage discussion follow each scenario. Includes teacher's guide.

Title: *Being an Explorer*
Producer: New Castle Communications
Series: Not Applicable
Year Released: 1996
Call Number: Biography
Length: 30 minutes
Price: $99.00
Reviewed in: *Booklist*
Grade Level: K–3
Keywords: Explorers

Children define the word "explorer" and talk about why they would like to be explorers. The expedition of Lewis and Clark is covered along with the expeditions of Will Steger, a modern-day explorer of the Arctic. Includes teacher's guide.

Title: *Berenstain Bears Forget Their Manners/Berenstain Bears and the Wicked Weasel Spell*
Producer: Cates Films/Random House Home Video
Series: Berenstain Bears First Time Video
Year Released: 1989
Call Number: Easy Fiction
Length: 25 minutes

Price: $7.00
Reviewed in: *Video Rating Guide for Libraries*
Grade Level: K–3
Keywords: Bears; Behavior; Manners

The first story teaches children manners that Papa finds hard to learn. In the second, the cubs foil Archweasel McGreed's plan to take over bear country.

Title: *Berenstain Bears Get Stage Fright/Go Bonkers*
Producer: Random House Home Video
Series: The Berenstain Bears Collection
Year Released: 1989
Call Number: Easy Fiction
Length: 30 minutes
Price: $7.00
Reviewed in: *Video Rating Guide for Libraries*
Grade Level: K–4
Keywords: Bears; Behavior; Theater

Sister is nervous about her part in the play; Brother is boasting. But on opening night, who is nervous and who is prepared? Also includes "Berenstain Bears Go Bonkers over Honkers."

Title: *Between the Walls*
Producer: National Film Board of Canada/Bullfrog Films
Series: Look Again, Vol. 1
Year Released: 1990
Call Number: 591.52
Length: 10 minutes
Price: $150.00
Reviewed in: *Video Rating Guide for Libraries*
Grade Level: PreK–6
Keywords: Ecology; Mice

A girl discovers a mouse living between the walls of her home, and builds a better trap when the mouse is threatened. Students can predict what she might do and observe how she removes the mouse in a sensible, sensitive way. Includes teacher's guide.

Title: *Beyond the Stacks: Finding Fun in the Library*
Producer: Cheshire Book Companions
Series: Not Applicable
Year Released: 1992
Call Number: 028.55
Length: 11 minutes
Price: $90.00
Reviewed in: *Emergency Librarian*
Grade Level: 5–6
Keywords: Library Skills; Reading

> This program is a first step in showing students that the library is filled with hundreds of resources to enjoy. Follow a thirteen year old as she tours the library and discovers paperback books for recreational reading, videos, CDs, books on tape, and other fun things that are there for the borrowing.

Title: *Big Bird Gets Lost*
Producer: Sony Wonder
Series: Sesame Street Kids' Guide to Life
Year Released: 1997
Call Number: Easy Fiction
Length: 41 minutes
Price: $12.95
Reviewed in: *School Library Journal*
Grade Level: PreK–1
Keywords: Early Childhood; Safety

> Big Bird loses his way while shopping for birdseed for his nest-warming party.

Title: *Big Cable Bridges*
Producer: Segments of Knowledge
Series: Not Applicable
Year Released: 1995
Call Number: 624.5
Length: 30 minutes
Price: $20.00

Reviewed in: *Booklist, School Library Journal, Video Librarian*
Grade Level: 3–6
Keywords: Bridges; Construction; Technology

Children take an up-close look at the making of the big cable bridges through live-action footage of powerful machines at work and educational information from bridge designers themselves. Shows how cable-stayed bridges are built, from start to finish.

Title: *Big Cats of the World*
Producer: ABC/Kane Productions/AIMS Media
Series: Wildlife Tales
Year Released: 1994
Call Number: 599.74
Length: 25 minutes
Price: $100.00
Reviewed in: *School Library Journal*
Grade Level: 4–6
Keywords: Animals; Cats

Large cats spend enormous amounts of time and effort in their daily search for food. Although all cats display a similarity in movement and personality, in the wild their hunting techniques span a remarkable range, even within the same environment. This program explores the hunting life of these exceptional animals, a life that is far more difficult than we can ever imagine. Includes guide.

Title: *Big Plane Trip, The*
Producer: Little Mammoth Media
Series: Not Applicable
Year Released: 1994
Call Number: 387.7
Length: 45 minutes
Price: $13.00
Reviewed in: *Booklist, Forbes, Video Librarian*
Grade Level: PreK–3
Keywords: Airplanes; Transportation

A live-action adventure for children that presents a behind-the-scenes look at the operations of an international flight and offers the experience of what it's like to fly on a big plane.

Title: *Big Red*
Producer: Fire Dog Pictures/Tapeworm Video Distributors
Series: Not Applicable
Year Released: 1993
Call Number: 363.37
Length: 28 minutes
Price: $20.00
Reviewed in: *Booklist, Video Rating Guide for Libraries*
Grade Level: PreK–2
Keywords: Fire Fighters; Safety

Children get a real-life adventure into the world of everyday heroes: the brave people and mighty equipment that fight fires. Students learn about the preparation, the tools, and the big trucks that fight the big fires, learning valuable lessons about fire safety.

Title: *Big Shot*
Producer: Pyramid Film & Video
Series: Not Applicable
Year Released: 1994
Call Number: 363.3
Length: 20 minutes
Price: $295.00
Reviewed in: *Booklist*
Grade Level: 5–6
Keywords: Gun Safety; Safety

Guns can kill by accident, and these accidents often involve young children. How do we educate children and protect them from this cycle? In this drama, two teenagers "borrow" a gun in order to practice shooting at targets, and an accident unfolds.

Title: *Bigmama's*
Producer: Reading Adventures
Series: Friends and Neighbors Multicultural Story Videos
Year Released: 1993
Call Number: Biography
Length: 6 minutes
Price: $45.00
Reviewed in: *School Library Journal*

Grade Level: K–4
Keywords: African Americans; Families; Literature

This video is based on the book by Caldecott Honor winner Donald Crews. When the train arrived in Cottondale, the summer at Bigmama's house in Florida began. Crews brilliantly evokes the sights, sounds, and emotions of a memorable childhood experience.

Title: *Bird*
Producer: BBC Wildvision, BBC Lionheart TV, Dorling Kindersley Vision in association with Oregon Public Broadcasting/Dorling Kindersley/Houghton Mifflin
Series: Eyewitness Video
Year Released: 1995
Call Number: 598
Length: 35 minutes
Price: $13.00
Reviewed in: *Booklist, School Library Journal*
Grade Level: PreK–6
Keywords: Animals; Birds

Viewers will journey into a three-dimensional "virtual museum" where live-action wildlife photography creates the sensation of being there. This program presents a completely different view of the marvels and mysteries of the natural world as they have never been seen before. Also includes behind-the-scenes, "making of the series" footage. Narrated by Martin Sheen.

Title: *Birthday Basket for Tia, A*
Producer: Reading Adventures
Series: Friends and Neighbors Multicultural Story Videos
Year Released: 1993
Call Number: Easy Fiction
Length: 10 minutes
Price: $45.00
Reviewed in: *School Library Journal*
Grade Level: K–6
Keywords: Families; Mexican Americans; Multicultural

In this video of the book by Pat Mora, illustrated by Cecily Lang, Cecilia knows that today is a special day—her great aunt Tia's ninetieth birthday—and wonders what gift could be important enough to give to Tia. This is an intergenerational story about a Mexican American family.

Title: *Black Is My Color: The African American Experience*
Producer: Rainbow Educational Media
Series: Multicultural History Series
Year Released: 1992
Call Number: 305.896
Length: 15 minutes
Price: $89.00
Reviewed in: *School Library Journal*
Grade Level: 4–6
Keywords: African Americans; Multicultural

Students explore the story of the African American people, from their roots in Africa to their important place in modern American society. Rare images and original music describe the many ways that black Americans responded to the New World and to the opportunities created by the Civil War and freedom. The program depicts the contributions of Dr. Martin Luther King Jr. and the leading personalities of our own era. Includes teacher's guide.

Title: *Body's Defenses against Disease, The*
Producer: Cochran Communications/Rainbow Educational Media
Series: Not Applicable
Year Released: 1996
Call Number: 613
Length: 24 minutes
Price: $89.00
Reviewed in: *Booklist, School Library Journal*
Grade Level: 4–6
Keywords: Disease; Health; Human Body

The body has several lines of defense against disease. The skin, mucous membranes, and immune system are explored. The program also looks at the pathogens that threaten it, particularly bacteria and viruses. Allergies, vaccinations, antibodies, and AIDS are covered. Includes teacher's guide.

Title: *Bollo Caper, The*
Producer: ABC/AIMS Media
Series: ABC Weekend Special
Year Released: 1990
Call Number: Fiction
Length: 23 minutes
Price: $50.00
Reviewed in: *Video Rating Guide for Libraries*
Grade Level: K–6
Keywords: Endangered Species; Leopards; Literature

In this animated adaptation of the book by Art Buchwald, viewers will delight in the story about Bollo, a rare golden leopard, who makes a daring escape from fur hunters and travels to Washington, DC, to have his species included on the endangered species list.

Title: *Booker T. Washington*
Producer: Schlessinger Video Productions
Series: Black Americans of Achievement Video Collection 1
Year Released: 1992
Call Number: Biography
Length: 30 minutes
Price: $40.00
Reviewed in: *School Library Journal, Video Librarian, Video Rating Guide for Libraries*
Grade Level: 4–6
Keywords: African Americans; Biographies; Washington, Booker T.

This video biography contains interviews with authorities on the subject's life, accompanied by archival footage, photographs, and period music. Topics include basic biographical information, the inspirational and motivational factors in his life, his message, and the significance of Booker T. Washington in society today.

Title: *Born to Be Wild*
Producer: BMG Video
Series: OWL/TV
Year Released: 1994
Call Number: 591.52
Length: 28 minutes
Price: $10.00
Reviewed in: *School Library Journal*

Grade Level: K–6
Keywords: Animals; Bears; Primates

Meet Winnie, the mischievous bear cub; visit with pandas from China; and join the expedition as you radio track koala bears in Australia. Take a close-up look at the endangered woolly monkey and explore the intelligence of chimpanzees.

Title: *Bread: From Farm to Table*
Producer: Eager Outdoor Video Productions/AIMS Media
Series: Not Applicable
Year Released: 1994
Call Number: 641.8
Length: 15 minutes
Price: $100.00
Reviewed in: *School Library Journal*
Grade Level: K–3
Keywords: Bread; Food; Health

Undeniably the world's most popular food, bread has been synonymous with healthy and hearty since biblical times. This program takes a tour of the bread-making process, from the time the wheat is planted to the moment the loaf arrives on the kitchen table. Includes guide.

Title: *Breaking Out of the Under Achievement Trap*
Producer: Cambridge Career Products
Series: Not Applicable
Year Released: 1990
Call Number: 152.4
Length: 25 minutes
Price: $98.00
Reviewed in: *Video Rating Guide for Libraries*
Grade Level: 6
Keywords: Behavior

Looks at techniques that students, teachers, and parents can use to help students break out of the under-achiever trap.

Title: *Building Skyscrapers*
Producer: Building Skyscrapers
Series: Not Applicable
Year Released: 1994
Call Number: 725
Length: 40 minutes
Price: $20.00
Reviewed in: *Booklist*
Grade Level: PreK–3
Keywords: Buildings; Construction; Technology

Kids love to see explosions, swinging steel, and mixing concrete, and that's what they get in this live-action program that takes them on and above the scene of a skyscraper construction site.

Title: *Built for Speed: A High Speed Live Action Adventure at the Racetrack*
Producer: WhiteTree Pictures
Series: Not Applicable
Year Released: 1994
Call Number: 796.7
Length: 30 minutes
Price: $15.00
Reviewed in: *School Library Journal*
Grade Level: PreK–3
Keywords: Cars; Race Cars; Stock Cars; Transportation

This video lets kids see inside a real stock car and then go onto the racetrack to see some live race-car action.

Title: *By the Light of the Halloween Moon*
Producer: Weston Woods
Series: Not Applicable
Year Released: 1997
Call Number: Easy Fiction
Length: 6 minutes
Price: $12.95
Reviewed in: *Booklist, School Library Journal*
Grade Level: PreK–2
Keywords: Halloween; Literature

Adapted from the book by Caroline Stutson. In this cumulative story, a cat's pursuit of a toe sets off a chain of events involving a girl, a sprite, a ghost, a ghoul, a bat, a witch, and the Halloween moon.

Title: *Cambodia*
Producer: White Mountain Entertainment
Series: Cultures of the World
Year Released: 1993
Call Number: 959.6
Length: 18 minutes
Price: $79.00
Reviewed in: *School Library Journal*
Grade Level: 4–6
Keywords: Asia; Cambodia; Social Studies

The people of Kampuchea live their lives with remarkable optimism considering the internal conflicts that still rage within this country. Students will see the Cambodian Ballet and the Lunar New Year celebration, and will visit the Royal Palace. In addition, they will tour the ancient capital of Angkor Thom and marvel at the majesty of the famous Angkor Wat temple. Includes teacher's guide.

Title: *Careers in Math: From Architects to Astronauts*
Producer: Human Relations Media
Series: Not Applicable
Year Released: 1994
Call Number: 331.7
Length: 28 minutes
Price: $175.00
Reviewed in: *Booklist, Video Rating Guide for Libraries*
Grade Level: 5–6
Keywords: Careers; Mathematics; Occupations

Students are taken on a whirlwind tour through some exciting careers where they see professionals using math on the job. Art, cooking, even cosmetology are just some of the fields in which students will see math in action. Students will gain an understanding of how algebra and geometry are applied to real-life situations, as well as insights into their own potential. Includes teacher's guide.

Title: *Casey's Revenge*
Producer: InnerVisions Productions/Kids' Media Group
Series: Human Race Club
Year Released: 1990
Call Number: 152.4
Length: 25 minutes
Price: $59.00
Reviewed in: *Video Rating Guide for Libraries*
Grade Level: K–4
Keywords: Behavior; Brothers and Sisters; Families; Revenge

When Casey can't stop Theresa from embarrassing him, he decides to "pay her back" during a special slide presentation at her birthday party. Theresa discovers his plans at the last minute and tries to stop him. The tape shows children why revenge doesn't work and how everyone wins when brothers and sisters respect one another. Includes guide.

Title: *Cat*
Producer: BBC Wildvision, BBC Lionheart TV, Dorling Kindersley Vision in association with Oregon Public Broadcasting/Dorling Kindersley/Houghton Muifflin
Series: Eyewitness Video Series
Year Released: 1995
Call Number: 599.74
Length: 35 minutes
Price: $13.00
Reviewed in: *Booklist, School Library Journal*
Grade Level: PreK–6
Keywords: Animals; Cats

Viewers will journey into a three-dimensional "virtual museum" where live-action wildlife photography creates the sensation of being there. This program presents a completely different view of the marvels and mysteries of the natural world as they have never been seen before. Also includes behind-the-scenes, "making of the series" footage. Narrated by Martin Sheen.

Title: *Cat in the Hat Comes Back, The*
Producer: Praxis Media/Random House Home Video
Series: Dr. Seuss's Beginner Book Videos
Year Released: 1989

Call Number: Easy Fiction
Length: 30 minutes
Price: $10.00
Reviewed in: *Video Rating Guide for Libraries*
Grade Level: 1–4
Keywords: Cats; Literature; Stories in Rhyme

Would you let him in? Sally and her brother don't have much choice, and they soon learn that C-A-T spells trouble! This favorite story of the mischievous cat has delighted generations of readers. Also includes two more Dr. Seuss titles: "There's a Wocket in My Pocket" and "Fox in Socks."

Title: *Celebrate 100 Kit: Everything Your Class Needs to Count Up to the 100th Day of School*
Producer: Robert Mack Productions/Scholastic, Inc.
Series: Not Applicable
Year Released: 1997
Call Number: Easy Fiction
Length: 10 minutes
Price: $14.95
Reviewed in: *School Library Journal*
Grade Level: K–2
Keywords: Counting; Mathematics; School

Children learn 100 spelling words, plant 100 seeds, bake 100 cookies, and do everything 100 ways to celebrate the 100th day of school. Paperback book, activity book, and poster are included with video.

Title: *Cell Division*
Producer: Rainbow Educational Media
Series: Cell Series
Year Released: 1995
Call Number: 574.87
Length: 19 minutes
Price: $99.00
Reviewed in: *Booklist, School Library Journal*
Grade Level: 4–6
Keywords: Cells; Science—Life

This program focuses on cell division. It explains the role of chromosomes and genes and how they affect hereditary characteristics as well as the differences between asexual and sexual reproduction and terms of cell division. Students will understand how cells divide (reproduce) through mitosis and how sex cells divide through meiosis. It also goes over cell differentiation.

Title: *Challenging Geography: Explorers Discover America*
Producer: Rainbow Educational Media
Series: Not Applicable
Year Released: 1992
Call Number: 973
Length: 22 minutes
Price: $89.00
Reviewed in: *School Library Journal, Video Rating Guide for Libraries*
Grade Level: 4–6
Keywords: Geography; Social Studies; U.S. History

Students learn how the story of the United States is in many ways the story of geography. After Christopher Columbus sighted an unknown land, our country started its geographic struggle. Explorers, settlements, and the forming of the thirteen colonies were all a part of the slow exploration of the New World. The mountains and plains needed to be crossed and the wilderness explored. Live-action footage is accompanied by historical stills and art photography. Includes teacher's guide.

Title: *Cherokee, The*
Producer: Schlessinger Video Productions
Series: Indians of North America Video Collection 1
Year Released: 1993
Call Number: 970.3
Length: 30 minutes
Price: $40.00
Reviewed in: *Booklist, School Library Journal*
Grade Level: 4–6
Keywords: Cherokee Indians; Indians of North America; Native Americans

Leading Native American scholars discuss the specific history of the Cherokee, including myths and stereotypes. There are interviews, combined with archival photographs and film footage, tribal music, crafts, and ceremonies to help students examine the spiritual relationship with nature, the role of women in Indian society, and the role of the U.S. government in Indian affairs.

Title: *Chewing Gum*
Producer: TVOntario/Films for the Humanities and Sciences
Series: Here's How
Year Released: 1991
Call Number: 664
Length: 10 minutes
Price: $49.00
Reviewed in: *Video Rating Guide for Libraries*
Grade Level: 1–3
Keywords: Gum; Inventions; Technology

The video first compares several cultures' chewing habits, then looks at the components of chewing gum and the manufacture of pellet and stick gum. Teacher's guide available for purchase.

Title: *Children of Other Lands: Andres Orozoco of Mexico*
Producer: Colman Communications/Rainbow Educational Media
Series: Not Applicable
Year Released: 1995
Call Number: 305.2
Length: 12 minutes
Price: $80.00
Reviewed in: *School Library Journal, Video Rating Guide for Libraries*
Grade Level: 1–4
Keywords: Families; Mexico; Multicultural; Social Studies

As viewers watch the program, they see how a child of an economically emerging country such as Mexico lives in two worlds—one modern, the other traditional. Andres's hometown, dramatically set in a valley surrounded by the mountains of central Mexico, is both a modern industrial city and a beautiful, picturesque reminder of old, colonial Mexico. Includes guide.

Title: *Christianity*
Producer: Rabbit Ears Productions
Series: Greatest Stories Ever Told
Year Released: 1993
Call Number: 280
Length: 30 minutes
Price: $13.00
Reviewed in: *Video Rating Guide for Libraries*
Grade Level: 4–8
Keywords: Christianity; Creation; Religion

This video presents the biblical story about how God created the world. It complements Bible study and the study of comparative religions.

Title: *Cicadas: The 17–Year Invasion*
Producer: TVOntario/Journal Films
Series: World of Nature 2
Year Released: 1993
Call Number: 595.7
Length: 15 minutes
Price: $49.00
Reviewed in: *Video Rating Guide for Libraries*
Grade Level: 4–6
Keywords: Cicadas; Insects; Science—Life

In a Chicago suburb, residents prepare for the invasion of millions of cicadas that emerge en masse from the ground once every seventeen years. The nymphs crawl out at night to the nearest tree, where they transform themselves into adult cicadas. Teacher's guide available for purchase.

Title: *Cinderella . . . Frozen in Time: Ice Capades*
Producer: Evocation Publishing Company/Sony Wonder
Series: Not Applicable
Year Released: 1995
Call Number: Easy Fiction
Length: 60 minutes
Price: $13.00
Reviewed in: *School Library Journal*
Grade Level: 2–6
Keywords: Dance; Ice Skating; Physical Education

Dorothy Hamill leads this adaptation of a familiar fairy tale that features state-of-the-art special effects, new characters, and an original score. Narrated by Lloyd Bridges.

Title: *Circle of Water*
Producer: National Geographic Society Educational Services
Series: On Nature's Trail
Year Released: 1995
Call Number: 574.5
Length: 23 minutes
Price: $99.00
Reviewed in: *Booklist*
Grade Level: 1–3
Keywords: Science—Earth; Water Cycle

Learn the principles of evaporation, condensation, and precipitation as young explorers follow the cycle of water. In their fantasies, the explorers rise with morning fog, fly through clouds, fall with rain and snow, and explore underground caves until they return to their own river and find they have been going in circles. Includes teacher's guide.

Title: *Circulatory and Respiratory Systems*
Producer: National Geographic Society Educational Services
Series: Your Body
Year Released: 1994
Call Number: 611
Length: 19 minutes
Price: $79.00
Reviewed in: *School Library Journal*
Grade Level: 4–6
Keywords: Circulatory Systems; Human Body; Respiratory Systems; Science—Life

Explore the biological systems that gather and distribute the oxygen and nutrients our bodies need for energy production. Animation and medical photography show the major parts of both the circulatory and respiratory systems: the heart, blood vessels and cells, nasal passages, diaphragm, and lungs. Includes teacher's guide.

Title: *Clarissa*
Producer: MarshMedia
Series: Key Concepts in Self-Esteem
Year Released: 1992
Call Number: 152.4
Length: 13 minutes
Price: $80.00
Reviewed in: *School Library Journal, Video Rating Guide for Libraries*
Grade Level: K–4
Keywords: Behavior; Cows; Dairy Farms; Self-esteem

A plain, brown cow rescues a troupe of prize farm animals and proves her worth to herself and everyone else. Helps students appreciate their own special talents and realize the inherent value of each person while they learn about dairy farms and the state of Wisconsin. Includes teacher's guide, hard-cover storybook.

Title: *Clocks and Watches*
Producer: TVOntario/Films for the Humanities and Sciences
Series: Here's How
Year Released: 1991
Call Number: 609
Length: 10 minutes
Price: $49.00
Reviewed in: *Video Rating Guide for Libraries*
Grade Level: 1–3
Keywords: Clocks; Inventions; Technology; Watches

Viewers learn about the history of timepieces and their role in daily life, and visit clock factories. Children take some clocks apart and design clock faces. Teacher's guide available for purchase.

Title: *Colin Powell*
Producer: Schlessinger Video Productions
Series: Black Americans of Achievement Video Collection 1
Year Released: 1992
Call Number: Biography
Length: 30 minutes
Price: $40.00
Reviewed in: *School Library Journal, Video Librarian, Video Rating Guide for Libraries*

Grade Level: 4–6
Keywords: African Americans; Biographies; Powell, Colin

This video biography contains interviews, archival footage, photographs, and period music. Topics include basic biographical information, the inspirational and motivational factors in Powell's life, his message, and the significance of Colin Powell in society today.

Title: *Collage*
Producer: NBT Enterprises/Rainbow Educational Media
Series: Art Start
Year Released: 1995
Call Number: 702
Length: 22 minutes
Price: $79.00
Reviewed in: *Booklist, School Library Journal*
Grade Level: 4–6
Keywords: Art; Collage

Assembling a collage made of both torn and cut pieces of paper demonstrates the use of descriptive edges. Learn how to use paper as a medium.

Title: *Colors*
Producer: Crystalroe Productions/DK Publishing
Series: Hullaballoo
Year Released: 1995
Call Number: 372
Length: 30 minutes
Price: $10.00
Reviewed in: *School Library Journal*
Grade Level: PreK–K
Keywords: Colors; Early Childhood

This program combines animation, puppetry, games, and songs to teach children about colors.

Title: *Colt Called Lucky, A*
Producer: Alan Sloan, Inc./AIMS Media
Series: Wild World
Year Released: 1989
Call Number: Fiction
Length: 15 minutes
Price: $50.00
Reviewed in: *Video Rating Guide for Libraries*
Grade Level: K–6
Keywords: Horses; Values

This story of a wild mustang living in the spectacular Southwest combines nature photography with a lesson in values. The story is followed by reading and language lessons.

Title: *Comanche, The*
Producer: Schlessinger Video Productions
Series: Indians of North America Video Collection 1
Year Released: 1993
Call Number: 970.3
Length: 30 minutes
Price: $40.00
Reviewed in: *Booklist, School Library Journal, Video Rating Guide for Libraries*
Grade Level: 4–6
Keywords: Comanche Indians; Indians of North America; Native Americans

Leading Native American scholars discuss the history of the Comanche, including myths and stereotypes. There are interviews combined with archival photographs and film footage, tribal music, crafts, and ceremonies to help students examine the spiritual relationship with nature, the role of women in Indian society, and the role of the U.S. government in Indian affairs.

Title: *Come Fly with Us*
Producer: Adventure Video/Paragon Home Video
Series: Not Applicable
Year Released: 1994
Call Number: 629.13
Length: 30 minutes
Price: $20.00

Reviewed in: *Booklist, School Library Journal*
Grade Level: K–6
Keywords: Airplanes; Transportation

> Three youngsters dream about flying some of the great planes of history and get a treat when their grandfather takes them up on a real flight.

Title: *Come Join Our Multicultural Band,* Vol. 1
Producer: Wagner's World of Music/Sherry Nelson Productions
Series: Professor Music
Year Released: 1994
Call Number: 780
Length: 30 minutes
Price: $30.00
Reviewed in: *Booklist, School Library Journal, Video Rating Guide for Libraries*
Grade Level: K–5
Keywords: Multicultural; Music

> Explores the music of different cultures. Also explains musical notation and provides viewer participation in a song or dance from each culture.

Title: *Communities of Living Things*
Producer: Centre Communications/Barr Films
Series: Not Applicable
Year Released: 1991
Call Number: 574.5
Length: 24 minutes
Price: $100.00
Reviewed in: *Video Rating Guide for Libraries*
Grade Level: 4–6
Keywords: Ecology; Habitats; Science—Life

> Viewers learn the location, special characteristics, plants, and animals of each of the six North American biomes. The effect of human use on the natural balance of these communities and the need to protect this equilibrium are presented.

Title: *Computers: Where They Come From and How They Work*
Producer: Disney Educational
Series: Not Applicable
Year Released: 1990
Call Number: 004.16
Length: 9 minutes
Price: $79.00
Reviewed in: *Video Rating Guide for Libraries*
Grade Level: 4–6
Keywords: Computers; Technology

This video presents a history of computers, from the simple calculating devices to the large, primitive, and cumbersome computers of the 1940s, and finally, to the present.

Title: *Concrete Trucking*
Producer: Pique Productions
Series: Big Truck
Year Released: 1994
Call Number: 629.3
Length: 30 minutes
Price: $15.00
Reviewed in: *Booklist*
Grade Level: PreK–2
Keywords: Concrete; Construction; Technology

In this real-life, video field trip, young viewers see all facets of the concrete-making process.

Title: *Connections*
Producer: National Film Board of Canada/Bullfrog Films
Series: Look Again, Vol. 1
Year Released: 1990
Call Number: 362.29
Length: 10 minutes
Price: $150.00
Reviewed in: *Video Rating Guide for Libraries*
Grade Level: PreK–6
Keywords: Environmental Concerns; Rivers; Science

The discovery of an animal skeleton in a riverbed stimulates a girl to imagine the many connections among the structures and functions of living creatures and machines. The film provides a springboard for exploring patterns and relationships among many elements of the environment. Includes teacher's guide.

Title: *Continents Adrift: An Introduction to Continental Drift and Plate Tectonics*
Producer: Rainbow Educational Media
Series: Earth Science
Year Released: 1995
Call Number: 551.2
Length: 27 minutes
Price: $99.00
Reviewed in: *School Library Journal*
Grade Level: 5–6
Keywords: Geology; Science—Earth

This program explores the causes of land masses splitting. Topics covered include: plate tectonics; divergent, convergent, and transformed boundaries; seafloor spreading; midocean ridge; subduction zone; faults and seismic waves. Includes teacher's guide.

Title: *Cool Cats, Raindrops, and Things that Live in Holes*
Producer: National Geographic Society Educational Services
Series: GeoKids
Year Released: 1994
Call Number: 591
Length: 33 minutes
Price: $15.00
Reviewed in: *Booklist*
Grade Level: PreK–1
Keywords: Animals; Dwellings

During a game of hide-and-seek, Sunny Honey-Possum and Bobby Bushbaby discover a tree hole, prompting Balzac de Chameleon to tell them about the variety of animals that live in holes.

Title: *Cool Creatures: Reptiles*
Producer: Rainbow Educational Media
Series: Not Applicable
Year Released: 1994
Call Number: 597.9

Length: 22 minutes
Price: $89.00
Reviewed in: *Booklist, School Library Journal*
Grade Level: 4–6
Keywords: Reptiles; Science—Life

Cold-blooded, three-chambered heart, scales—these are just a few characteristics of reptiles. This full-motion video examines reptiles, noting the above characteristics along with others. Reptiles identified and discussed are: turtles, lizards, snakes, crocodilians (crocodiles, alligators, gharials, and caimans). Different reptile habitats are explored, along with the reptiles' mechanisms for survival. Includes teacher's guide.

Title: *Coot Club*
Producer: BBC-TV in association with Primetime Television and Theatre Projects/Janson Associates
Series: Swallows and Amazons
Year Released: 1995
Call Number: Fiction
Length: 90 minutes
Price: $20.00
Reviewed in: *Booklist, School Library Journal*
Grade Level: 4–6
Keywords: Animals; Literature

This live-action production based on the children's book series by Arthur Ransome tells the story of a group of six young friends who share adventures on the backwater lakes of England in the 1930s.

Title: *Cops Are Tops: Our Police at Work*
Producer: Video Dialog/Rainbow Educational Media
Series: Community Helpers
Year Released: 1994
Call Number: 352.2
Length: 15 minutes
Price: $89.00
Reviewed in: *Booklist, School Library Journal, Video Rating Guide for Libraries*
Grade Level: 1–3
Keywords: Community; Police; Social Studies

This video shows a wide variety of services performed by police for their communities. It emphasizes the hard work police do and how community members, especially school children, are helped by the police.

Title: *Cougar: King of the Mountain*
Producer: Adventure Productions
Series: Mother Nature's World of Wildlife
Year Released: 1991
Call Number: 599.74
Length: 30 minutes
Price: $20.00
Reviewed in: *Video Rating Guide for Libraries*
Grade Level: K–6
Keywords: Animals; Cats; Cougars

Join the children of Camp Wilderness as they see a cougar. Learn about the cougar in its wilderness home as John Byner tells the story to photography and music.

Title: *Cougars and How They Live*
Producer: ABC/Kane Productions/AIMS Media
Series: Animals and How They Live
Year Released: 1994
Call Number: 599.74
Length: 27 minutes
Price: $100.00
Reviewed in: *School Library Journal*
Grade Level: 5–6
Keywords: Cats; Cougars; Families

This video looks at a mother cougar and her three offspring in the Sawtooth Mountains of Idaho. Viewers will see the mother train her young to communicate with her, to eat meat, to hunt, to elude other predators, and to develop competiveness—even with each other. Includes teacher's guide.

Title: *Count with Me!*
Producer: Dorling Kindersley
Series: Hullaballoo
Year Released: 1995
Call Number: 513.2
Length: 30 minutes
Price: $10.00
Reviewed in: *Booklist, Publishers Weekly, Video Librarian*
Grade Level: PreK–1
Keywords: Counting; Early Childhood; Mathematics; Numbers

Games, magical puppetry, international music and dance, and Ted Bear help children develop a fundamental understanding of abstract ideas such as counting.

Title: *Country Mouse and the City Mouse, The: A Christmas Tale*
Producer: Michael Sporn/Random House Home Video
Series: Not Applicable
Year Released: 1994
Call Number: Easy Fiction
Length: 25 minutes
Price: $10.00
Reviewed in: *Booklist, School Library Journal*
Grade Level: K–3
Keywords: Christmas; Holidays; Mice

Emily, the simple country mouse, goes for a Christmas visit to her worldly cousin Alexander, who lives in the city. Their adventures bring home the warmth and wonder of the season. Stars the voices of Crystal Gayle and John Lithgow. Parents' Choice Award.

Title: *Cows!* (2d ed.)
Producer: Churchill Video Ventures/Churchill Media
Series: Not Applicable
Year Released: 1995
Call Number: 636.2
Length: 9 minutes
Price: $50.00
Reviewed in: *School Library Journal*
Grade Level: K–5
Keywords: Cows; Science—Life

This video is an exploration of cows—the texture of noses, shapes of bodies, grinding of jaws, and swishing of tails.

Title: *Creating Cultural Diversity*
Producer: Cheshire Book Companions
Series: Book Connection
Year Released: 1992
Call Number: 394.2
Length: 23 minutes
Price: $75.00
Reviewed in: *School Library Journal, Video Rating Guide for Libraries*
Grade Level: 4–6
Keywords: Customs; Holidays; Multicultural

Viewers learn about the holidays, languages, customs, and traditions of various cultures.

Title: *Creation*
Producer: Rabbit Ears Productions
Series: Not Applicable
Year Released: 1993
Call Number: 291.1
Length: 30 minutes
Price: $13.00
Reviewed in: *School Library Journal*
Grade Level: 1–4
Keywords: Creation; Religion

This video presents the biblical version of the creation of the world. Narration includes the first three chapters of the Book of Genesis.

Title: *Creek, The*
Producer: Schlessinger Video Productions
Series: Indians of North America Video Collection 2
Year Released: 1994
Call Number: 971.2
Length: 30 minutes
Price: $40.00
Reviewed in: *Booklist, School Library Journal*

Grade Level: 4–6
Keywords: Creek Indians; Indians of North America; Native Americans

Leading Native American scholars discuss the history of the Creek, including myths and stereotypes. There are interviews combined with archival photographs and film footage, tribal music, crafts, and ceremonies to help students examine the spiritual relationship with nature, the role of women in Indian society, and the role of the U.S. government in Indian affairs.

Title: *Creepy Creatures and Slimy Stuff*
Producer: Children's Group
Series: OWL/TV
Year Released: 1994
Call Number: 595.7
Length: 30 minutes
Price: $10.00
Reviewed in: *School Library Journal*
Grade Level: 3–6
Keywords: Animals; Insects; Science—Life; Snakes

The kids of OWL/TV take a close-up look at "slugs, snakes, and other slimy stuff." This video covers environments from the Seychelles rainforest to the desert of Arizona. Features children from all over the globe interacting with the different environments in a combination of animated segments and live-action footage.

Title: *Critter Songs: A Celebration of Children and Wildlife*
Producer: Clara Pincus/Video Project
Series: Not Applicable
Year Released: 1994
Call Number: 591.52
Length: 12 minutes
Price: $40.00
Reviewed in: *Booklist*
Grade Level: K–6
Keywords: Animals; Music

This video features two songs and a mixture of live-action visuals and children's artwork. It also encourages kids to learn about animal behavior and to work on behalf of animals, as well as to think about how all animals, including humans, are interdependent and valuable, each with a unique "voice." Includes teacher's guide.

Title: *Cubs and Kittens*
Producer: Adventure Productions
Series: Mother Nature's World of Wildlife
Year Released: 1991
Call Number: 591.3
Length: 32 minutes
Price: $20.00
Reviewed in: *Video Rating Guide for Libraries*
Grade Level: K–6
Keywords: Animals; Babies; Families

Students will see close-ups of playful baby bear cubs, cougars, badgers, ducks, bobcats, red foxes, and more. John Byner narrates as mothers lovingly protect and pamper the babies.

Title: *Dairy Farm*
Producer: TVOntario/Films for the Humanities and Sciences
Series: Take a Look 2
Year Released: 1991
Call Number: 637
Length: 10 minutes
Price: $49.00
Reviewed in: *Video Rating Guide for Libraries*
Grade Level: 2–5
Keywords: Cows; Dairy Farms; Farms

Kate visits Jamie at his uncle's dairy farm when a new calf is born, and she learns how the cows are fed, milked, and cared for. Viewers follow the route that milk takes from the cow to the consumer. Teacher's guide available for purchase.

Title: *Daisy Discovers the World*
Producer: Alan Sloan, Inc./AIMS Media
Series: Wild World
Year Released: 1989
Call Number: Fiction
Length: 15 minutes

Price: $100.00
Reviewed in: *Video Rating Guide for Libraries*
Grade Level: K–6
Keywords: Sea Lions; Values

The curiosity of a young sea lion takes her on an exciting adventure in this story that combines nature photography with a lesson in values. The story is followed by reading and language lessons.

Title: *Dancing with the Indians*
Producer: Live Oak Media
Series: Not Applicable
Year Released: 1993
Call Number: Easy Fiction
Length: 8 minutes
Price: $38.00
Reviewed in: *School Library Journal, Video Rating Guide for Libraries*
Grade Level: K–4
Keywords: Indians of North America; Native Americans; Seminole Indians

Based on the book by Angela Shelf Medearis, with illustrations by Samuel Byrd, the video depicts a young black girl's recounting of her family's annual visit to and participation in the ceremonies of the Seminole tribe that, during the Civil War some seventy years earlier, had given sanctuary to her grandfather, an escaped slave. Includes teacher's guide.

Title: *Decimals to Be Exact, Part One*
Producer: Allied Video
Series: Assistant Professor
Year Released: 1993
Call Number: 513.2
Length: 20 minutes
Price: $30.00
Reviewed in: *School Library Journal, Video Rating Guide for Libraries*
Grade Level: 4–6
Keywords: Decimals; Mathematics

This video describes the functions of the decimal point, extends place value to the right of the decimal point, and explains how to read and write decimals correctly. Includes book list.

Title: *Digital Environment, The*
Producer: California Academy of Sciences/Video Project
Series: Kids from CAOS
Year Released: 1995
Call Number: 004.16
Length: 32 minutes
Price: $60.00
Reviewed in: *Booklist, School Library Journal*
Grade Level: 6
Keywords: Computers; Technology

This three-parter looks at how computers and other technologies are helping us better understand and preserve our planet—and re-create the past. "Mission to Planet Earth" profiles astronauts and students who teamed up using radar and computers to help assess the endangered habitat of the Ruwandan gorilla. "Digital Dinosaurs" reveals how scientists and computer artists worked together to create the perfect raptor for the *Jurassic Park* movie. "Visualizing the Environment" shows how computer experts create amazing 3–D effects to demonstrate the workings of our planet and our environment. Includes teacher's guide.

Title: *Dingles, The*
Producer: National Film Board of Canada/Bullfrog Films
Series: Not Applicable
Year Released: 1989
Call Number: Easy Fiction
Length: 8 minutes
Price: $145.00
Reviewed in: *Video Rating Guide for Libraries*
Grade Level: PreK–4
Keywords: Crisis; Literature; Safety; Storms

Les Dew has made an animated adaptation of Helen Levchuk's book about a caring, grandmotherly figure, Doris Dingle, and her three cats. Suddenly a ferocious storm bursts violently into the family's life. Includes study guide.

Title: *Dinosaurs: Lessons from Bones*
Producer: Double Diamond Corporation/American School
 Publishers
Series: Not Applicable
Year Released: 1991
Call Number: 567.9
Length: 25 minutes
Price: $138.00
Reviewed in: *Booklist, Video Rating Guide for Libraries*
Grade Level: 3–6
Keywords: Dinosaurs; Science—Earth

This two-part, live-action video takes students on site to Colorado
for an exploration of the process of examining fossils. Students learn
what a fossil is, how it is formed, and how it is removed from a
site.

Title: *Do the Alphabet*
Producer: Children's Television Workshop/Sony Wonder
Series: My Sesame Street
Year Released: 1995
Call Number: 372.4
Length: 45 minutes
Price: $13.00
Reviewed in: *School Library Journal*
Grade Level: PreK–1
Keywords: Alphabet Skills; Early Childhood

Join Big Bird, Kermit, Ernie, Bert, Cookie Monster, and the gang as
they help Baby Bear learn the alphabet. Includes a variety of Sesame
Street alphabet songs.

Title: *Dog*
Producer: BBC Wildvision, BBC Lionheart TV, Dorling Kindersley
 Vision in association with Oregon Public Broadcasting/Dorling
 Kindersley/Houghton Mifflin
Series: Eyewitness Video
Year Released: 1995
Call Number: 636.7
Length: 35 minutes
Price: $13.00
Reviewed in: *Booklist, School Library Journal*

Grade Level: PreK–6
Keywords: Animals; Dogs

Viewers will journey into a three-dimensional "virtual museum" where live-action, wildlife photography creates the sensation of being there. This program presents a view of the marvels and mysteries of the natural world. Also included is behind-the-scenes, "making of the series" footage. Narrated by Martin Sheen.

Title: *Dog and His Boy, A*
Producer: Pyramid Film and Video
Series: Not Applicable
Year Released: 1993
Call Number: Easy Fiction
Length: 30 minutes
Price: $225.00
Reviewed in: *Booklist, Video Rating Guide for Libraries*
Grade Level: 1–4
Keywords: Imagination; Language Arts

Without a word of dialogue, this drama depicts how a young boy's ho-hum day is transformed through the awakening of his imagination. With the help of a friendly dog and some simple props, he becomes Robin Hood, an Old West gunslinger, and a swashbuckling finder of buried treasure. He returns to reality with his own priceless treasures: a new friend and the knowledge of the limitless power of his imagination. Includes teacher's guide.

Title: *Dr. Seuss's ABC*
Producer: Praxis Media/Random House Home Video
Series: Dr. Seuss's Beginner Book Videos
Year Released: 1989
Call Number: Easy Fiction
Length: 30 minutes
Price: $10.00
Reviewed in: *Video Rating Guide for Libraries*
Grade Level: 1–4
Keywords: Alphabet Skills; Early Childhood

The zaniest alphabet ever! Only Dr. Seuss could illustrate an alphabet with such imaginative and descriptive characters. Also includes two more Dr. Seuss titles: "I Can Read with My Eyes Shut!" and "Mr. Brown Can Moo! Can You?"

Title: *Dr. Zed's Brilliant Science Activities*
Producer: Children's Group
Series: Not Applicable
Year Released: 1994
Call Number: 507.8
Length: 30 minutes
Price: $10.00
Reviewed in: *School Library Journal*
Grade Level: 2–6
Keywords: Experiments; Science

Follow Dr. Zed through the world of science. See experiments you can do at home using everyday materials. Build your own bugsucker and create your own molecular art.

Title: *Dragonfly*
Producer: TVOntario
Series: Nature Watch
Year Released: 1989
Call Number: 595.7
Length: 25 minutes
Price: $49.00
Reviewed in: *Video Rating Guide for Libraries*
Grade Level: 2–6
Keywords: Dragonfly; Life Cycle; Science—Life

Viewers follow the life cycle of the dragonfly, and learn about its habitat and unique characteristics. One of the oldest winged insects on earth, the dragonfly's basic design has not changed in 300 million years. Teacher's guide available for purchase.

Title: *Drawing*
Producer: NBT Enterprises/Rainbow Educational Media
Series: Art Start
Year Released: 1995
Call Number: 743
Length: 20 minutes
Price: $79.00
Reviewed in: *School Library Journal*
Grade Level: 4–6
Keywords: Art; Drawing

The focus is on observation skills and on developing the ability to reduce images to either straight or curved lines for basic contour drawing.

Title: *Durwin's World*
Producer: Lucerne Media
Series: Not Applicable
Year Released: 1994
Call Number: 398.2
Length: 24 minutes
Price: $149.00
Reviewed in: *School Library Journal*
Grade Level: 1–3
Keywords: Folk Tales; Literature

Durwin the dragon reads three folktales: Native American, Dutch, and English.

Title: *Early Settlers*
Producer: Schlessinger Video Productions/Library Video Company
Series: American History for Children
Year Released: 1996
Call Number: 978
Length: 25 minutes
Price: $30.00
Reviewed in: *Booklist*
Grade Level: 1–5
Keywords: Pilgrims; Social Studies

Explains the passage of the Mayflower, the Pilgrims, Plymouth Rock, the Mayflower Compact, Squanto and the first Thanksgiving, and life in colonial Williamsburg.

Title: *Earthquakes: Our Restless Planet*
Producer: Rainbow Educational Media
Series: Not Applicable
Year Released: 1995
Call Number: 551.2
Length: 22 minutes
Price: $99.00
Reviewed in: *Booklist, School Library Journal*

Grade Level: 5–6
Keywords: Earthquakes; Science—Earth

The destruction created by earthquakes is a reminder that our planet is in a constant state of change. In this program students see how earthquakes are triggered by movements in the great plates that form a shell around our Earth and learn related terms.

Title: *Easter Egg Farm, The*
Producer: Live Oak Media
Series: Not Applicable
Year Released: 1995
Call Number: Easy Fiction
Length: 10 minutes
Price: $38.00
Reviewed in: *Booklist*
Grade Level: PreK–3
Keywords: Easter; Holidays; Literature

The video is based on the book by Mary Jane Auch, in which Pauline the Hen is perplexed by her inability to lay eggs. She becomes even more perplexed when her most concentrated efforts produce eggs with images on their shells of objects she was looking at when she was concentrating. Although the eggs prove just the ticket for Easter, they become even more interesting when they hatch. Includes teacher's guide.

Title: *Eco-Rap: Voices from the Hood*
Producer: Tides Foundation/Video Project
Series: Not Applicable
Year Released: 1994
Call Number: 363.72
Length: 40 minutes
Price: $60.00
Reviewed in: *Booklist, School Library Journal*
Grade Level: 6
Keywords: Ecology; Environmental Concerns

This video follows a multiethnic group of young people as they learn about local environmental hazards and express their concerns using the urban poetry of rap music. Environmental experts take them on "toxic tours" to see the hazards in their communities. Includes study guide.

Title: *Electing a President: The Process*
Producer: Cochran Communications
Series: Our Federal Government
Year Released: 1993
Call Number: 324.6
Length: 22 minutes
Price: $99.00
Reviewed in: *The Book Report, Booklist, School Library Journal, Video Rating Guide for Libraries*
Grade Level: 5–8
Keywords: Elections; Presidents; Social Studies

Focusing on presidential elections, this program includes information about presidential politics relating to elections, primaries, conventions, and campaigns. Coverage includes examples of past elections as well as changes in election campaigning over the years. Includes teacher's guide.

Title: *Electricity and Electrical Safety*
Producer: Bennett Marine Video
Series: Tell Me Why, Vol. 22
Year Released: 1991
Call Number: 537
Length: 30 minutes
Price: $20.00
Reviewed in: *Video Rating Guide for Libraries*
Grade Level: 3–6
Keywords: Electricity; Science—Physical

This video encyclopedia answers questions about electricity. The video is divided into short segments about a variety of topics relating to electricity.

Title: *Emperor's New Clothes, The*
Producer: Hanna-Barbera Home Video
Series: Timeless Tales from Hallmark
Year Released: 1990
Call Number: 398.2
Length: 30 minutes
Price: $95.00
Reviewed in: *Video Rating Guide for Libraries*

Grade Level: K–6
Keywords: Fairy Tales; Literature; Values

This is a live-action dramatization of one of Hans Christian Andersen's best-known and most popular tales. Of moral and symbolic significance, it involves a king who has questionable values.

Title: *Eureeka's Castle: Sing Along with Eureeka*
Producer: Baker and Taylor
Series: Nickelodeon Jr.
Year Released: 1995
Call Number: 782.42
Length: 30 minutes
Price: $13.00
Reviewed in: *Booklist*
Grade Level: PreK–1
Keywords: Friendship; Music; Values

Designed for kids to learn through play, dance, and sing-along fun, this program blends live-action characters and puppets who teach about friendship and values in a world full of discovery.

Title: *European Folktales, Vol. 10*
Producer: Halas and Batchelor/AIMS Media
Series: European Folktales
Year Released: 1993
Call Number: 398.2
Length: 35 minutes
Price: $50.00
Reviewed in: *Video Rating Guide for Libraries*
Grade Level: K–4
Keywords: Europe; Folk Tales; Literature

The animated program includes the stories "The Ungrateful Snake," "The Leaves and the Roots," and "Prince Phoenix." Includes study guide.

Title: *Evening Things Out: Understanding Averages*
Producer: Children's Television Workshop/PBS Video
Series: Math Talk
Year Released: 1995

Call Number: 513.2
Length: 15 minutes
Price: $40.00
Reviewed in: *School Library Journal*
Grade Level: 4–6
Keywords: Mathematics; Number Sense

Cartoon characters, music videos, quiz shows, carnival games, and soap operas all work together to teach mathematics. Includes teacher's guide.

Title: *Every Stone Has a Story*
Producer: National Geographic Society Educational Services
Series: Not Applicable
Year Released: 1995
Call Number: 549
Length: 20 minutes
Price: $79.00
Reviewed in: *School Library Journal*
Grade Level: 4–6
Keywords: Minerals; Rocks; Science—Earth

Join scientist and rock hound Rolf Johnson as he examines rocks and leads students in experiments to determine the content and structure of rocks, minerals, and crystals. Includes teacher's guide.

Title: *Everything Grows*
Producer: Crystalroe Productions/DK Publishing
Series: Hullaballoo
Year Released: 1995
Call Number: 372
Length: 30 minutes
Price: $10.00
Reviewed in: *School Library Journal*
Grade Level: PreK–1
Keywords: Animals; Early Childhood; Growth

This program combines animation, puppetry, games, and songs to teach children about the growth of animals and humans.

Title: *Exploring Our Solar System*
Producer: AIMS Media
Series: Not Applicable
Year Released: 1989
Call Number: 523.2
Length: 15 minutes
Price: $103.00
Reviewed in: *Video Rating Guide for Libraries*
Grade Level: 4–6
Keywords: Science—Space; Solar System; Space

This program combines live-action photography, footage from space, artwork, and three-dimensional models to present an introduction to the solar system.

Title: *Fall Brings Changes*
Producer: Churchill Media
Series: Not Applicable
Year Released: 1991
Call Number: 525
Length: 12 minutes
Price: $80.00
Reviewed in: *Video Rating Guide for Libraries*
Grade Level: K–4
Keywords: Fall; Seasons

A musical of a 1961 production about fall, featuring songs, new scenes of Halloween and Thanksgiving, and scenes of fall colors. Students learn what the cold weather brings from descriptions and drawings by children. No adult narration.

Title: *Ferret Husbandry*
Producer: Instructional Video
Series: Not Applicable
Year Released: 1995
Call Number: 599.74
Length: 12 minutes
Price: $24.50
Reviewed in: *Booklist*
Grade Level: 4–6
Keywords: Animals; Ferrets; Pets

A concise and thorough review of basic ferret husbandry, this video is designed to answer the most common questions and concerns.

Title: *Fiber*
Producer: NBT Enterprises/Rainbow Educational Media
Series: Art Start
Year Released: 1995
Call Number: 702
Length: 20 minutes
Price: $79.00
Reviewed in: *Booklist, School Library Journal*
Grade Level: 4–6
Keywords: Art; Fiber

The difference between art and craft is explored in this lesson. Students work as craftsmen, learning different knots and using two to four strands of fiber on their projects.

Title: *Field Trip to the Oil Refinery*
Producer: AIMS Media
Series: Not Applicable
Year Released: 1994
Call Number: 333.79
Length: 17 minutes
Price: $100.00
Reviewed in: *School Library Journal*
Grade Level: 4–6
Keywords: Oil Production; Petroleum; Social Studies

Jason is preparing a book report on the many uses of petroleum when a picture of a dinosaur suddenly comes to life and explains to him how petroleum was originally formed millions of years ago. The friendly dinosaur takes Jason on an imaginary field trip to an oil refinery, where he learns how crude oil is transformed into fuels and petrochemicals. Includes guide.

Title: *Finding It Fast in the Library*
Producer: Cheshire Book Companions
Series: Not Applicable
Year Released: 1991

Call Number: 028.55
Length: 28 minutes
Price: $75.00
Reviewed in: *Booklist, School Library Journal, Video Rating Guide for Libraries*
Grade Level: 4–6
Keywords: Library Skills; Technology

This video is an overview of the library of the 1990s for upper elementary students.

Title: *Finding Your Way: Using Maps and Globes*
Producer: Rainbow Educational Media
Series: Not Applicable
Year Released: 1990
Call Number: 912
Length: 20 minutes
Price: $89.00
Reviewed in: *Media and Methods, School Library Journal, Science Books and Films, Video Rating Guide for Libraries*
Grade Level: 4–6
Keywords: Globes; Maps; Social Studies

Maps convey many different kinds of information. The program shows examples of the different types of maps, defines and explains related terms, and discusses key concepts. It also explains the differences between maps and globes, giving the advantages and disadvantages of each. Includes teacher's guide.

Title: *Fire and Rescue*
Producer: Focus Video Productions/Instructional Video, Inc.
Series: Not Applicable
Year Released: 1993
Call Number: 628.9
Length: 30 minutes
Price: $15.00
Reviewed in: *Video Librarian, Video Rating Guide for Libraries*
Grade Level: 1–6
Keywords: Fire; Fire Fighters; Safety

Fred Levine connects with a childhood fascination and also helps children know what may happen in a crisis.

Title: *Fire in the Forest*
Producer: United Learning
Series: Not Applicable
Year Released: 1994
Call Number: 978.7
Length: 12 minutes
Price: $80.00
Reviewed in: *Booklist*
Grade Level: 5–6
Keywords: Fire; Forest Fires; Safety; Yellowstone National Park

The program follows scientists in the field as they explore the role of forest fires in Yellowstone National Park's complex ecosystem. Includes teacher's guide, blackline masters.

Title: *Fire Safety: Hall of Flame*
Producer: Mazzarella Communications/AIMS Media
Series: Not Applicable
Year Released: 1991
Call Number: 363.3
Length: 12 minutes
Price: $100.00
Reviewed in: *School Library Journal, Video Rating Guide for Libraries*
Grade Level: K–6
Keywords: Fire; Museums; Safety

In this program, host Ashley Burns illustrates fire safety rules by taking young viewers on a guided tour of the Hall of Flame museum. He explains that fire can be a warm and cozy friend or a hazardous foe. Ashley uses the museum exhibits to demonstrate several important dos and don'ts.

Title: *First Ladies*
Producer: ABC News/MPI Home Video
Series: Not Applicable
Year Released: 1990
Call Number: 973
Length: 60 minutes
Price: $30.00
Reviewed in: *Video Rating Guide for Libraries*

Grade Level: 6
Keywords: First Ladies; Social Studies

In this history of First Ladies from the turn of the century, the viewer "meets" Eleanor Roosevelt, Lady Bird Johnson, Pat Nixon, Betty Ford, Nancy Reagan, Barbara Bush, and many more.

Title: *First Look at Birds, A*
Producer: Sno River Productions/AIMS Media
Series: A First Look At
Year Released: 1993
Call Number: 598
Length: 15 minutes
Price: $100.00
Reviewed in: *Video Rating Guide for Libraries*
Grade Level: K–3
Keywords: Birds; Science—Life

The video gives an introduction to the world of birds and the special features that make them unique creatures. The migration, breeding, communication, and feeding patterns of various species give viewers a look at birds as they live in their natural habitats. Includes teacher's guide.

Title: *First Look at Mammals, A*
Producer: AIMS Media
Series: A First Look At
Year Released: 1994
Call Number: 599
Length: 13 minutes
Price: $100.00
Reviewed in: *School Library Journal*
Grade Level: K–3
Keywords: Mammals; Science—Life

Mammals may live on land, in water, or fly through the air, but they all have some common characteristics. This program explores the common traits that set mammals apart from other animals: their warm body temperature, body hair, and the nursing of and caring for their young. Includes guide.

Title: *Fish*
Producer: BBC Wildvision, BBC Lionheart TV, Dorling Kindersley Vision in association with Oregon Public Broadcasting/Dorling Kindersley/Houghton Mifflin
Series: Eyewitness Video
Year Released: 1995
Call Number: 591
Length: 35 minutes
Price: $13.00
Reviewed in: *Booklist, School Library Journal*
Grade Level: PreK–6
Keywords: Fish; Science—Life

Viewers will journey into a three-dimensional "virtual museum" where wildlife footage creates the sensation of being there. This program presents a view of the marvels and mysteries of the natural world. Also includes behind-the-scenes, "making of the series" footage. Narrated by Martin Sheen.

Title: *Fish, Amphibians, and Reptiles*
Producer: United Learning
Series: Junior Zoologist
Year Released: 1992
Call Number: 597
Length: 16 minutes
Price: $55.00
Reviewed in: *Video Rating Guide for Libraries*
Grade Level: 1–4
Keywords: Amphibians; Animals; Fish; Reptiles

The unique characteristics of fish, amphibians, and reptiles are explored. The anatomy and life cycles of these animals are discussed and illustrated. Includes teacher's guide, blackline masters.

Title: *Fisherman and His Wife, The*
Producer: Rabbit Ear Productions/SVS, Inc.
Series: Rabbit Ears Storybook Classics
Year Released: 1989
Call Number: 398.2
Length: 30 minutes
Price: $20.00
Reviewed in: *Video Rating Guide for Libraries*

Grade Level: K–3
Keywords: Fairy Tales; Literature; Values

Narrated by Jodie Foster, this story from the Brothers Grimm tells of an enchanted flounder who can grant any wish imaginable. The fisherman would rather leave well enough alone, but his greedy wife wants more.

Title: *Flight*
Producer: Bennett Marine Video
Series: Tell Me Why, Vol. 19
Year Released: 1989
Call Number: 629.13
Length: 30 minutes
Price: $20.00
Reviewed in: *Video Rating Guide for Libraries*
Grade Level: 3–6
Keywords: Flight; Technology

This video encyclopedia answers questions about all aspects of flight: birds, planes, insects, the mechanics of mechanical flight, space programs, satellites, etc.

Title: *Flying, Trying, and Honking Around*
Producer: National Geographic Society Educational Services
Series: GeoKids
Year Released: 1994
Call Number: 629.133
Length: 33 minutes
Price: $15.00
Reviewed in: *Booklist*
Grade Level: PreK–1
Keywords: Animals; Flight

Ever wish you could fly? Sunny Honey-Possum wants to, Bobby Bushbaby wants to help, and Balzac de Chameleon knows just the feathery creatures to tell them about.

Title: *Focus on Friendship*
Producer: Bronson Films/AIMS Media
Series: Ethics and Values

Year Released: 1992
Call Number: 177.6
Length: 17 minutes
Price: $150.00
Reviewed in: *Video Rating Guide for Libraries*
Grade Level: K–8
Keywords: Behavior; Friendship

Loyalty, trust, sharing, and understanding are discussed. The frustration, conflict, and disappointment that may be encountered with friends are also brought to light.

Title: *Focus on Honesty*
Producer: Bronson Films/AIMS Media
Series: Ethics and Values
Year Released: 1992
Call Number: 177.9
Length: 17 minutes
Price: $150.00
Reviewed in: *Video Rating Guide for Libraries*
Grade Level: K–6
Keywords: Behavior; Honesty; Values

This video addresses honesty and its relation to trust and self-esteem. The fact that dishonesty requires a conscious choice is emphasized.

Title: *Focus on Responsibility*
Producer: Bronson Films/AIMS Media
Series: Ethics and Values
Year Released: 1992
Call Number: 177.9
Length: 17 minutes
Price: $150.00
Reviewed in: *Video Rating Guide for Libraries*
Grade Level: K–6
Keywords: Behavior; Responsibility

The ideas of personal, family, and social responsibility are discussed. The program stresses the benefits of discipline, and shows that being responsible brings great personal rewards.

Title: *Food*
Producer: TVOntario/Films for the Humanities and Sciences
Series: Zardip's Search for Healthy Wellness
Year Released: 1990
Call Number: 612
Length: 15 minutes
Price: $49.00
Reviewed in: *Video Rating Guide for Libraries*
Grade Level: 2–5
Keywords: Food; Health; Nutrition

Zardip develops a fondness for junk food, so the kids try to cure him by explaining the importance of proper nutrition and the four basic food groups. Teacher's guide available for purchase.

Title: *Food Chain* (AIMS)
Producer: AIMS Media
Series: Not Applicable
Year Released: 1992
Call Number: 574.5
Length: 20 minutes
Price: $103.00
Reviewed in: *School Library Journal*
Grade Level: 1–6
Keywords: Food Chain; Science—Life

This video illustrates how each part of a food chain depends on and nourishes other parts, starting with single-celled algae and ending with humans.

Title: *Food Chain* (NGS)
Producer: National Geographic Society Educational Services
Series: On Nature's Trail
Year Released: 1995
Call Number: 574.5
Length: 23 minutes
Price: $99.00
Reviewed in: *Booklist*
Grade Level: 1–3
Keywords: Food Chain; Science—Life

A foursome discovers how neighborhood creatures find food and learns how local food chains may connect with others far away.

Using their imaginations, the explorers travel from forest treetops to the deep, cold waters of Alaska to the steaming Okefenokee Swamp, tracing a web of food and life. Includes teacher's guide.

Title: *Food for Thought*
Producer: TVOntario/Journal Films
Series: Many Voices
Year Released: 1992
Call Number: 305.8
Length: 15 minutes
Price: $49.00
Reviewed in: *Video Rating Guide for Libraries*
Grade Level: 4–6
Keywords: Holidays; Islamic Religion; Multicultural

Isa worries about how others will react when she practices the traditions of her Muslim faith and fasts during Ramadan. When her friend Ashley makes light of her fasting, Isa feels isolated. Students learn some aspects and differences of Islamic religion. Teacher's guide available for purchase.

Title: *Fool of the World and the Flying Ship, The*
Producer: Cosgrave Hall Productions/Churchill Media
Series: None
Year Released: 1992
Call Number: 398.2
Length: 54 minutes
Price: $100.00
Reviewed in: *School Library Journal, Video Rating Guide for Libraries*
Grade Level: 1–6
Keywords: Folk Tales; Literature; Russia

An animated Russian folktale. Magically gifted with a flying ship of sparkling ice, a peasant boy and his friends journey to the czar's palace to complete three impossible tasks, and in doing so prove that even the most humble of people can defeat power and greed.

Title: *Formation of Continents and Mountains*
Producer: United Learning
Series: Not Applicable
Year Released: 1990
Call Number: 551.1
Length: 2 videos, 10 minutes each
Price: $135.00
Reviewed in: *Media and Methods, Video Rating Guide for Libraries*
Grade Level: 5–6
Keywords: Geology; Science—Earth

This two-part introduction to geology looks at the diversity of our planet's surface, its internal structure, definitions of geology, and historical developments. It also covers mountains, volcanoes, and earthquakes. Includes teacher's guide, blackline masters.

Title: *Fractions and All Their Parts, 1*
Producer: Allied Video
Series: Assistant Professor
Year Released: 1993
Call Number: 513.2
Length: 23 minutes
Price: $30.00
Reviewed in: *Video Rating Guide for Libraries*
Grade Level: 4–6
Keywords: Fractions; Mathematics

This video defines fractions and presents everyday examples. It illustrates numerator and denominator, and demonstrates how to find the fraction of a whole or a set. Includes book list.

Title: *Fractions and All Their Parts, 2*
Producer: Allied Video
Series: Assistant Professor
Year Released: 1993
Call Number: 513.2
Length: 23 minutes
Price: $30.00
Reviewed in: *School Library Journal, Video Rating Guide for Libraries*
Grade Level: 4–6
Keywords: Fractions; Mathematics

This video defines equivalent fractions and then builds on the understanding to explain simplifying fractions. It uses memorable examples of simple and improper fractions, and demonstrates how improper fractions are renamed as mixed numbers. Includes book list.

Title: *Fractions and All Their Parts, 3*
Producer: Allied Video
Series: Assistant Professor
Year Released: 1993
Call Number: 513.2
Length: 23 minutes
Price: $30.00
Reviewed in: *School Library Journal, Video Rating Guide for Libraries*
Grade Level: 4–6
Keywords: Fractions; Mathematics

Students see how to add and subtract fractions with the same denominator and with different denominators, and how to add and subtract mixed numbers. Includes book list.

Title: *Fractions: Multiplication and Division*
Producer: Educational Video Resources
Series: Basic Mathematical Skills
Year Released: 1993
Call Number: 513.2
Length: 28 minutes
Price: $50.00
Reviewed in: *Library Journal, Video Rating Guide for Libraries*
Grade Level: 5–6
Keywords: Mathematics; Multiplication

Teacher Elayne Gay presents definitions, problems, and real-life examples of the multiplication and division of fractions.

Title: *From East to West: The Asian-American Experience*
Producer: Video Dialog
Series: Multicultural History
Year Released: 1993

Call Number: 305.895
Length: 24 minutes
Price: $89.00
Reviewed in: *School Library Journal*
Grade Level: 4–6
Keywords: Asian Americans; Multicultural

Describes the historical reasons for Asian Americans leaving their native lands and settling in the United States. Key concepts relating to the migration, struggle, and assimilation into the American mainstream are examined. Asian contributions to American culture in art, music, clothing, cuisine, and architecture are reflected throughout the program. Includes teacher's guide.

Title: *Frosty Returns*
Producer: Bill Melendez Productions/Lucerne Media
Series: Christmas Classics
Year Released: 1995
Call Number: Easy Fiction
Length: 25 minutes
Price: $195.00
Reviewed in: *School Library Journal*
Grade Level: PreK–3
Keywords: Environmental Concerns; Snow

A greedy tycoon arrives in Beansboro selling an aerosol spray that removes snow. The townspeople think it's a great idea. But with the help of a little girl and boy, Frosty enlightens the folks about the wonders of snow and the importance of protecting the environment. Jonathan Winters narrates and John Goodman is the voice of Frosty.

Title: *Galimoto*
Producer: Reading Adventures
Series: Friends and Neighbors Multicultural Story Videos
Year Released: 1993
Call Number: Easy Ficiton
Length: 9 minutes
Price: $45.00
Reviewed in: *School Library Journal, Video Rating Guide for Libraries*
Grade Level: K–4
Keywords: Africa; Literature; Multicultural; Toy-making

Karen Lynn Williams's book is brought to video. Kondi, a seven-year-old African boy, decides to make a galimoto—a toy vehicle—out of scraps of wire. Words and watercolors capture the essence of life in a contemporary African village.

Title: *Gangs: Decisions and Options*
Producer: United Learning
Series: What about Gangs?
Year Released: 1993
Call Number: 158.1
Length: 18 minutes
Price: $90.00
Reviewed in: *Video Rating Guide for Libraries*
Grade Level: 6
Keywords: Behavior; Gangs

This video shows how three youngsters from different backgrounds grapple with their decision to join a gang or reject membership. Issues of low self-esteem, dysfunctional families, and fears of gang violence and reprisal are covered. Includes teacher's guide.

Title: *Garbage Day!*
Producer: ChildVision Educational Films
Series: Not Applicable
Year Released: 1994
Call Number: 363.7
Length: 25 minutes
Price: $15.00
Reviewed in: *Booklist, School Library Journal, Video Business*
Grade Level: PreK–3
Keywords: Ecology; Garbage

Join garbageman Gus as he takes Billy and his Dad on an excursion through the world of garbage. They see the automated machinery used to collect trash from residential neighborhoods and dumpster sites, along with landfills and recycling centers and the enormous equipment used to process everyday trash.

Title: *George Washington Carver*
Producer: Schlessinger Video Productions
Series: Black Americans of Achievement Video Collection 1
Year Released: 1992
Call Number: Biography
Length: 30 minutes
Price: $40.00
Reviewed in: *School Library Journal, Video Librarian, Video Rating Guide for Libraries*
Grade Level: 4–6
Keywords: African Americans; Biographies; Carver, George Washington

This video biography contains interviews with leading authorities on the subject's life, accompanied by archival footage, photographs, and period music. Topics include basic biographical information, the inspirational and motivational factors in his life, his message, and the significance of George Washington Carver in society today.

Title: *German Americans*
Producer: Schlessinger Video Productions
Series: Multicultural Peoples of North America
Year Released: 1993
Call Number: 305.8
Length: 30 minutes
Price: $40.00
Reviewed in: *Booklist, School Library Journal*
Grade Level: 4–6
Keywords: German Americans; Multicultural

Celebrate the cultural heritage of German Americans by tracing the history of their emigration to North America, the unique traditions they brought, and who they are today. A three-generation portrait is provided, with the older generation describing their motivations for emigrating and the younger generation describing the importance of cultural identity, how it is maintained, and how it changes.

Title: *Germs*
Producer: TVOntario/Films for the Humanities and Sciences
Series: Zardip's Search for Healthy Wellness
Year Released: 1990
Call Number: 616.9

Length: 15 minutes
Price: $49.00
Reviewed in: *Video Rating Guide for Libraries*
Grade Level: 2–5
Keywords: Germs; Health

The importance of cleanliness is emphasized when Zardip discovers that he is not well equipped to fight off nasty earthly germs of human beings. Teacher's guide available for purchase.

Title: *Getting to Know William Steig*
Producer: Weston Woods
Series: Not Applicable
Year Released: 1995
Call Number: Biography
Length: 20 minutes
Price: $30.00
Reviewed in: *Booklist*
Grade Level: 3–6
Keywords: Authors; Biographies; Steig, William

In a visit to the former Connecticut home of author and illustrator William Steig, Steig discusses his childhood, the influence of his parents, and his relationship with his wife and best friend, Jeane.

Title: *Ghost Story*
Producer: Children's Television Workshop/GPN
Series: GhostWriter
Year Released: 1993
Call Number: 428
Length: 150 minutes
Price: $50.00
Reviewed in: *Booklist*
Grade Level: 3–6
Keywords: Language Arts; Mystery

In this video the GhostWriter team forms and starts working on its first case, a series of backpack thefts. They solve it in five episodes, decoding secret messages, organizing ideas, and carefully interpreting text. Includes guide.

Title: *Gingerbread Man, The*
Producer: Live Oak Media
Series: Not Applicable
Year Released: 1994
Call Number: Easy Fiction
Length: 8 minutes
Price: $38.00
Reviewed in: *School Library Journal*
Grade Level: PreK–2
Keywords: Fairy Tales; Literature

From the book by Eric A. Kimmel, with illustrations by Megan Lloyd, this is the classic tale of the freshly baked gingerbread man who sets out to make his way in the world. Convinced that he can outrun any danger that may confront him, he fails to appreciate that a very fast runner is no match for a very sly fox. Includes teacher's guide.

Title: *Giraffes and How They Live*
Producer: ABC/Kane Productions/AIMS Media
Series: Animals and How They Live/ Wildlife Tales
Year Released: 1994
Call Number: 599.74
Length: 19 minutes
Price: $100.00
Reviewed in: *School Library Journal*
Grade Level: 4–6
Keywords: Africa; Giraffes

A lofty view of Africa's Serengeti is the giraffe's greatest asset, yet it is only one attribute of the tallest animal on earth. This film examines the giraffe's world: its predators, its traveling companions, and its daily struggle to survive. Includes guide.

Title: *Girl's World, A*
Producer: Laurie Hepburn Productions
Series: Not Applicable
Year Released: 1995
Call Number: 331.7
Length: 45 minutes
Price: $20.00
Reviewed in: *Booklist*

Grade Level: 2–6
Keywords: Artists; Careers; Pilots; Veterinarians

This program is designed to introduce young girls to future career possibilities through discussions and on-the-job tours with three career women: a real-life veterinarian, artist, and pilot, each of whom explains her work, tells how she became inspired, and answers questions about her occupation. Parent's Choice Award Winner.

Title: *Glaciers: Nature's Conveyor Belt*
Producer: United Learning
Series: Not Applicable
Year Released: 1994
Call Number: 551.3
Length: 15 minutes
Price: $90.00
Reviewed in: *Booklist*
Grade Level: 5–6
Keywords: Geology; Glaciers

Viewers will see and hear why the midwestern farmland is so fertile, why rocks are sculpted in various ways, and how the lochs of Scotland, the fjords of Norway, and the Great Lakes came into existence. Viewers will also go rafting through some of the glaciated areas of Alaska. Includes teacher's guide, blackline masters.

Title: *Goblin Mischief*
Producer: TVOntario/GPN
Series: Magic Library
Year Released: 1990
Call Number: Easy Fiction
Length: 15 minutes
Price: $49.00
Reviewed in: *Video Rating Guide for Libraries*
Grade Level: 2–3
Keywords: Literature; Mice; Sequencing

The mice come to the Magic Library wearing shirts with words on them, and an evil goblin is so envious that he uses a scheme found in "Bill and the Google-eyed Goblins" (by Alice Shertle) to try to steal one for himself. But the mice match the goblin's reading skills to outsmart him. Guide available for purchase.

Title: *Good Thing about Spots, A*
Producer: Alan Sloan, Inc./AIMS Media
Series: Wild World
Year Released: 1989
Call Number: 599.74
Length: 15 minutes
Price: $50.00
Reviewed in: *Video Rating Guide for Libraries*
Grade Level: K–6
Keywords: Language Arts; Leopards

This is an adventure story about a shy leopard cub learning to appreciate his spots. The lesson in values is combined with nature photography. The story is followed by reading and language lessons.

Title: *Grandpa Worked on the Railroad*
Producer: Fast Forward Video/Ingram Library Services
Series: Not Applicable
Year Released: 1994
Call Number: 629
Length: 30 minutes
Price: $15.00
Reviewed in: *Booklist*
Grade Level: K–3
Keywords: Careers; Railroads

The video contains original songs, play activities, games, stories, demonstrations by engine crews, and reenactments of railroading history and fable.

Title: *Great Kapok Tree, The*
Producer: SRA/McGraw-Hill
Series: Children's Literature
Year Released: 1995
Call Number: Easy Fiction
Length: 10 minutes
Price: $42.00
Reviewed in: *School Library Journal*
Grade Level: K–3
Keywords: Ecology; Rain Forest; South America; Trees

This animated version of Lynne Cherry's "The Great Kapok Tree: A Tale of the Amazon Rain Forest" features a beautiful story and lush paintings of the diversity of life in the rain forest. Includes teacher's guide.

Title: *Great Snake*
Producer: Churchill Media
Series: Not Applicable
Year Released: 1991
Call Number: 398.2
Length: 6 minutes
Price: $60.00
Reviewed in: *School Library Journal, Video Rating Guide for Libraries*
Grade Level: K–7
Keywords: Africa; Fables; Literature

From Matabeleland in Zimbabwe comes this animated tale of a small boy who outwits a great snake to become chief of his tribe. Includes teacher's guide.

Title: *Growing Pains*
Producer: Cheshire Book Companions
Series: Not Applicable
Year Released: 1992
Call Number: Fiction
Length: 22 minutes
Price: $75.00
Reviewed in: *Video Rating Guide for Libraries*
Grade Level: 4–6
Keywords: Literature; Reading

The video reviews themes in classic titles that relate to the real-life experiences of the middle-grade student. Titles discussed include: "Summer of the Swans," "Slake's Limbo," "The Cat Ate My Gymsuit," "The Great Gilly Hopkins," "It's Like This, Cat," "Harriet the Spy," and others. Serves as an introduction to young adult reading.

Title: *Growing Up! For Boys*
Producer: Marsh Media
Series: Growing Up!
Year Released: 1994
Call Number: 612.6
Length: 18 minutes
Price: $60.00
Reviewed in: *Booklist*
Grade Level: 5–6
Keywords: Health; Human Body; Puberty

This takes a look at the basics of male anatomy and development. The narrator—a musician at work in his studio—provides useful advice on health, hygiene, and good grooming and points to sources of reliable information during the confusing times of puberty.

Title: *Growing Up! For Girls*
Producer: Marsh Media
Series: Growing Up!
Year Released: 1994
Call Number: 612.6
Length: 19 minutes
Price: $60.00
Reviewed in: *Booklist*
Grade Level: 5–6
Keywords: Health; Human Body; Puberty

Information about the female reproductive system, the emotional and physical transformations of puberty, and the importance of good health and hygiene is geared toward encouraging a positive body image and sense of personal worth.

Title: *Gullah Gullah Island: Sing Along with Binyah Binyah*
Producer: Baker and Taylor/Sony Wonder
Series: Nickelodeon Jr.
Year Released: 1995
Call Number: 782.42
Length: 30 minutes
Price: $13.00

Reviewed in: *Booklist, Children's Video Report, School Library Journal*
Grade Level: PreK–1
Keywords: Friendship; Music; Values

Designed for kids to learn through play, dance, and sing-along fun, this program blends live-action characters and puppets who teach about friendship and values in a world full of discovery.

Title: *Hailstones and Halibut Bones*
Producer: Pied Piper/AIMS Media
Series: Not Applicable
Year Released: 1993
Call Number: 811
Length: 16 minutes
Price: $50.00
Reviewed in: *School Library Journal*
Grade Level: 4–6
Keywords: Literature; Poetry

Based on the book by Mary O'Neill, this video takes viewers on a journey into the world of color with this interpretation of Mary O'Neill's poetry.

Title: *Hair Scare*
Producer: TVOntario/Journal Films
Series: Many Voices
Year Released: 1992
Call Number: 305.8
Length: 15 minutes
Price: $49.00
Reviewed in: *Video Rating Guide for Libraries*
Grade Level: 4–6
Keywords: Culture; Multicultural; Sikh Culture

Amar, a Sikh boy, is harassed at his new school and turned away from a community pool for wearing a turban. Hoping to avoid further confrontation, he will not remove his turban even to dry his hair. Teacher's guide available for purchase.

Title: *Harriet Tubman*
Producer: Schlessinger Video Productions
Series: Black Americans of Achievement Video Collection 1
Year Released: 1992
Call Number: Biography
Length: 30 minutes
Price: $40.00
Reviewed in: *School Library Journal, Video Librarian, Video Rating Guide for Libraries*
Grade Level: 4–6
Keywords: African Americans; Biographies; Tubman, Harriet

This video biography contains interviews with leading authorities on the subject's life, accompanied by archival footage, photographs, and period music. Topics include basic biographical information, the inspirational and motivational factors in her life, her message, and the significance of Harriet Tubman in society today.

Title: *Harry and the Lady Next Door*
Producer: Barr Films
Series: Harry the Dog
Year Released: 1989
Call Number: Easy Fiction
Length: 20 minutes
Price: $100.00
Reviewed in: *Video Rating Guide for Libraries*
Grade Level: K–4
Keywords: Dogs; Literature

Harry, the lively white-and-black border collie, stars in this live-action adaptation of a book by Gene Zion. Harry likes most of his neighbors, except the opera singer who lives next door. The high-pitched noises hurt Harry's ears and he will try anything to get the Lady Next Door to stop singing. Find out what happens when Harry and his family attend a concert in the park where the Lady Next Door is singing.

Title: *Harry, the Dirty Dog*
Producer: Weston Woods
Series: Not Applicable
Year Released: 1997
Call Number: Easy Fiction

Length: 9 minutes
Price: $60
Reviewed in: *Booklist*
Grade Level: PreK–3
Keywords: Dogs; Humor—Literature; Language Arts

Adapted from the book by Gene Zion. Tells the story of Harry, a white dog with black spots, who runs away from home because he hates getting a bath. After many adventures and visits to dirty places, Harry returns home only to be recognized as a black dog with white spots.

Title: *Heat, Temperature and Energy*
Producer: Rainbow Educational Media
Series: Not Applicable
Year Released: 1995
Call Number: 536
Length: 23 minutes
Price: $89.00
Reviewed in: *Booklist, School Library Journal, Video Rating Guide for Libraries*
Grade Level: 4–6
Keywords: Energy; Science—Physical

Students learn that heat is a form of energy, that substances contain thermal energy, and that there is a molecular basis for such energy. They will also be made aware of the differences between heat and temperature, and that there are three basic ways heat is transferred. The importance of insulators in terms of energy conservation is also explored.

Title: *Heli-Kids: A Helicopter Adventure for Kids*
Producer: Heli-Kids/Video Information
Series: Not Applicable
Year Released: 1995
Call Number: 629.133
Length: 30 minutes
Price: $20.00
Reviewed in: *School Library Journal*
Grade Level: PreK–3
Keywords: Helicopters; Transportation

Children soar above the ocean, chase a moving train, and put out a forest fire when they experience the live-action excitement of flying in a helicopter.

Title: *Help Wanted*
Producer: TVOntario/Journal Films
Series: Mathica's Mathshop 1
Year Released: 1994
Call Number: 510
Length: 15 minutes
Price: $49.00
Reviewed in: *Video Rating Guide for Libraries*
Grade Level: K–1
Keywords: Estimating; Geometry; Mathematics

Mathica answers a help-wanted ad for "someone to solve problems," and finds herself in the math magician's Mathshop. A witch applies, too, but Mathica emerges the better problem solver and gets the job. This video covers the following math skills: estimation of numbers; counting by 2s, 5s, and 10s to 25; number facts of 7; and solids and their properties—cube, cone. Teacher's guide available for purchase.

Title: *Henry and Mudge in Puddle Trouble*
Producer: Random House/American School Publishers
Series: Not Applicable
Year Released: 1989
Call Number: Easy Fiction
Length: 11 minutes
Price: $43.00
Reviewed in: *Video Rating Guide for Libraries*
Grade Level: K–3
Keywords: Dogs; Literature

In this animated adaptation of book by Cynthia Rylant, springtime brings new adventures for these best friends as they encounter the first spring flower, a gigantic puddle, and a box of kittens.

Title: *Henry Wadsworth Longfellow*
Producer: SRA School Group
Series: Meet the Author
Year Released: 1993
Call Number: Biography
Length: 19 minutes
Price: $83.00
Reviewed in: *Video Rating Guide for Libraries*
Grade Level: 5–6
Keywords: Authors; Biographies; Longfellow, Henry Wadsworth

"Paul Revere's Ride" and other Longfellow poems offer an opportunity to combine social studies with language arts. This program shows how a quiet boy from Portland, Maine, became an international celebrity by telling the story of American history in stirring words.

Title: *Heritage of the Black West*
Producer: National Geographic Society Educational Services
Series: Not Applicable
Year Released: 1995
Call Number: 978
Length: 25 minutes
Price: $99.00
Reviewed in: *School Library Journal*
Grade Level: 4–6
Keywords: African Americans; U.S. History

As students visit with a modern-day cowboy and his family, viewers learn the story of black frontiersmen and women and their relationship with Native Americans, and about popular folk heroes, including buffalo soldiers. Includes teacher's guide.

Title: *Hiawatha*
Producer: Weston Woods Studios
Series: Not Applicable
Year Released: 1995
Call Number: 811
Length: 12 minutes
Price: $90.00

Reviewed in: *Booklist, School Library Journal*
Grade Level: K–4
Keywords: Literature; Native Americans; Poetry

Hiawatha's childhood is brought to life against a background of authentic Native American music in this excerpt from Longfellow's classic poem.

Title: *Hill of Fire*
Producer: GPN
Series: Reading Rainbow
Year Released: 1989
Call Number: Easy Fiction
Length: 30 minutes
Price: $44.00
Reviewed in: *Video Rating Guide for Libraries*
Grade Level: K–4
Keywords: Literature; Science—Earth; Volcanoes

Rumbling earthquakes, molten lava, fountains of fire—a volcano is born in a poor farmer's corn field. The story is narrated by Fernando Escandon, written by Thomas P. Lewis, and illustrated by Joan Sandlin. *Hill of Fire* is based on the true story of the eruption of Paricutin Volcano in Mexico. It also includes a scene of LeVar Burton perched 2,000 feet from a major eruption of Kilauea Volcano at Volcanoes National Park in Hawaii. Teacher's guide available.

Title: *Hip-Hop Kidz: Learn to Hip-Hop Dance*
Producer: M.A.D. Degrees Productions
Series: Not Applicable
Year Released: 1995
Call Number: 782.42
Length: 30 minutes
Price: $20.00
Reviewed in: *Booklist, School Library Journal*
Grade Level: 2–6
Keywords: Dance; Physical Education

Kids can learn the latest, hottest dance moves on this video that features kids instructing kids.

Title: *Holiday Facts and Fun: Halloween*
Producer: Colman Communications
Series: Holiday Facts and Fun
Year Released: 1993
Call Number: 394.2
Length: 12 minutes
Price: $70.00
Reviewed in: *Booklist, School Library Journal*
Grade Level: K–4
Keywords: Halloween; Holidays

Children learn how Halloween began and how, over hundreds of years, it developed into the fun-filled yet spooky holiday of today. Youngsters will find out why jack-o-lanterns are carved from pumpkins, and learn games to play and safety rules to follow. Includes teacher's guide.

Title: *Holiday Facts and Fun: Kwanzaa*
Producer: Rainbow Educational Media
Series: Holiday Facts and Fun
Year Released: 1994
Call Number: 394.2
Length: 10 minutes
Price: $70.00
Reviewed in: *Booklist, School Library Journal, Video Rating Guide for Libraries*
Grade Level: 1–3
Keywords: African Americans; Holidays; Kwanzaa

Kwanzaa, a holiday celebrated by African Americans in late December, is explained. The program shows Kwanzaa's founder, Dr. Maulana Kerenga, and tells why he began the holiday. The seven symbols, their significance, and the seven principles of Kwanzaa are covered. Viewers see a family celebrate Kwanzaa as the holiday unfolds over a seven-day period. Includes teacher's guide.

Title: *Holiday Facts and Fun: Martin Luther King Day*
Producer: Colman Communications
Series: Holiday Facts and Fun
Year Released: 1992
Call Number: 394.2
Length: 10 minutes

Price: $70.00
Reviewed in: *ALA Booklist, School Library Journal, Midwest Book Review, Video Rating Guide for Libraries*
Grade Level: 1–4
Keywords: African Americans; Biographies; Holidays; King, Martin Luther Jr.

This live-action video highlights the career of Dr. Martin Luther King Jr. and explains his contributions to the people of the United States and throughout the world. Martin Luther King Jr.'s first experience with prejudice, as a six-year-old child, is discussed, as are his early years in school. Dr. King's unwavering belief in nonviolence as the best way to solve human problems is given special attention. Viewers see congressional passage of Dr. King's birthday as a national holiday and are taken to joyous celebrations and programs that honor Dr. King. Includes teacher's guide.

Title: *Holiday Facts and Fun: Valentine's Day*
Producer: Colman Communications
Series: Holiday Facts and Fun
Year Released: 1993
Call Number: 394.2
Length: 10 minutes
Price: $70.00
Reviewed in: *School Library Journal, Video Rating Guide for Libraries*
Grade Level: K–4
Keywords: Holidays; Valentine's Day

Why do we send cards and flowers to loved ones on Valentine's Day? Who is Dan Cupid, and why does he shoot arrows at unsuspecting victims? Why is the red heart a symbol of love? These, and many other questions, are answered in this program. The program traces Valentine's Day back to ancient Rome and recounts the story of the person many believe was the first Valentine (there were fourteen in all)—a cleric who defied Roman law by marrying young soldiers about to be sent into battle. Includes teacher's guide.

Title: *Horses . . . Close Up and Very Personal*
Producer: Stage Fright Productions
Series: Not Applicable
Year Released: 1995

Call Number: 636.1
Length: 30 minutes
Price: $15.00
Reviewed in: *Booklist*
Grade Level: PreK–2
Keywords: Animals; Horses

Children meet such breeds as Appaloosas, Palominos, quarter horses, Arabians, draft horses, ponies, and more. Relying solely on visuals, sound effects, and minimal music, the program presents images of horses in their environment.

Title: *Horton Hatches the Egg*
Producer: Green Light Media/Random House Home Video
Series: Dr. Seuss Video Classics
Year Released: 1992
Call Number: Easy Ficiton
Length: 30 minutes
Price: $10.00
Reviewed in: *Video Rating Guide for Libraries*
Grade Level: K–3
Keywords: Animals; Elephants; Literature

Horton, a rhyming elephant, helps out Mayzie, the lazy bird, by sitting on her egg while she takes a vacation. Based on the book by Dr. Seuss.

Title: *How a Car Is Built*
Producer: Think Media
Series: How Do They Do That?
Year Released: 1995
Call Number: 629.222
Length: 30 minutes
Price: $15.00
Reviewed in: *Booklist*
Grade Level: 1–6
Keywords: Automobiles; Transportation

In this live-action video, IQ Parrot takes kids on location to show the manufacturing of the Ford Mustang from its start as a sheet of steel until it rolls off the nine-mile assembly line.

Title: *How Animals Survive*
Producer: AIMS Media
Series: Animal Life
Year Released: 1990
Call Number: 591.5
Length: 15 minutes
Price: $100.00
Reviewed in: *Video Rating Guide for Libraries*
Grade Level: 4–6
Keywords: Animals; Camouflage; Science—Life

This video shows the diverse methods of protection that have been developed throughout the varied species of the animal kingdom. Among the methods are the specialized uses of the five basic senses, camouflage, mimicry, hibernation, migration, species cooperation, "safety in numbers," and communication. Includes teacher's guide.

Title: *How Do You Do Your How Do You Dos?*
Producer: Swenson Green Productions
Series: Amazing Advantage for Kids
Year Released: 1994
Call Number: 395
Length: 20 minutes
Price: $15.00
Reviewed in: *Booklist, School Library Journal, Video Rating Guide for Libraries*
Grade Level: 1–6
Keywords: Behavior; Etiquette; Manners

This video teaches children lessons in manners and etiquette to help them feel confident and at ease in social situations. Explains proper introductions.

Title: *How Does the Land Build Up?*
Producer: Creative Adventure/United Learning
Series: Junior Geologist
Year Released: 1993
Call Number: 551
Length: 8 minutes
Price: $55.00

Reviewed in: *Video Rating Guide for Libraries*
Grade Level: 2–4
Keywords: Geology; Science—Earth

The focus is on the effects of plate tectonics and how forces in nature cause the land to rise. Segments addressed include: What is plate tectonics? What is a volcano? How are mountains made? and What causes an earthquake? Includes teacher's guide, blackline masters.

Title: *How Does the Land Wear Down?*
Producer: Creative Adventure/United Learning
Series: Junior Geologist
Year Released: 1993
Call Number: 551
Length: 9 minutes
Price: $55.00
Reviewed in: *Video Rating Guide for Libraries*
Grade Level: 2–4
Keywords: Geology; Science—Earth

This video illustrates and explains the effects of water, wind, and gravity on our planet's surface. Segments addressed include: How does moving water wear down the land? How does ice wear down the land? How does wind wear down the land? and What other forces can wear down the land? Includes teacher's guide, blackline masters.

Title: *How Things Work*
Producer: Bennett Marine Video
Series: Tell Me Why, Vol. 20
Year Released: 1990
Call Number: 620
Length: 30 minutes
Price: $20.00
Reviewed in: *Video Rating Guide for Libraries*
Grade Level: 3–6
Keywords: Science—Physical; Technology

This video encyclopedia answers questions about telescopes, television, seismographs, dams, refrigerators, engines, windmills, oil derricks, etc.

Title: *How to Chinese Jumprope*
Producer: MelAimee Productions/Instructional Video
Series: Not Applicable
Year Released: 1995
Call Number: 796.2
Length: 28 minutes
Price: $15.00
Reviewed in: *Booklist, School Library Journal, Video Librarian*
Grade Level: K–6
Keywords: Jumprope; Physical Education

Students learn how to do eleven jumprope games for three or four people. All games are shown step-by-step.

Title: *How to Make Your Own Great Video with Just a Camcorder*
Producer: Noodlehead Network/Film Ideas
Series: Not Applicable
Year Released: 1993
Call Number: 778.5
Length: 25 minutes
Price: $110.00
Reviewed in: *School Library Journal*
Grade Level: 3–6
Keywords: Technology; Theater; Video Production

From script development to acting to editing, kids continually offer their wit and insight, creating a video everyone can learn from and enjoy.

Title: *How to Use a Microscope*
Producer: United Learning
Series: Not Applicable
Year Released: 1989
Call Number: 502.8
Length: 20 minutes
Price: $95.00
Reviewed in: *Elementary School Library Collection, Video Rating Guide for Libraries*
Grade Level: 6
Keywords: Microscopes; Technology

Developed in the seventeenth century, the microscope opened up a totally new world of objects never before seen by humans. Since that time, advancements in this scientific instrument have resulted in a wide range of applications and explorations. Includes teacher's guide, blackline masters.

Title: *How We're Different and Alike*
Producer: Colman Communications Corp./Rainbow Educational Media
Series: Not Applicable
Year Released: 1994
Call Number: 158
Length: 10 minutes
Price: $70.00
Reviewed in: *School Library Journal, Video Rating Guide for Libraries*
Grade Level: 1–3
Keywords: Multicultural; Prejudice

Featuring music, animation, and live-action sequences, this program tells how and why all people are different and alike. Body shapes; colors of eyes, hair, and skin; likes and dislikes; mental and artistic differences—all are depicted as ways of making our world interesting and exciting. The program also shows that while many differences exist, people are also very much alike—all need love and attention, food and water, clothing and shelter. Sometimes the differences may cause anger or hatred, but the video concludes it's always better to see the similarities and work cooperatively. Includes teacher's guide.

Title: *Hummingbirds and How They Live*
Producer: ABC/Kane Productions/AIMS Media
Series: Animals and How They Live
Year Released: 1994
Call Number: 598.8
Length: 25 minutes
Price: $100.00
Reviewed in: *School Library Journal*
Grade Level: 4–6
Keywords: Birds; Hummingbirds; Science—Life

This show focuses on the ingenious methods by which the tiny hummingbird, a miniature high-performance machine, copes with its environment. In Belize—with the help of ultra-slow-motion photography—viewers are able to observe several species as they feed, establish territory, build nests, bathe, and fight off an attack by snakes. Includes teacher's guide.

Title: *Hungary: Between East and West*
Producer: Camera Q.
Series: Not Applicable
Year Released: 1989
Call Number: 943.9
Length: 17 minutes
Price: $90.00
Reviewed in: *School Library Journal, Video Rating Guide for Libraries*
Grade Level: 4–6
Keywords: Europe; Hungary; Social Studies

Students learn about the history and struggles for freedom and their profound impact on Hungary. They also explore the physical, cultural, and economic geographies of Hungary. Insights into the everyday lives of typical Hungarians and the attractions of Budapest are shown. Includes teacher's guide.

Title: *Hurricanes, Tornadoes, and Thunderstorms*
Producer: Peter Matulavich Productions/Rainbow Educational Media
Series: Not Applicable
Year Released: 1997
Call Number: 551.55
Length: 27 minutes
Price: $99.00
Reviewed in: *School Library Journal*
Grade Level: 4–6
Keywords: Science; Weather

The power of hurricanes, tornadoes, and thunderstorms is surveyed and the atmospheric conditions that cause them are examined.

Title: *Hurtful Words*
Producer: Film Ideas
Series: Life Lessons
Year Released: 1993
Call Number: 152.4
Length: 12 minutes
Price: $135.00
Reviewed in: *Childhood Education, Video Rating Guide for Libraries*
Grade Level: 1–4
Keywords: Behavior

A theme of thinking about what we say before we say it is maintained throughout this culturally diverse video as students learn the ways to "stop" and "think" in order to avoid using unkind actions or hurtful words. Includes teacher's guide.

Title: *I Am Joe's Hand*
Producer: Pyramid Film and Video
Series: I Am Joe
Year Released: 1990
Call Number: 612
Length: 20 minutes
Price: $245.00
Reviewed in: *Video Rating Guide for Libraries*
Grade Level: 3–6
Keywords: Hands; Health; Human Body

This program demonstrates the complex interaction of bones, ligaments, tendons, and muscles of the hand. Sports and on-the-job injuries, and basic first aid procedures for cuts and frostbite are demonstrated.

Title: *I Can Build!*
Producer: Can Too! Tapes
Series: Can Too
Year Released: 1994
Call Number: 690
Length: 25 minutes
Price: $15.00
Reviewed in: *Booklist, Publishers Weekly, School Library Journal*

Grade Level: PreK–4
Keywords: Construction; Sequencing; Technology

From designing to building, kids watch as a playhouse is constructed in this video using time-lapse photography and 3–D animation. Children learn how things are done and the important steps necessary to complete any task.

Title: *I Can Make Good Choices*
Producer: Sunburst Communications
Series: Not Applicable
Year Released: 1995
Call Number: 155.2
Length: 18 minutes
Price: $99.00
Reviewed in: *Booklist, School Library Journal*
Grade Level: 2–4
Keywords: Behavior; Self-esteem

Learning to make their own choices can boost children's self-esteem, but, like any other skill, making good decisions takes thought and practice. This program helps students learn to evaluate their options, predict outcomes, and accept the consequences of their choices. Two "You Make the Choice" scenarios provide opportunities for practice. Includes teacher's guide, worksheets.

Title: *I Dig Fossils: A Real Life Adventure for Children of All Ages*
Producer: Mazon Productions
Series: Not Applicable
Year Released: 1993
Call Number: 560
Length: 25 minutes
Price: $25.00
Reviewed in: *Booklist, Video Rating Guide for Libraries*
Grade Level: 1–6
Keywords: Fossils; Science—Earth

Teach students about the science of digging for fossils. The program shows a young student and his father as they excavate an abandoned coal mine. Students learn dozens of helpful hints about digging for fossils: the kinds of rocks to look for, where these rocks are likely to be found, and how to break the rocks open. Includes bibliography.

Title: *I Get So Mad!*
Producer: Sunburst Communications
Series: Not Applicable
Year Released: 1993
Call Number: 152.4
Length: 13 minutes
Price: $99.00
Reviewed in: *Video Rating Guide for Libraries*
Grade Level: K–2
Keywords: Anger; Behavior

When children get angry, their strong feelings can propel them into inappropriate or destructive behavior. This program makes students aware that anger is a natural emotion everyone experiences at times. It shows them that it's not the getting angry that counts, but what they decide to do about it. Ways to cope with anger are shown. Includes teacher's guide, student worksheets, audiocassette.

Title: *I Hate My Brother Harry*
Producer: Churchill Media
Series: Not Applicable
Year Released: 1994
Call Number: Easy Fiction
Length: 16 minutes
Price: $100.00
Reviewed in: *Booklist*
Grade Level: K–6
Keywords: Behavior; Brothers and Sisters; Families; Literature

From the book by Crescent Dragonwagon comes a live-action story about a little girl and her older brother, Harry. Harry teases her, tells her improbable stories about frogs in the green icing and snakes in the bed, but other times is as nice as can be. Does she really hate her brother Harry, or is it all a part of growing up together?

Title: *I Love Big Machines*
Producer: TM Books/Video
Series: I Love Toy Trains and Big Machines
Year Released: 1994
Call Number: 629.004
Length: 30 minutes
Price: $15.00

Reviewed in: *School Library Journal*
Grade Level: PreK–3
Keywords: Machines; Transportation

This video explains how things kids see everyday are made, how they work, and the role big machines play in the process—road construction, big cranes, tugboats, railroad bridges, hot-air balloons, and much more is explained. All mixed with music and humor.

Title: *I'll Fix Anthony*
Producer: Bernard Wilets Productions/AIMS Media
Series: Not Applicable
Year Released: 1990
Call Number: Easy Fiction
Length: 14 minutes
Price: $70.00
Reviewed in: *Video Rating Guide for Libraries*
Grade Level: 1–5
Keywords: Brothers and Sisters; Literature; Self-esteem

Based on the book by Judith Viorst, in this video Anthony, Nicholas's older brother, can read books but won't read them to Nicholas. Nicholas dreams of the day when he will have his revenge, when he is older just like Anthony . . . when he is six!

Title: *Ice Cream and Popsicles*
Producer: TVOntario/Films for the Humanities and Sciences
Series: Here's How
Year Released: 1991
Call Number: 637
Length: 10 minutes
Price: $49.00
Reviewed in: *Video Rating Guide for Libraries*
Grade Level: 1–3
Keywords: Ice Cream; Inventions; Technology

Kids learn about the "water ices" of the ancient Chinese. Then they make their own ice cream, and visit a plant that makes Popsicles and ice cream. Teacher's guide available for purchase.

Title: *In the Month of Kislev*
Producer: Paul Gagne/Weston Woods Studios
Series: Not Applicable
Year Released: 1994
Call Number: 394.2
Length: 13 minutes
Price: $90.00
Reviewed in: *Booklist, School Library Journal*
Grade Level: K–2
Keywords: Hanukkah; Holidays; Jewish Americans; Literature

A wealthy, arrogant merchant learns the true meaning of Hanukkah when he takes the family of a poor peddler to court for savoring the smell of his wife's pancakes from outside their window. Adapted from Nina Jaffe's book with illustrations by Louise August, the video is narrated by Theodore Bikel. Includes teacher's guide.

Title: *Indonesia*
Producer: Lucerne Media
Series: Changing Face of Asia
Year Released: 1994
Call Number: 959.8
Length: 10 minutes
Price: $195.00
Reviewed in: *School Library Journal*
Grade Level: 5–6
Keywords: Asia; Indonesia

Not fully united until early in this century, Indonesia comprises some 13,500 islands. A great oil wealth has contributed to a stable economy, but politically Indonesia has had an unstable history. This video covers the history, geography, and industry of Indonesia as well as the culture of the people.

Title: *Information Please! Your Library in Action*
Producer: Rainbow Educational Media
Series: Community Helpers
Year Released: 1995
Call Number: 028.55
Length: 15 minutes
Price: $89.00

Reviewed in: *Booklist, School Library Journal, Video Rating Guide for Libraries*
Grade Level: 1–3
Keywords: Community; Libraries; Social Studies

The library still provides quiet study areas but is bustling with other activities as well. Youngsters will identify with Mark as he discovers that some libraries have their card catalogs on computers. After that, he finds that computers, CD-ROM, audiocassettes, and videocassettes are all part of the library, and the library personnel are trained to help find the information needed.

Title: *Insect Disguises*
Producer: TVOntario/Journal Films
Series: World of Nature 2
Year Released: 1993
Call Number: 591.57
Length: 15 minutes
Price: $49.00
Reviewed in: *Video Rating Guide for Libraries*
Grade Level: 4–6
Keywords: Camouflage; Insects; Science—Life

Insects found in rain forests show how an effective disguise can help ward off predators and attract "dinner." These tiny creatures make use of color, shape, and movement to camouflage themselves. Teacher's guide available for purchase.

Title: *Insects*
Producer: Penguin Home Video/Bennett Marine Video
Series: Tell Me Why, Vol. 5
Year Released: 1989
Call Number: 595.7
Length: 30 minutes
Price: $20.00
Reviewed in: *Video Rating Guide for Libraries*
Grade Level: 3–6
Keywords: Insects; Science—Life

This video encyclopedia answers questions about insects.

Title: *Insects and Spiders: The Private World of Jean Henri Fabre*
Producer: Digital Nutshell/Lucerne Media
Series: Science in Your Own Backyard
Year Released: 1995
Call Number: 595.7
Length: 10 minutes
Price: $145.00
Reviewed in: *School Library Journal*
Grade Level: 5–6
Keywords: Insects; Science—Life

This video looks at world-famous entomologist Jean Henri Fabre, whose universe was the intimate world of insects in his garden and surrounding countryside. Many of the observations of butterfly, beetle, dragonfly, mantid, and spider behaviors are narrated in Fabre's own words.

Title: *Introducing the Cell*
Producer: Rainbow Educational Media
Series: Cell
Year Released: 1995
Call Number: 574.8
Length: 21 minutes
Price: $99.00
Reviewed in: *Booklist, School Library Journal*
Grade Level: 5–6
Keywords: Biology; Cells; Science—Life

All living things are composed of cells. The objectives of this program are that students will understand that the cell is the basic unit of life; be able to name and describe several single-celled organisms; be able to name basic cell parts; be able to describe the differences between animal and plant cells; and will learn that similar cells are grouped together to form tissue.

Title: *Inventors and Inventions*
Producer: National Geographic Society Educational Services
Series: Not Applicable
Year Released: 1995
Call Number: 609.73
Length: 22 minutes
Price: $99.00

Reviewed in: *Booklist*
Grade Level: 4–6
Keywords: Inventions; Inventors; Technology

From compact discs and cellular telephones to improved containers for household cleansers and automatic pancake-making machines, new inventions affect our lives. They can help us live longer, learn better, increase productivity, or better enjoy our leisure time. Students learn about inventions and the people who make them. Includes teacher's guide.

Title: *Irish Americans*
Producer: Schlessinger Video Productions
Series: Multicultural Peoples of North America
Year Released: 1993
Call Number: 973.004
Length: 27 minutes
Price: $40.00
Reviewed in: *Booklist, School Library Journal, Video Rating Guide*
Grade Level: 4–6
Keywords: Families; Irish Americans; Multicultural

Viewers meet a variety of Irish American families, learning their traditions, exploring their culture, and understanding their history.

Title: *Iroquois, The*
Producer: Schlessinger Video Productions
Series: Indians of North America Video Collection 1
Year Released: 1994
Call Number: 970.3
Length: 30 minutes
Price: $40.00
Reviewed in: *Booklist, School Library Journal, Video Rating Guide for Libraries*
Grade Level: 4–6
Keywords: Indians of North America; Iroquois Indians; Native Americans

Leading Native American scholars discuss the history of the Iroquois people, including myths and stereotypes. There are interviews combined with archival photographs and film footage, tribal music, crafts, and ceremonies to help students examine the spiritual relationship with nature, the role of women in Indian society, and the role of the U.S. government in Indian affairs.

Title: *It's Chemical: Phase Changes*
Producer: AIMS Media
Series: Not Applicable
Year Released: 1989
Call Number: 530.4
Length: 26 minutes
Price: $130.00
Reviewed in: *Video Rating Guide for Libraries*
Grade Level: 5–6
Keywords: Chemistry; Matter; Science—Physical

This video explores the phase changes of the three states of matter: liquid, solid, and gas. Includes teacher's guide.

Title: *It's Your Body*
Producer: Health Education Systems/Lucerne Media
Series: Safe Child Program 1–3
Year Released: 1989
Call Number: 362.7
Length: 29 minutes
Price: $395.00
Reviewed in: *Video Rating Guide for Libraries*
Grade Level: K
Keywords: Personal Safety; Safety

Divided into five segments of four to seven minutes each, this video teaches children personal skills for the prevention of abuse. Curriculum guide available.

Title: *Italian Americans*
Producer: Schlessinger Video Productions
Series: Multicultural Peoples of North America
Year Released: 1993
Call Number: 973.004
Length: 27 minutes
Price: $40.00

Reviewed in: *Booklist, School Library Journal, Video Rating Guide for Libraries*
Grade Level: 4–6
Keywords: Families; Italian Americans; Multicultural

Viewers meet a variety of Italian American families, learning their traditions, exploring their culture, and understanding their history.

Title: *Jackie Robinson*
Producer: Schlessinger Video Productions
Series: Black Americans of Achievement Video Collection 1
Year Released: 1992
Call Number: Biography
Length: 30 minutes
Price: $40.00
Reviewed in: *School Library Journal, Video Librarian, Video Rating Guide for Libraries*
Grade Level: 4–6
Keywords: African Americans; Biographies; Robinson, Jackie

This video biography contains interviews with leading authorities on the subject's life, accompanied by archival footage, photographs, and period music. Topics include basic biographical information, the inspirational and motivational factors in his life, his message, and the significance of Jackie Robinson in society today.

Title: *Japanese Americans*
Producer: Schlessinger Video Productions
Series: Multicultural Peoples of North America
Year Released: 1993
Call Number: 973.004
Length: 27 minutes
Price: $40.00
Reviewed in: *Booklist, School Library Journal, Video Rating Guide for Libraries*
Grade Level: 4–6
Keywords: Families; Japanese Americans; Multicultural

Viewers meet a variety of Japanese American families, learning their traditions, exploring their culture, and understanding their history.

Title: *Jesse Owens*
Producer: Schlessinger Video Productions
Series: Black Americans of Achievement Video Collection 2
Year Released: 1994
Call Number: Biography
Length: 30 minutes
Price: $40.00
Reviewed in: *School Library Journal, Video Librarian, Video Rating Guide for Libraries*
Grade Level: 4–6
Keywords: African Americans; Biographies; Owens, Jesse

This video biography contains interviews with leading authorities on the subject's life, accompanied by archival footage, photographs, and period music. Topics include basic biographical information, the inspirational and motivational factors in his life, his message, and the significance of Jesse Owens in society today.

Title: *Job of a TV Meteorologist*
Producer: United Learning
Series: Exploring Weather
Year Released: 1993
Call Number: 551.6
Length: 18 minutes
Price: $55.00
Reviewed in: *Video Rating Guide for Libraries*
Grade Level: 5–6
Keywords: Careers; Meteorologists; Weather

A well-known meteorologist explains how he gathers information and data from a number of sophisticated sources to determine forecasts and weather bulletins for the viewing audience. Includes teacher's guide, blackline masters.

Title: *Johnny Tremain*
Producer: Disney Educational Productions
Series: Not Applicable
Year Released: 1997
Call Number: Fiction
Length: 81 minutes
Price: $99.00
Reviewed in: *School Library Journal*

Grade Level: 4–6
Keywords: Colonial America; Social Studies

Based on the book by Esther Forbes. After injuring his hand, a silversmith's apprentice in Boston becomes a messenger for the Sons of Liberty in the days before the American Revolution.

Title: *Jomo and Mata*
Producer: Great Plains Television/MarshMedia
Series: Key Concepts in Personal Development
Year Released: 1993
Call Number: Easy Fiction
Length: 20 minutes
Price: $80.00
Reviewed in: *Video Rating Guide for Libraries*
Grade Level: K–4
Keywords: Africa; Brothers and Sisters; Elephants; Literature

When the riverbed dries up, Jomo the elephant learns that helping to dig a well is more important than besting his brother, and that each member of a family can be honored for his or her special talents. This tale presents a view of the East African savannah. Includes teacher's guide.

Title: *Journey of the Blob*
Producer: National Film Board of Canada/Bullfrog Films
Series: Look Again, Vol. 2
Year Released: 1990
Call Number: 333.91
Length: 10 minutes
Price: $150.00
Reviewed in: *Video Rating Guide for Libraries*
Grade Level: K–6
Keywords: Ecology; Environmental Concerns; Hazardous Waste

A boy makes a decision about how to dispose of a green glob he has concocted. What will happen if he dumps it into a stream? This film illustrates the water cycle and raises questions about environmental responsibility and the consequences of our decisions. Includes teacher's guide.

Title: *Journey through Jazz*, Parts 1 and 2
Producer: Rick Levy Management
Series: Not Applicable
Year Released: 1994
Call Number: 781.65
Length: 2 videos, 60 minutes each
Price: $100.00
Reviewed in: *Booklist, School Library Journal*
Grade Level: 3–6
Keywords: Jazz; Music

Presented by members of the Dan Jordan Trio, a versatile jazz group, this film relates the history and principal characteristics of jazz. The concepts and components of jazz are related to everyday life. Topics intertwined with music include music as emotion, goals, problem solving, experimentation, and cooperation. Includes teacher's guide.

Title: *Jungle for Joey, A*
Producer: Alan Sloan, Inc./AIMS Media
Series: Wild World
Year Released: 1989
Call Number: Fiction
Length: 15 minutes
Price: $100.00
Reviewed in: *Video Rating Guide for Libraries*
Grade Level: K–6
Keywords: Language Arts; Primates; Reading; Values

A baby orangutan finds a new home in this story that combines nature photography with a lesson in values. The story is followed by reading and language lessons. Teacher's manual included.

Title: *Just the Facts (for Boys)*
Producer: Lucerne Media
Series: Just the Facts
Year Released: 1995
Call Number: 612
Length: 10 minutes
Price: $130.00

Reviewed in: *School Library Journal*
Grade Level: 1–3
Keywords: Anatomy; Health; Human Body

Sitting with their child, a mother and father explain male and female body parts, how the sexual act joins sperm and egg to create a baby, and how the baby is born. Simple diagrams illustrate their explanations.

Title: *Just the Facts (for Girls)*
Producer: Lucerne Media
Series: Just the Facts
Year Released: 1995
Call Number: 612
Length: 10 minutes
Price: $130.00
Reviewed in: *School Library Journal*
Grade Level: 1–3
Keywords: Anatomy; Health; Human Body

Sitting with their child, a mother and father explain male and female body parts, how the sexual act joins sperm and egg to create a baby, and how the baby is born. Simple diagrams illustrate their explanations.

Title: *KangaZoo Club 1: Baboons-Sea Lions-Tigers*
Producer: Raymond International/Crocus Entertainment
Series: KangaZoo Club
Year Released: 1990
Call Number: 596
Length: 40 minutes
Price: $10.00
Reviewed in: *Video Rating Guide for Libraries*
Grade Level: K–4
Keywords: Animals; Zoos

Songs and presentations about different animals and how they are taken care of in zoos, animal parks, and aquariums.

Title: *KangaZoo Club 2: Monkeys-Crocodiles-Lions*
Producer: Raymond International/Crocus Entertainment
Series: KangaZoo Club
Year Released: 1990
Call Number: 596
Length: 40 minutes
Price: $10.00
Reviewed in: *Video Rating Guide for Libraries*
Grade Level: K–4
Keywords: Animals; Zoos

Songs and presentations about different animals and how they are taken care of in zoos, animal parks, and aquariums.

Title: *KangaZoo Club 3: Gorillas-Dolphins-Cheetahs*
Producer: Raymond International/Crocus Entertainment
Series: KangaZoo Club
Year Released: 1990
Call Number: 596
Length: 40 minutes
Price: $10.00
Reviewed in: *Video Rating Guide for Libraries*
Grade Level: K–4
Keywords: Animals; Zoos

Songs and presentations about different animals and how they are taken care of in zoos, animal parks, and aquariums.

Title: *Keeping Your Community Clean*
Producer: Rainbow Educational Media
Series: Community Helpers
Year Released: 1995
Call Number: 363.72
Length: 15 minutes
Price: $89.00
Reviewed in: *Booklist, School Library Journal, Video Rating Guide for Libraries*
Grade Level: 1–3
Keywords: Community; Garbage; Social Studies

In this program, youngsters see how sanitation workers help a community by collecting and disposing of garbage. They also see how recycling workers use special trucks to pick up materials that can be recycled. Other types of community helpers, such as street cleaners, are also introduced.

Title: *Kid's Guide to Divorce, A*
Producer: Learning Tree Publishing/SVE
Series: Not Applicable
Year Released: 1989
Call Number: 306.85
Length: 36 minutes
Price: $125.00
Reviewed in: *School Library Journal, Video Rating Guide for Libraries*
Grade Level: K–3
Keywords: Behavior; Divorce; Families

Today's children are confronted with a wide variety of family situations, from single-parent homes to blended families to families in the process of separation and divorce. This program helps children cope with these situations and provides information and sources for help and advice. A teacher's guide is included.

Title: *Kid's Guide to Feeling Good about Yourself, A*
Producer: Learning Tree Publishing/SVE
Series: Not Applicable
Year Released: 1989
Call Number: 152.4
Length: 35 minutes
Price: $125.00
Reviewed in: *Video Rating Guide for Libraries*
Grade Level: K–3
Keywords: Behavior; Self-esteem

Students can overcome the limitations of shyness, loneliness, feeling different, or just being scared. This program shows students that they have control over who they are and how they feel about who they are, and that they can feel better through their own individual efforts.

Title: *Kid's Guide to Friendship, A*
Producer: Learning Tree Publishing/SVE
Series: Not Applicable
Year Released: 1989
Call Number: 155.4
Length: 23 minutes
Price: $105.00

Reviewed in: *Video Rating Guide for Libraries*
Grade Level: K–3
Keywords: Behavior; Friendship

Students learn why friends are important, how they can show others that they want to make friends, and how they can make friends for a lifetime.

Title: *Kid's Guide to Manners, A*
Producer: Learning Tree Publishing/SVE
Series: Not Applicable
Year Released: 1989
Call Number: 177
Length: 16 minutes
Price: $85.00
Reviewed in: *Video Rating Guide for Libraries*
Grade Level: K–3
Keywords: Behavior; Manners

Broad areas where good manners are especially important—when eating, when meeting someone new, and other social occasions—are covered.

Title: *Kid's Guide to Personal Behavior 1: Tattling, Disobeying, and Fibbing*
Producer: Learning Tree Publishing/SVE
Series: Not Applicable
Year Released: 1989
Call Number: 170
Length: 25 minutes
Price: $105.00
Reviewed in: *Video Rating Guide for Libraries*
Grade Level: K–2
Keywords: Behavior; Responsibility; Values;

Introduce youngsters to the concepts of personal responsibility and acceptable social behavior. Students see the negative consequences of undesirable behavior in this video.

Title: *Kid's Guide to Personal Behavior 2: Rudeness, Whining, and Bickering*
Producer: Learning Tree Publishing/SVE
Series: Not Applicable
Year Released: 1989
Call Number: 170
Length: 26 minutes
Price: $105.00
Reviewed in: *Video Rating Guide for Libraries*
Grade Level: K–2
Keywords: Behavior; Responsibility; Values

Introduce youngsters to the concepts of personal responsibility and acceptable social behavior. Students see the negative consequences of undesirable behavior in this video.

Title: *Kid's Guide to Personal Hygiene, A*
Producer: Learning Tree Publishing/SVE
Series: Not Applicable
Year Released: 1989
Call Number: 613
Length: 17 minutes
Price: $85.00
Reviewed in: *Video Rating Guide for Libraries*
Grade Level: K–3
Keywords: Health; Personal Hygiene

Bill Harley, a writer and performer of children's songs and stories, uses his wit to teach personal hygiene.

Title: *Kid's Guide to School Safety, A*
Producer: Learning Tree Publishing/SVE
Series: Not Applicable
Year Released: 1989
Call Number: 371.7
Length: 18 minutes
Price: $85.00
Reviewed in: *Booklist, Video Rating Guide for Libraries*
Grade Level: K–3
Keywords: Safety; School Safety

The importance of thinking ahead and of thinking about the safety of others is demonstrated. This program shows that safety is a habit, an attitude, and a way of living. It stresses the value of a positive attitude toward personal safety and the safety of others. Includes guide.

Title: *Kid's Guide to Self-Protection, A*
Producer: Learning Tree Publishing/SVE
Series: Not Applicable
Year Released: 1989
Call Number: 362.76
Length: 51 minutes
Price: $165.00
Reviewed in: *School Library Journal, Video Rating Guide for Libraries*
Grade Level: K–3
Keywords: Molestation; Safety; Self-protection

This video deals with the subject of child molestation. It is designed for a very young audience and treats this issue sensitively. Includes guide.

Title: *Kids Make Music*
Producer: Bogner Entertainment
Series: Not Applicable
Year Released: 1995
Call Number: 780
Length: 45 minutes
Price: $15.00
Reviewed in: *Booklist, School Library Journal*
Grade Level: PreK–1
Keywords: Early Childhood; Music

An instructor and her puppet friend lead children in a series of songs to teach children the basics of music through singing, dancing, rhyming, and clapping. Also features discussion on the benefits of music for children and its effect on developmental skills, while including suggestions for expanding these lessons in the classroom.

Title: *Kiki and the Cuckoo*
Producer: Great Plains Television/MarshMedia
Series: Key Concepts in Self-Esteem
Year Released: 1993
Call Number: Fiction
Length: 15 minutes
Price: $80.00
Reviewed in: *Video Rating Guide for Libraries*
Grade Level: K–4
Keywords: Competition; Literature

A Kansas meadowlark gets into a senseless rivalry with a cuckoo clock and loses sight of his real goals. The prairie grasslands and wildlife are depicted in watercolors. Includes teacher's guide.

Title: *King Comes Calling, The*
Producer: TVOntario/Journal Films
Series: Mathica's Mathshop 1
Year Released: 1994
Call Number: 513.2
Length: 15 minutes
Price: $49.00
Reviewed in: *Video Rating Guide for Libraries*
Grade Level: K–1
Keywords: Geometry; Mathematics; Problem Solving; Sorting

King Scowl of Scorn comes to visit and disdainfully allows Mathica to help him with some problems. The Mathmagician imprisons him in the Mathshop, allowing him to leave only when he shows more consideration for others. Includes the following math skills: counting by 10s; sorting; plane figures—rectangle and triangle. Teacher's guide available for purchase.

Title: *Knight School*
Producer: LSB Productions/Churchill Media
Series: Not Applicable
Year Released: 1992
Call Number: 152.4
Length: 20 minutes
Price: $80.00
Reviewed in: *Video Rating Guide for Libraries*
Grade Level: 2–6
Keywords: Behavior; Knights; Values

Young Kevin is about to cheat on a test when he's suddenly whisked from his classroom to an open field. There he is confronted by Sir Sisal, a medieval (and somewhat accident-prone) knight who turns out to be none other than Kevin. In a series of vignettes, Sir Sisal teaches Kevin some basic rules of conduct that will help him—and young viewers—do the right thing and treat others with respect. Includes teacher's guide.

Title: *Knight-Time Tale, A*
Producer: TVOntario/GPN
Series: Return to the Magic Library
Year Released: 1991
Call Number: 428
Length: 15 minutes
Price: $49.00
Reviewed in: *Video Rating Guide for Libraries*
Grade Level: 3–4
Keywords: Knights; Language Arts; Literature

While Zazi reads "The Sceptre of Aldric" by Ian Ritchie, Leon and Norbert prefer to look at pictures of knights in shining armor. Suddenly, a knight emerges from the bookshelves, bringing Zazi's medieval adventure to life. Literature skills covered include: conflict; formal and informal language. Teacher's guide available for purchase.

Title: *Koko's Kitten*
Producer: Churchill Media
Series: Not Applicable
Year Released: 1989
Call Number: 599.88
Length: 17 minutes
Price: $70.00
Reviewed in: *Booklist, Video Rating Guide for Libraries*
Grade Level: PreK–3
Keywords: Cats; Friendship; Gorillas; Kittens; Literature

From the popular book, *Koko*, this is the true story about the gentle gorilla who has learned to express thoughts and feelings in sign language. It tells of how she loved and cared for the kitten she named All-Ball; how she lost it, grieved, and grew from the experience. Includes teacher's guide.

Title: *Komodo Dragon: The Largest Lizard*
Producer: TVOntario/Journal Films
Series: World of Nature 2
Year Released: 1993
Call Number: 597.95
Length: 15 minutes
Price: $49.00
Reviewed in: *Video Rating Guide for Libraries*
Grade Level: 4–6
Keywords: Animals; Lizards; Reptiles

The Komodo dragon is characterized by a large mouth, dry skin, and sharp claws, but its most outstanding feature is size. Identified only in 1912, the dragon has carried on its hunting and breeding rituals on Komodo Island for centuries. Teacher's guide available for purchase.

Title: *Korean Americans*
Producer: Schlessinger Video Productions
Series: Multicultural Peoples of North America
Year Released: 1993
Call Number: 973.004
Length: 27 minutes
Price: $40.00
Reviewed in: *Booklist, School Library Journal, Video Rating Guide for Libraries*
Grade Level: 4–6
Keywords: Families; Korean Americans; Multicultural

In this video, viewers meet a variety of Korean American families, learn their traditions, explore their culture, and understand their history.

Title: *Kuwait*
Producer: White Mountain Entertainment
Series: Cultures of the World
Year Released: 1993
Call Number: 953
Length: 18 minutes
Price: $80.00
Reviewed in: *School Library Journal*

Grade Level: 4–6
Keywords: Asia; Kuwait; Social Studies

Completed just before the invasion by Iraq, this program shows students Kuwait as it was and may never be again. It describes the education and health care systems, archaeological excavations that date to the Roman Empire, and the dominant oil industry. Includes teacher's guide.

Title: *Kylie's Concert*
Producer: Great Plains Television/MarshMedia
Series: Key Concepts in Self-Esteem
Year Released: 1993
Call Number: Easy Fiction
Length: 14 minutes
Price: $80.00
Reviewed in: *Video Rating Guide for Libraries*
Grade Level: K–4
Keywords: Ecology; Endangered Species; Koalas

Kylie the Australian koala helps students explore questions about endangered species and habitats and demonstrates how a single voice can make a difference. Includes teacher's guide.

Title: *Land of Dinosaurs*
Producer: Lucerne Media
Series: Not Applicable
Year Released: 1993
Call Number: 567.91
Length: 15 minutes
Price: $225.00
Reviewed in: *School Library Journal*
Grade Level: 1–3
Keywords: Dinosaurs; Fossils; Science—Earth

An animated adventure teaches Jimmy about fossils and the sciences behind them that enable us to gain knowledge of the past.

Title: *Langston Hughes*
Producer: Schlessinger Video Productions
Series: Black Americans of Achievement Video Collection 2
Year Released: 1994
Call Number: Biography
Length: 30 minutes
Price: $40.00
Reviewed in: *School Library Journal, Video Librarian, Video Rating Guide for Libraries*
Grade Level: 4–6
Keywords: African Americans; Authors; Biographies; Hughes, Langston

This video biography contains interviews with leading authorities on the subject's life, accompanied by archival footage, photographs, and period music. Topics include basic biographical information, the inspirational and motivational factors in his life, his message, and the significance of Langston Hughes in society today.

Title: *Laos*
Producer: White Mountain Entertainment
Series: Cultures of the World
Year Released: 1993
Call Number: 959.404
Length: 18 minutes
Price: $80.00
Reviewed in: *Booklist, School Library Journal*
Grade Level: 4–6
Keywords: Asia; Laos; Social Studies

This least developed country in Southeast Asia is a study in basic economics. Students will learn that the Mekong River is the main means of transportation and the source of economic activity for the villages along its banks. The modern capital of Vientiane and the ancient capital of Luang Prabang are visited. Includes teacher's guide.

Title: *Lasers: The Special Light*
Producer: Lucerne Media
Series: Science and Technology—Today and Tomorrow
Year Released: 1994
Call Number: 621.36
Length: 20 minutes

Price: $195.00
Reviewed in: *Booklist*
Grade Level: 6
Keywords: Lasers; Science—Physical; Technology

Lasers have already revolutionized many areas of the modern world and may have still wider potential in the future. This program examines the various types of lasers and their application in communications, medicine, manufacturing, construction, and weaponry. The fundamental principals of laser operations, including the difference between coherent and incoherent light, and stimulated and spontaneous light emissions are explained. Includes teacher's guide.

Title: *Last Hit, The: Children and Violence*
Producer: Children's Hospital of Michigan/Film Ideas
Series: Not Applicable
Year Released: 1994
Call Number: 303.6
Length: 20 minutes
Price: $150.00
Reviewed in: *Booklist, School Library Journal*
Grade Level: K–6
Keywords: Safety; Violence

This culturally diverse video focuses on children ages six to twelve who share their experiences with violence along with viewpoints on what constitutes violence and the best ways to avoid it.

Title: *Lean Mean Machine, The—A Story about Handling Emotions*
Producer: InnerVisions Productions/Kids' Media Group
Series: Human Race Club
Year Released: 1990
Call Number: 152.4
Length: 23 minutes
Price: $25.00
Reviewed in: *Video Rating Guide for Libraries*
Grade Level: K–4
Keywords: Behavior; Feelings

Maggie mistakenly assumes that she will represent the Human Race Club in the home-town go-cart derby. Then her runaway emotions steer her on a collision course into trouble. Students learn how to handle strong emotions and uncomfortable feelings. Includes guide.

Title: *Legend of the Bluebonnet*
Producer: Dimensions Films
Series: Not Applicable
Year Released: 1991
Call Number: 398.2
Length: 20 minutes
Price: $75.00
Reviewed in: *School Library Journal, Video Rating Guide for Libraries*
Grade Level: K–6
Keywords: Bluebonnets; Comanche Indians; Literature; Native Americans

Join a group of schoolchildren as a Native American carver shares an old Comanche story. This story, based on the book by Tomie dePaola, illustrates a famous Texas legend about a girl who gives away what is most important to her so that others can eat. This program teaches about Native American culture and the rewards of giving.

Title: *Lenny the Lumberjack*
Producer: Can-U Imagine Productions in association with Lion Gibby/411 Video Information
Series: Not Applicable
Year Released: 1995
Call Number: 331.7
Length: 50 minutes
Price: $15.00
Reviewed in: *School Library Journal*
Grade Level: K–6
Keywords: Careers; Forests; Occupations

Kids can watch real lumberjacks operate their powerful and gigantic machinery.

Title: *Let's Be Friends*
Producer: Sunburst Communications
Series: Not Applicable
Year Released: 1994
Call Number: Easy Fiction
Length: 14 minutes
Price: $99.00

Reviewed in: *Booklist, School Library Journal*
Grade Level: K–2
Keywords: Behavior; Friendship; Human Relations

The ability to make and keep friends plays a critical role in children's socialization. Using songs, age-appropriate scenarios, and a storyteller to move the action along, the program presents typical friendship problems and their solutions to help the students improve their social skills and discover the joys and rewards of being a friend. Includes teacher's guide, worksheets.

Title: *Let's Create for Halloween*
Producer: Let's Create, Inc.
Series: Let's Create
Year Released: 1995
Call Number: 745.594
Length: 60 minutes
Price: $25.00
Reviewed in: *Booklist, Children's Video Report*
Grade Level: 1–5
Keywords: Art; Behavior; Halloween

Halloween is a fun time, full of tricks and treats, and this tape is for children who like to get into the spirit of the holiday. Children create six Halloween art projects.

Title: *Let's Explore . . . Furry, Fishy, Feathery Friends*
Producer: Braun Film and Video, Inc.
Series: Not Applicable
Year Released: 1995
Call Number: 636
Length: 30 minutes
Price: $15.00
Reviewed in: *Booklist, School Library Journal, Video Librarian*
Grade Level: PreK–3
Keywords: Animals; Pets

Kids can get a close-up look at pets that can be purchased from a pet store, like puppies, fish, birds, turtles, and many more.

Title: *Let's Go to the Farm with Mac Parker*
Producer: Vermont Story Works
Series: Not Applicable
Year Released: 1994
Call Number: 630
Length: 60 minutes
Price: $15.00
Reviewed in: *Booklist, School Library Journal*
Grade Level: K–5
Keywords: Dairy Farms; Social Studies

This video looks at a year on a large, working dairy farm. From silage to maple syrup, from a country fair to logging, this picture of farm life allows children to witness the clean and messy aspects of raising cows and making milk.

Title: *Let's Play Games*
Producer: A and M Video
Series: Shari Lewis: Lamb Chop's Play Alongs
Year Released: 1994
Call Number: 793
Length: 30 minutes
Price: $10.00
Reviewed in: *Booklist*
Grade Level: PreK–1
Keywords: Early Childhood; Music

This play-along program features songs, poems and stories.

Title: *Let's See*
Producer: TVOntario/Films for the Humanities and Sciences
Series: Art's Place
Year Released: 1990
Call Number: 740
Length: 15 minutes
Price: $49.00
Reviewed in: *Video Rating Guide for Libraries*
Grade Level: K–3
Keywords: Art; Artists; Games

While Jessie and Mrs. Hooter, Leo's old art teacher, go sightseeing, Leo plays some looking games with Doodles and Art. Mirror tells the story of Little Tommy Tum, and the art of Marc Chagall is featured. Includes guide.

Title: *Libre Quiero Ser (I Want to Be Free)*
Producer: Human Relations Media
Series: Not Applicable
Year Released: 1995
Call Number: 613.85
Length: 12 minutes
Price: $119.00
Reviewed in: *School Library Journal*
Grade Level: 4–6
Keywords: Health; Tobacco

This Spanish-language video is aimed at Latino youth. A music video format is used and incorporates Latin and hip-hop music with interviews of kids to approach the deadly subject of tobacco use.

Title: *Living in Space*
Producer: TVOntario
Series: Look Up
Year Released: 1990
Call Number: 629.45
Length: 15 minutes
Price: $49.00
Reviewed in: *Video Rating Guide for Libraries*
Grade Level: 3–6
Keywords: Astronauts; Science—Space; Space

Filmed in a space shuttle, astronaut Sally Ride describes the challenges of living in space. Related learning activities include designing clothes for space and eating pudding while standing on your head. Includes guide.

Title: *Louisa May Alcott*
Producer: American School Publishers
Series: Meet the Newbery Author
Year Released: 1992
Call Number: Biography
Length: 40 minutes
Price: $85.00
Reviewed in: *School Library Journal, Video Rating Guide for Libraries*
Grade Level: 4–6
Keywords: Alcott, Louisa May; Authors; Biographies

This live-action video looks at the life story and works of Louisa May Alcott. The video shows Alcott's home in Concord, Massachusetts, now a museum, and gives students insight into the family that inspired the famous characters in *Little Women, Little Men* and *Jo's Boys*. Includes teacher's guide.

Title: *Made for Art*
Producer: TVOntario/Films for the Humanities and Sciences
Series: Art's Place
Year Released: 1990
Call Number: 745.594
Length: 15 minutes
Price: $49.00
Reviewed in: *Video Rating Guide for Libraries*
Grade Level: K–3
Keywords: Art; Birthdays; Language Arts

It is Art's birthday, so his friends use a variety of media to create art for him. Leo is determined to make something unique. Mirror tells Art a special story, and Jessie brings him a surprise from the bakery. Includes guide.

Title: *Making a Difference*
Producer: California Academy of Sciences/Video Project
Series: Kids from CAOS
Year Released: 1995
Call Number: 363.72
Length: 29 minutes
Price: $60.00
Reviewed in: *Booklist, School Library Journal*

Grade Level: 6
Keywords: Ecology; Environmental Concerns

This video profiles students putting science into action to make a difference on behalf of the environment. "Wild Mustangs" travels to a ranch that is helping save wild horses from extinction. "The Tree Musketeers" profiles a group started and run by kids that is planting trees to counter urban pollution. "The Salmon Project" shows concerned teens working with scientists to bring back endangered salmon in a local stream. Includes teacher's guide.

Title: *Making It Happen: Masters of Invention*
Producer: Bob Oliver Communications/Churchill Media
Series: Not Applicable
Year Released: 1995
Call Number: 607
Length: 22 minutes
Price: $150.00
Reviewed in: *Booklist, School Library Journal*
Grade Level: 4–6
Keywords: African Americans; Inventors; Technology

African American inventors who made major contributions to the progress of society are featured. Archival footage documents their creativity and science, communications, transportation, and more. Hosted by Glynn Turman.

Title: *Malaysia*
Producer: Lucerne Media
Series: Changing Face of Asia
Year Released: 1994
Call Number: 915
Length: 12 minutes
Price: $195.00
Reviewed in: *School Library Journal*
Grade Level: 5–6
Keywords: Asia; Malaysia

This New Mexico–sized region on the southeastern tip of Asia was under British control from 1867 to 1963. The current government, a federal democracy with a constitutional monarch, is a unique blend of western and Asian influences. This video provides information on the history, geography, and industry of Malaysia as well as a look at the culture of the people.

Title: *Manor House Mystery, The: Problem-Solving in Geometry*
Producer: Human Relations Media
Series: Detective Stories for Math Problem Solving
Year Released: 1991
Call Number: 516
Length: 30 minutes
Price: $175.00
Reviewed in: *School Library Journal, Video Rating Guide for Libraries*
Grade Level: 5–6
Keywords: Geometry; Mathematics; Problem Solving

Billy and Jodie have been hired by a shady-looking detective to help unravel a mystery involving a haunted house. The clues begin to unfold when they find the handbook of a secret society: the Sigma Delta Society. It lays out a series of tasks that will eventually lead them to a treasure . . . and a secret passage. Includes teacher's resource book, student clue kits.

Title: *Many Moons*
Producer: Rembrandt Films/Churchill Media
Series: Not Applicable
Year Released: 1995
Call Number: Easy Fiction
Length: 10 minutes
Price: $60.00
Reviewed in: *School Library Journal*
Grade Level: K–6
Keywords: Fairy Tales; Literature; Moons; Princesses

From the Caldecott Medal winner by James Thurber comes the tale of Princess Lenore, who falls ill and needs the moon to be well again. When none of the king's councillors can figure out a way to get it for her, it is the court jester who realizes that the Princess has had the answer all along. Includes teacher's guide.

Title: *Marc Brown*
Producer: Northern Light Productions/American School Publishers
Series: Meet the Author
Year Released: 1990
Call Number: Biography
Length: 19 minutes

Price: $85.00
Reviewed in: *School Library Journal, Video Rating Guide for Libraries*
Grade Level: 4–6
Keywords: Authors; Biographies; Brown, Marc

In conversations with his aardvark character Arthur, Marc Brown reveals where he finds the inspiration for his stories, characters, and art in this live-action video. Sequences dramatize some of Marc's early experiences as a short-order cook, truck driver, and college teacher, before discovering what he really wanted to do. Includes teacher's guide.

Title: *Marc Brown Does Play Rhymes*
Producer: American School Publishers
Series: Not Applicable
Year Released: 1989
Call Number: 372
Length: 14 minutes
Price: $53.00
Reviewed in: *Video Rating Guide for Libraries*
Grade Level: PreK–1
Keywords: Early Childhood; Finger Play; Music

Here is another live-action video, filmed in Marc's studio and then on a school playground. Marc and the children play and sing to the music and songs of "John Brown's Body," "I'm a Little Teapot," "The Counting Game," "Do Your Ears Hang Low?" and more.

Title: *Mars, the Red Planet*
Producer: Space Smart Inc.
Series: Not Applicable
Year Released: 1992
Call Number: 523.43
Length: 28 minutes
Price: $40.00
Reviewed in: *School Library Journal*
Grade Level: 5–6
Keywords: Mars; Science—Space; Space

Combines dramatization and animation with launch and space flight footage to present data about Mars and man's attempts to learn about it. Includes teacher's guide.

Title: *Mary McLeod Bethune*
Producer: Schlessinger Video Productions
Series: Black Americans of Achievement Video Collection 2
Year Released: 1994
Call Number: Biography
Length: 30 minutes
Price: $40.00
Reviewed in: *School Librarian Journal, Video Librarian, Video Rating Guide for Libraries*
Grade Level: 4–6
Keywords: African Americans; Bethune, Mary McLeod; Biographies

This video biography contains interviews with leading authorities on the subject's life, accompanied by archival footage, photographs, and period music. Topics include basic biographical information, the inspirational and motivational factors in her life, her message, and the significance of Mary McLeod Bethune in society today.

Title: *Math . . . Who Needs It?*
Producer: FASE Productions/Instructional Video, Inc.
Series: Futures
Year Released: 1991
Call Number: 510
Length: 58 minutes
Price: $20.00
Reviewed in: *School Library Journal, Video Rating Guide for Libraries*
Grade Level: 4–6
Keywords: Careers; Mathematics

A PBS special designed to motivate students to study mathematics by showing them that a world of opportunities is open to those with good math skills. Reproducible activity sheets included.

Title: *Matter*
Producer: TVOntario/Films for the Humanities and Sciences
Series: Take a Look 2
Year Released: 1991
Call Number: 530.4
Length: 10 minutes
Price: $49.00
Reviewed in: *Video Rating Guide for Libraries*

Grade Level: 2–5
Keywords: Matter; Science—Physical

Kate defines matter for Jamie and then shows him how it can take the form of solid, liquid, or gas. To demonstrate how liquids and gases take up space and have mass, Kate fills a glass with lemonade, and blows up a balloon. Teacher's guide available for purchase.

Title: *Maya Art and Architecture*
Producer: Alarion Press
Series: Not Applicable
Year Released: 1995
Call Number: 972.81
Length: 54 minutes
Price: $124.00
Reviewed in: *School Library Journal*
Grade Level: 5–6
Keywords: Art; Mayans

In this look at the Maya temples, palaces, sculptures, and paintings, learn how archeologists have only now been able to decipher their mysterious writings. Includes teacher's guide, poster, workbook.

Title: *McGruff and the Dangerous Stranger*
Producer: AIMS Media
Series: Not Applicable
Year Released: 1994
Call Number: 363.1
Length: 15 minutes
Price: $195.00
Reviewed in: *School Library Journal*
Grade Level: 1–3
Keywords: Personal Safety; Safety

McGruff the Crime Dog and his nephew Scruff are concerned about the disappearance of a neighborhood child. This sparks a discussion about the definition of "stranger" and prompts McGruff to review practical ways children can stay safe on the way home from school. The story ends happily when the missing child is found unharmed.

Title: *McGruff on Halloween*
Producer: AIMS Media
Series: McGruff the Crime Dog
Year Released: 1990
Call Number: 614.8
Length: 14 minutes
Price: $80.00
Reviewed in: *Video Rating Guide for Libraries*
Grade Level: K–6
Keywords: Halloween; Holidays; Safety

With examples from his files, McGruff gives plenty of tips to make Halloween both safe and fun. Attending a club or neighborhood party is the best way to celebrate Halloween, but for those who do go trick or treating, McGruff recommends some important dos and don'ts to follow.

Title: *McGruff's Self-Care Alert*
Producer: AIMS Media
Series: McGruff the Crime Dog
Year Released: 1990
Call Number: 614.8
Length: 17 minutes
Price: $80.00
Reviewed in: *Video Rating Guide for Libraries*
Grade Level: K–6
Keywords: Personal Safety; Safety

To help youngsters feel safe from crime when they're alone, McGruff gives some important and useful advice. He illustrates his self-care message with the experiences of four children who have learned how to protect themselves. McGruff also offers suggestions to help children deal successfully with loneliness.

Title: *Me and My Body*
Producer: MarshMedia
Series: All about Me
Year Released: 1990
Call Number: 612
Length: 12 minutes

Price: $60.00
Reviewed in: *Media and Methods, Video Rating Guide for Libraries*
Grade Level: K–2
Keywords: Health; Human Body

This live-action video introduces students to the wonders of the human body: its main parts, how it moves, how the brain controls the body and the bones and muscles hold it up, how the five senses help us enjoy the world, and the importance of eating right and exercising. Melodies, lyrics, and on-screen children bring these concepts to life. Correlating computer software available. Includes teacher's guide.

Title: *Me and My Family*
Producer: MarshMedia
Series: All about Me
Year Released: 1990
Call Number: 306.85
Length: 9 minutes
Price: $60.00
Reviewed in: *Video Rating Guide for Libraries, Wilson Library Bulletin*
Grade Level: K–2
Keywords: Early Childhood; Families

Use this live-action video to explore with young students the nature of families—their many sizes and kinds, the way family members share responsibilities and care for each other. Heather Forest and a group of youngsters share their thoughts about families through song, pantomime, games and discussion. Correlating computer software available. Includes guide.

Title: *Meal Planning: The Food Pyramid in Action*
Producer: Learning Seed
Series: Not Applicable
Year Released: 1996
Call Number: 642
Length: 18 minutes
Price: $89.00
Reviewed in: *Booklist*

Grade Level: 4–6
Keywords: Food; Health; Nutrition

This video shows how to put the food pyramid into action for everyday meal planning. Two teens chide mom for using the old "four food groups" and end up planning the family's meals for a week.

Title: *Meet Jack Prelutsky*
Producer: American School Publishers
Series: Meet the Author
Year Released: 1991
Call Number: Biography
Length: 22 minutes
Price: $85.00
Reviewed in: *School Library Journal, Video Rating Guide for Libraries*
Grade Level: 4–6
Keywords: Authors; Biographies; Prelutsky, Jack

Jack Prelutsky presents his poems and songs before an elementary audience in this live-action video. At home in Olympia, Washington, Prelutsky explains how he uses rhyme, alliteration, and onomatopoeia to enhance his poems. He recreates the day that he wrote "The Ballad of the Boneless Chicken." Includes teacher's guide.

Title: *Meet Leo Lionni*
Producer: Nothern Light Productions/American School Publishers
Series: Meet the Author
Year Released: 1992
Call Number: Biography
Length: 19 minutes
Price: $85.00
Reviewed in: *School Library Journal, Video Rating Guide for Libraries*
Grade Level: 4–6
Keywords: Authors; Biographies; Lionni, Leo

This live-action video visits the four-time Caldecott Award winner at work in Tuscany, Italy. Lionni explains the inspiration for his books *Frederick* and *Swimmy* and talks about his hopes for young children. Includes teacher's guide.

Title: *Mercury, Venus and Mars*
Producer: TVOntario
Series: Look Up
Year Released: 1990
Call Number: 523.4
Length: 15 minutes
Price: $49.00
Reviewed in: *Video Rating Guide for Libraries*
Grade Level: 3–6
Keywords: Planets; Science—Space

Characteristics of Mercury, Venus, and Mars are studied, and terrestrial planets and biospheres are explained. Activities include creating a model of gravitational force with an eraser and pencil, making a biosphere in a jar, and designing aliens. Includes guide.

Title: *Merlin and the Dragons*
Producer: Lightyear Entertainment
Series: Not Applicable
Year Released: 1991
Call Number: Fiction
Length: 26 minutes
Price: $15.00
Reviewed in: *Video Rating Guide for Libraries*
Grade Level: K–6
Keywords: Arthur, King; Literature; Merlin

Told by film star Kevin Kline, this is the adventure of Merlin as a boy. Young Arthur doesn't understand why pulling a sword from a stone qualifies him for kingship. Old Merlin tells the boy a story that inspires Arthur with the confidence he will need to become a great king.

Title: *Metric System*
Producer: Educational Video Resources
Series: Basic Mathematical Skills Series
Year Released: 1993
Call Number: 530.8
Length: 28 minutes
Price: $50.00

Reviewed in: *Library Journal*
Grade Level: 5–6
Keywords: Mathematics; Measurement; Metric System

Definitions and conversions are presented and explained by instructor Elayne Gay. Sample problems are solved, step-by-step.

Title: *Mice in the Library*
Producer: TVOntario/GPN
Series: Return to the Magic Library
Year Released: 1991
Call Number: Fiction
Length: 15 minutes
Price: $49.00
Reviewed in: *Video Rating Guide for Libraries*
Grade Level: 3–4
Keywords: Language Arts; Literature; Mystery

A riddle on the computer screen leads Zazi and Leon to believe that today's story is a mystery. They are right; smooth-talking Sadie McSlueth shows up to read "Red Rocket" by Ian Ritchie and teaches them the mystery-story rules. Literature skills covered include using clues to make deductions. Teacher's guide available for purchase.

Title: *Mildred D. Taylor*
Producer: American School Publishers
Series: Meet the Author
Year Released: 1991
Call Number: Biography
Length: 21 minutes
Price: $85.00
Reviewed in: *School Library Journal, Video Rating Guide for Libraries*
Grade Level: 4–6
Keywords: African Americans; Authors; Biographies; Taylor, Mildred D.

Viewers journey to Colorado to meet this Newbery Award–winning author who is also the recipient of the 1991 Coretta Scott King Award for fiction. As a young girl, Mildred Taylor was angered and dismayed by the lack of information regarding the achievements of black people in America. She began to write to tell people about the black role models in stories told by her family and to share the richness of their history. Includes teacher's guide.

Title: *Milk and Cookies*
Producer: Kid Vids Educational Entertainment
Series: Show and Tell Series
Year Released: 1996
Call Number: 636.2
Length: 30 minutes
Price: $14.95
Reviewed in: *School Library Journal*
Grade Level: PreK-4
Keywords: Careers, Dairy Farms, Food

Two real-life kids research a show-and-tell for their class, gathering first-hand information at a farm, a dairy, and a bakery.

Title: *Milk Cow, Eat Cheese*
Producer: Real World Video
Series: Not Applicable
Year Released: 1995
Call Number: 636.214
Length: 30 minutes
Price: $15.00
Reviewed in: *Booklist, School Library Journal*
Grade Level: PreK–4
Keywords: Cows; Dairy Farms; Social Studies

Students look at the workings of a dairy farm, including milking cows and cheese production. All of the unique steps that are involved in milking a cow are shown.

Title: *Miss Christy's Dancin' Ballet*
Producer: PPI—Peter Pan Video
Series: Miss Christy's Dancin'
Year Released: 1994
Call Number: 792.8
Length: 35 minutes
Price: $13.00
Reviewed in: *School Library Journal*
Grade Level: 1–6
Keywords: Ballet; Dance; Physical Education

Celebrity choreographer and children's dance specialist Christy Curtis has developed this program for children to learn ballet.

Title: *Miss Christy's Dancin' Jazz*
Producer: PPI—Peter Pan Video
Series: Miss Christy's Dancin'
Year Released: 1994
Call Number: 792.8
Length: 35 minutes
Price: $13.00
Reviewed in: *School Library Journal*
Grade Level: 2–6
Keywords: Dance; Jazz; Physical Education

Celebrity choreographer and children's dance specialist Christy Curtis has developed this program for children to learn jazz.

Title: *Molly's Magic*
Producer: MarshMedia
Series: Key Concepts in Personal Development
Year Released: 1995
Call Number: 152.4
Length: 16 minutes
Price: $30.00
Reviewed in: *Booklist, School Library Journal*
Grade Level: K–4
Keywords: Behavior; Creative Thinking; Ireland

When the O'Malley family's plan for supplementing their farm income seems doomed to failure, a problem-solving pig named Molly shows that adversity may sometimes be overcome with a little creative thinking. Irish customs and geography are also shown. Includes teacher's guide.

Title: *Monkey Moves*
Producer: Stephen Rosenholtz/Rosewood Publications
Series: Exercise like the Animals for Kids
Year Released: 1994
Call Number: 613.71
Length: 25 minutes
Price: $15.00
Reviewed in: *Booklist, School Library Journal*
Grade Level: PreK–4
Keywords: Early Childhood; Exercise; Physical Education

This video depicts exercise set to music designed to stimulate a child's imagination about animals while developing balance, coordination, self-expression, and music appreciation.

Title: *More than Manners*
Producer: Lori Mahaley for New Leaf Media/Film Ideas
Series: Life Lessons
Year Released: 1994
Call Number: 177
Length: 16 minutes
Price: $135.00
Reviewed in: *Booklist*
Grade Level: 1–6
Keywords: Behavior; Etiquette; Manners

Manners are more than etiquette; they can also show our concern and respect for others. In this production children will see examples of "do" manners and "don't" manners and how "do" manners can most importantly show that we consider other people and their feelings.

Title: *Mose the Fireman*
Producer: Rabbit Ears Productions
Series: American Heroes and Legends
Year Released: 1993
Call Number: 398.2
Length: 30 minutes
Price: $10.00
Reviewed in: *Booklist, School Library Journal*
Grade Level: K–4
Keywords: Fire Fighters; Safety; Tall Tales

Michael Keaton adopts a broad New York accent for this history of Gotham's legendary fireman, whose outrageous exploits shape one of America's tallest tales. A jazz score accompanies the sights and sounds of the turn of the century.

Title: *Moses in Egypt*
Producer: Rabbit Ears Productions
Series: Greatest Stories Ever Told
Year Released: 1993
Call Number: 222
Length: 30 minutes
Price: $13.00
Reviewed in: *School Library Journal*
Grade Level: 1–4
Keywords: Moses; Religion

This video tells the story of Moses and how he is summoned by God to deliver his fellow Israelites from slavery in Egypt.

Title: *Moses the Lawgiver*
Producer: Rabbit Ears Productions
Series: Greatest Stories Ever Told
Year Released: 1993
Call Number: 222
Length: 30 minutes
Price: $10.00
Reviewed in: *School Library Journal*
Grade Level: K–6
Keywords: Moses; Religion

This video tells the story of how Moses receives God's commandments atop Mt. Sinai and leads the Israelites on their forty-year journey to the promised land.

Title: *Mosquito, The*
Producer: Greatest Tales/Barr Films
Series: Animals Families
Year Released: 1990
Call Number: 395.77
Length: 11 minutes
Price: $35.00
Reviewed in: *Video Rating Guide for Libraries*
Grade Level: 1–6
Keywords: Insects; Mosquitoes; Science—Life

In this introduction to the world of mosquitos, students learn about the insect's natural habitat, life cycles, eating habits, and much more. Includes teacher's guide.

Title: *Move like the Animals*
Producer: Stephen Rosenholtz/Rosewood Publications
Series: Exercise like the Animals for Kids
Year Released: 1994
Call Number: 372.86
Length: 25 minutes
Price: $20.00
Reviewed in: *Booklist, School Library Journal*
Grade Level: PreK–K
Keywords: Early Childhood; Exercise; Physical Education

This video shows exercise set to music designed to stimulate a child's imagination about animals while developing balance, coordination, self-expression, and music appreciation.

Title: *Moving the Mail: Postal Employees at Work*
Producer: Video Dialog/Rainbow Educational Media
Series: Community Helpers
Year Released: 1994
Call Number: 353.4
Length: 15 minutes
Price: $89.00
Reviewed in: *Booklist, School Library Journal, Video Rating Guide for Libraries*
Grade Level: K–3
Keywords: Community; Postal Service; Social Studies

A community is a place where people live; it might be a city, a farm area, or a suburb. Postal workers help people who live in one community keep in touch with people who live in different communities. Some postal workers collect mail, some deliver mail, and others sort mail. Their job is to make sure that when we mail a letter or package, it arrives at its destination.

Title: *Multi-Cultural Christmas, A*
Producer: Colman Communications Corporation/United Learning
Series: Holiday Facts and Fun
Year Released: 1993
Call Number: 394.2
Length: 22 minutes
Price: $70.00

Reviewed in: *Booklist, School Library Journal, Video Rating Guide for Libraries*
Grade Level: K–4
Keywords: Christmas; Holidays; Multicultural

Five children from distinctly different ethnic backgrounds tell how their families, friends, and neighbors celebrate the Christmas season. Northern European, African American, Hispanic, Native American, and Asian youngsters show and explain family and ethnic customs associated with their holiday celebrations. Includes teacher's guide.

Title: *Murky Water Caper, The*
Producer: CITE/Video Project
Series: Not Applicable
Year Released: 1993
Call Number: 333.91
Length: 30 minutes
Price: $60.00
Reviewed in: *Video Rating Guide for Libraries*
Grade Level: 1–4
Keywords: Ecology; Environmental Concerns; Pollution; Water

Follow the adventures of Billie Beaver, Molly Duck, Toots the Trout, and a host of other characters who seek the help of Detective Tuesday to find out who's been polluting the local stream. Taped before a live audience of young children, this video provides an introduction to water pollution and conservation. Includes educational kit from America's Clean Water Foundation.

Title: *My Body, My Buddy: Caring and Sharing*
Producer: Rainbow Educational Media
Series: My Body, My Buddy: Behavior
Year Released: 1995
Call Number: 158
Length: 18 minutes
Price: $89.00
Reviewed in: *School Library Journal, Video Rating Guide for Libraries*
Grade Level: 2–4
Keywords: Behavior; Feelings; Sharing

Buddy, his alter ego Body, and their young friends discover the importance of consideration for other people's feelings. Questions about feelings are explored dramatically, while Body lets us know how it feels to be left out or ignored or treated badly. The kids role play situations, giving the audience a blueprint for future behavior.

Title: *My Body, My Buddy: Healthy Food*
Producer: Jacoby-Storm Productions/Rainbow Educational Video
Series: My Body, My Buddy: Health
Year Released: 1993
Call Number: 613.2
Length: 16 minutes
Price: $89.00
Reviewed in: *School Library Journal, Video Rating Guide for Libraries*
Grade Level: 1–4
Keywords: Exercise; Health; Nutrition

It is necessary to understand, at an early age, the value of eating healthful foods. This video shows how a person's body is his or her best buddy and explains that our bodies need healthful food, not junk food, to grow properly. Includes teacher's guide.

Title: *My Body, My Buddy: Healthy Fun*
Producer: Jacoby-Storm Productions/Rainbow Educational Video
Series: My Body, My Buddy: Health
Year Released: 1993
Call Number: 796
Length: 15 minutes
Price: $89.00
Reviewed in: *School Library Journal, Video Rating Guide for Libraries*
Grade Level: 1–4
Keywords: Exercise; Physical Education; Safety

Everybody needs exercise to stay healthy. In this video, Buddy shows Talia and Evan the importance of exercise and the importance of safety in exercise, like using a helmet when biking, wearing proper clothes, and not horsing around. Healthy fun also includes extra rest after a lot of exertion. Includes teacher's guide.

Title: *My Body, My Buddy: Teasing and Bullying*
Producer: Rainbow Educational Media
Series: My Body, My Buddy: Behavior
Year Released: 1995
Call Number: 158
Length: 18 minutes
Price: $89.00
Reviewed in: *School Library Journal, Video Rating Guide for Libraries*
Grade Level: 2–4
Keywords: Behavior; Bullies; Self-esteem

In dramatic situations, Buddy, his alter ego Body, and their young friends learn not only what it feels like to be picked on, but how the bully often feels, too. The kids role play a variety of responses to teasing and bullying and talk about the pros and cons of each possibility. The audience also learns a number of ways to build strong self-images and to defuse potentially tough encounters.

Title: *My Body, My Buddy: Winning and Losing*
Producer: Rainbow Educational Media
Series: My Body, My Buddy: Behavior
Year Released: 1995
Call Number: 175
Length: 18 minutes
Price: $89.00
Reviewed in: *School Library Journal, Video Rating Guide for Libraries*
Grade Level: 2–4
Keywords: Behavior; Competition

Buddy, his alter ego Body, and their young friends illustrate dramatically the fun of participating and begin to understand that they can't win all the time. They realize that losers can have just as good of a time—and learn something, too. Body explains how anger and frustration and disappointment make you feel. The kids role play typical situations so that they—and the audience—can see how to respond to losing in the future.

Title: *My First Magic Video*
Producer: Baker and Taylor
Series: My First Video
Year Released: 1995
Call Number: 793.8
Length: 40 minutes
Price: $13.00
Reviewed in: *Booklist, School Library Journal*
Grade Level: 1–6
Keywords: Magic; Technology

This video is based on the book by the same name and includes activities.

Title: *My First Science Video*
Producer: Sony Kids
Series: My First Video
Year Released: 1992
Call Number: 507.8
Length: 45 minutes
Price: $15.00
Reviewed in: *Booklist, School Library Journal*
Grade Level: K–4
Keywords: Science; Science Experiments

This video shows sixteen simple science experiments that illustrate basic principles of science. Includes teacher's guide.

Title: *My Way Sally*
Producer: Murdock Communications/MarshMedia
Series: Not Applicable
Year Released: 1989
Call Number: Easy Fiction
Length: 19 minutes
Price: $80.00
Reviewed in: *Video Rating Guide for Libraries*
Grade Level: K–4
Keywords: Dogs; England; Self-esteem

Sally is a young English foxhound who learns to command the respect of the other hounds and turns trouble into a win-win situation. The sites of Great Britain are introduced. Includes teacher's guide.

Title: *Mysteries Revealed—Basic Research Skills*
Producer: Delphi Productions/United Learning
Series: Not Applicable
Year Released: 1995
Call Number: 028.7
Length: 17 minutes
Price: $95.00
Reviewed in: *School Library Journal*
Grade Level: 5–6
Keywords: Library Skills; Research Skills

This video uses the mysterious disappearance of the Anasazi Indians, ancient tribes of the Southwest, to demonstrate the use of the library computer catalog system, card catalog, *Reader's Guide to Periodical Literature*, microfilm/microfiche, and other data bases. Includes teacher's guide, blackline master.

Title: *Native American Life*
Producer: Schlessinger Video Productions/Library Video Company
Series: American History For Children
Year Released: 1996
Call Number: 973
Length: 25 minutes
Price: $30.00
Reviewed in: *Booklist*
Grade Level: 1–5
Keywords: Indians of North America; Native Americans

This video includes historical information on life in America before European contact, Mother Earth/Father Sky, Pocahontas, Tecumseh and the Trail of Tears, the diversity of various Native American cultures, and life today.

Title: *Nature Friends!*
Producer: Dorling Kindersley
Series: Hullaballoo
Year Released: 1995
Call Number: 590
Length: 30 minutes
Price: $10.00
Reviewed in: *Booklist, Publishers Weekly, Video Librarian*

Grade Level: PreK–1
Keywords: Animals; Nature

Games, puppetry, international music and dance, and Ted Bear help children develop fundamental understandings of abstract ideas such as nature.

Title: *Navajo, The*
Producer: Schlessinger Video Productions
Series: Indians of North America Video Collection 1
Year Released: 1993
Call Number: 970.1
Length: 30 minutes
Price: $40.00
Reviewed in: *Booklist, School Library Journal, Video Rating Guide for Libraries*
Grade Level: 4–6
Keywords: Indians of North America; Native Americans; Navajo Indians

Leading Native American scholars discuss the history of the Navajo people, including myths and stereotypes. There are interviews combined with archival photographs and film footage, tribal music, crafts, and ceremonies, to help students examine the spiritual relationship with nature, the role of women in Indian society, and the role of the U.S. government in Indian affairs.

Title: *Night*
Producer: National Film Board of Canada/Bullfrog Films
Series: Look Again, Vol. 2
Year Released: 1990
Call Number: 231.7
Length: 28 minutes
Price: $150.00
Reviewed in: *Video Rating Guide for Libraries*
Grade Level: K–6
Keywords: Night; Science—Earth

A girl views the city at night from her balcony, wondering about the sights and sounds of her familiar world after dark. Includes teacher's guide.

Title: *Nina's Strange Adventure*
Producer: Alan Sloan, Inc./AIMS Media
Series: Wild World
Year Released: 1989
Call Number: Fiction
Length: 15 minutes
Price: $50.00
Reviewed in: *Video Rating Guide for Libraries*
Grade Level: K–6
Keywords: Language Arts; Otters; Science—Life; Values

An adventure story that is also a lesson in values, the program shows a young otter in her natural habitat and traveling to the land of her dreams. Story is followed by reading and language lessons.

Title: *No More Teasing!*
Producer: Sunburst Communications
Series: Not Applicable
Year Released: 1995
Call Number: 158.1
Length: 16 minutes
Price: $99.00
Reviewed in: *School Library Journal*
Grade Level: 2–4
Keywords: Behavior; Bullies; Human Relations

This program presents strategies kids can use to protect themselves against teasing or bullying. The "No More Teasing Team"—peer hosts who introduce common teasing situations and offer solutions—shows how students can change their own behavior to lessen teasing or bullying's impact. Includes teacher's guide, student worksheets.

Title: *Oceans: Earth's Last Frontier*
Producer: Rainbow Educational Media
Series: Not Applicable
Year Released: 1995
Call Number: 551.46
Length: 24 minutes
Price: $89.00
Reviewed in: *Booklist, School Library Journal*
Grade Level: 4–6
Keywords: Oceans; Science—Life

Students discover that oceans are vital to the health of our planet, cover 70 percent of the earth's surface, and are incredibly interesting. Using graphics and student demonstrations, this program describes how oceans have mountain ranges thousands of miles long, trenches far deeper than the Grand Canyon, and are rich with life.

Title: *Officer Buckle and Gloria*
Producer: Weston Woods
Series: Not Applicable
Year Released: 1997
Call Number: Easy Fiction
Length: 11 minutes
Price: $60
Reviewed in: *Booklist, School Library Journal*
Grade Level: PreK–3
Keywords: Dogs; Literature; Safety

Based on the Caldecott Medal book by Peggy Rathmann. The children at Napville Elementary School always ignore Officer Buckle's safety tips until a police dog named Gloria accompanies him when he gives his safety speeches.

Title: *Oil Spills*
Producer: GPN
Series: Dr. Dad's Ph3
Year Released: 1994
Call Number: 363.73
Length: 15 minutes
Price: $30.00
Reviewed in: *Booklist*
Grade Level: 3–6
Keywords: Ecology; Environmental Concerns; Oil Spills

Olivia and her friends learn about cleaning oil spills the hard way when they accidentally create an environmental disaster of their own. They discover how sorbents work and how oil and water really don't mix. At the site of an industrial spill, Dr. Ralph Portier gives Dr. Dad a first-hand look at how microbes are used to clean up a land spill. Teacher's guide available for purchase.

Title: *Old Glory*
Producer: Colman Communications/Rainbow Educational Media
Series: Not Applicable
Year Released: 1994
Call Number: 929.9
Length: 10 minutes
Price: $70.00
Reviewed in: *Booklist, School Library Journal*
Grade Level: 2–5
Keywords: Flags; Social Studies; U.S. History

The story of the American flag is told from Revolutionary War days to the present. Viewers see many of the flags that have flown over this country while learning the historical background of each one. In addition, youngsters learn what the flag symbolizes, what the various parts of the flag mean, and how to properly maintain and display the American flag. Includes teacher's guide.

Title: *One World, Many Worlds: Hispanic Diversity in the United States*
Producer: Rainbow Educational Media
Series: Multicultural History
Year Released: 1993
Call Number: 305.86
Length: 22 minutes
Price: $89.00
Reviewed in: *School Library Journal, Video Rating Guide for Libraries*
Grade Level: 4–6
Keywords: Hispanic Americans; Multicultural

This video focuses first on historical background of the Hispanic American—the how and why Hispanics came to America. It then shows the location of Hispanic communities today—their struggle with discrimination and their contribution to American culture. While Hispanics maintain ties with their places of origin and culture, they continue the struggle for rights and acceptance here. Includes teacher's guide.

Title: *Oops! I Messed Up!*
Producer: Sunburst Communications
Series: Not Applicable
Year Released: 1995
Call Number: 158
Length: 22 minutes
Price: $99.00
Reviewed in: *School Library Journal*
Grade Level: 2–4
Keywords: Behavior; Self-esteem

With the help of an eccentric inventor who refuses to be discouraged by his blunders, this program demonstrates how important mistakes are to learning. Students are helped to understand that mistakes happen to everyone, and that even though they mess up, they can still turn failure around and learn from it. Includes teacher's guide, worksheets.

Title: *Otherwise Known as Sheila the Great*
Producer: Calico Films/Barr Films
Series: Judy Blume
Year Released: 1989
Call Number: Fiction
Length: 16 minutes
Price: $40.00
Reviewed in: *Video Rating Guide for Libraries*
Grade Level: 4–6
Keywords: Fear; Literature

Adapted from the book by Judy Blume, this video tells how an eventful summer and a straightforward friend help Sheila outgrow some foolish fears.

Title: *Our Changing Earth*
Producer: Rainbow Educational Media
Series: Not Applicable
Year Released: 1991
Call Number: 551.1
Length: 22 minutes
Price: $89.00
Reviewed in: *Booklist, School Library Journal, Video Rating Guide for Libraries*

Grade Level: 4–6
Keywords: Geology; Science—Earth

The Earth that we live on is made up of land, water, crust, mantle, and core. It rotates on its axis causing day and night; its revolutions around the sun cause the seasons. The earth has been built up by volcanoes and mountains; it has been worn down by the forces of weathering, erosion, glaciers, and earthquakes. These concepts are addressed and vocabulary is defined. Includes teacher's guide.

Title: *Our Federal Government: The Legislative Branch*
Producer: Cochran Communications
Series: Our Federal Government
Year Released: 1993
Call Number: 328.73
Length: 28 minutes
Price: $99.00
Reviewed in: *Booklist, School Library Journal*
Grade Level: 5–6
Keywords: Government; Social Studies

Live-action, historical prints, graphics, and documentary footage help tell the story of the creation and function of the legislative branch. Students learn the requirements for becoming a member of Congress, the process by which a bill becomes a law, the structure of the House of Representatives and Senate, the role of committees, the roles of the Speaker of the House and the vice president, the powers of Congress, and the interaction of the legislative branch with other branches of government.

Title: *Our Federal Government: The Presidency*
Producer: Rainbow Educational Media
Series: Our Federal Government
Year Released: 1993
Call Number: 353.73
Length: 22 minutes
Price: $99.00
Reviewed in: *Booklist, School Library Journal, Video Rating Guide for Libraries*
Grade Level: 5–6
Keywords: Government; Presidents; Social Studies

Students see how the Constitution established the executive branch, provided for the separation of powers, and determined the relationship of the executive branch to the legislative and judicial branches of the federal government. The powers granted to the executive branch are covered, also the requirements for holding the office of president. In addition, the program explains how the presidency has evolved in terms of its influence and exercise of power since the Constitution was ratified. Includes teacher's guide.

Title: *Our Federal Government: The Supreme Court*
Producer: Rainbow Educational Media
Series: Our Federal Government
Year Released: 1993
Call Number: 347
Length: 22 minutes
Price: $99.00
Reviewed in: *Booklist, School Library Journal, Video Rating Guide for Libraries*
Grade Level: 5–6
Keywords: Government; Social Studies; Supreme Court

The origins of the judicial branch and Supreme Court are addressed here, also an examination of the Supreme Court's power to influence American history and society in profound ways. The video shows how the exercise of this power has often been controversial—that the philosophy of the court can change as different justices are appointed and because of the political and social climates of the times. The Supreme Court's influence on other branches of the federal government is also revealed. Includes teacher's guide.

Title: *Our Internal Defender*
Producer: MarshMedia
Series: Immune System
Year Released: 1990
Call Number: 616
Length: 10 minutes
Price: $60.00
Reviewed in: *Video Rating Guide for Libraries*
Grade Level: 4–6
Keywords: Diseases; Health; Human Body

The video introduces students to the micro-organisms and minute foreign particles surrounding us at all times, including the infectious viruses and bacteria that threaten us, and explains how the immune system protects us when these foes break through the body's outer defenses. It explores the nature of immunity, from the recognition of the invader to the eventual showdown of the battle as the invader is defeated.

Title: *Our Planet Earth*
Producer: United Learning
Series: Junior Geologist
Year Released: 1993
Call Number: 551
Length: 9 minutes
Price: $55.00
Reviewed in: *Video Rating Guide for Libraries*
Grade Level: 2–4
Keywords: Geology; Science—Earth

From the views of the earth from a space shuttle, students begin their exploration of the science of geology. Footage of the many different land formations across our planet's surface helps teach students about the geology of our planet. Includes teacher's guide, blackline masters.

Title: *Our Solar System: The Inner Planets*
Producer: Allied Video Corp.
Series: Our Solar System
Year Released: 1992
Call Number: 523.4
Length: 26 minutes
Price: $30.00
Reviewed in: *Booklist, Video Rating Guide for Libraries*
Grade Level: 2–5
Keywords: Planets; Science—Space; Solar System

This voyage aboard an imaginary homemade spacecraft is packed with video footage, photography, and animation. It presents interesting facts about each planet.

Title: *Over a Barrel*
Producer: Children's Television Workshop/GPN
Series: GhostWriter
Year Released: 1993
Call Number: 428
Length: 30 minutes
Price: $50.00
Reviewed in: *Booklist*
Grade Level: 3–6
Keywords: Environmental Concerns; Language Arts; Mystery

When a mysterious illness sweeps the neighborhood, the team conducts a survey and discovers that toxic waste buried in the community garden is to blame. Next they figure out who dumped the waste, and make posters and write letters to attract the press and embarrass the culprit into cleaning up the mess. Includes guide.

Title: *Painting*
Producer: NBT Enterprises/Rainbow Educational Media
Series: Art Start
Year Released: 1995
Call Number: 751
Length: 20 minutes
Price: $79.00
Reviewed in: *Booklist, School Library Journal*
Grade Level: 4–6
Keywords: Art; Painting

The student experiments with different brush strokes while learning the parts and types of brushes. The focus extends to color mixing.

Title: Papa Piccolo
Producer: GPN/MarshMedia
Series: Key Concepts in Self-Esteem
Year Released: 1992
Call Number: Easy Fiction
Length: 17 minutes
Price: $80.00
Reviewed in: *Video Rating Guide for Libraries*

Grade Level: K–4
Keywords: Families; Italy; Language Arts

A free-spirited tomcat becomes a father figure to two orphaned kittens. Watercolor depictions of Venice provide the background to this story. Includes teacher's guide.

Title: *Pastels*
Producer: NBT Enterprises/Rainbow Educational Media
Series: Art Start
Year Released: 1995
Call Number: 751.4
Length: 20 minutes
Price: $79.00
Reviewed in: *Booklist, School Library Journal*
Grade Level: 4–6
Keywords: Art; Colors

In this video, complementary colors are introduced and used to enhance a picture depicting a sea creature's particular personality. Pastel techniques are explored.

Title: *Patrick Stewart Narrates "The Planets"*
Producer: BMG Video
Series: Not Applicable
Year Released: 1991
Call Number: 523.2
Length: 51 minutes
Price: $17.00
Reviewed in: *Video Rating Guide for Libraries*
Grade Level: 5–6
Keywords: Planets; Science—Space

This video discusses man's voyage into space with the Holst/Tomita score in the background.

Title: *Pattern Patrol*
Producer: TVOntario/Films for the Humanities and Sciences
Series: Art's Place
Year Released: 1990
Call Number: 702

Length: 15 minutes
Price: $49.00
Reviewed in: *Video Rating Guide for Libraries*
Grade Level: K–3
Keywords: Language Arts; Patterns

Kim and Leo play a pattern-spotting game and then learn to design their own patterns. Mirror tells a story about a hunter who tries to capture a beautifully patterned creature to please his maharajah. Includes guide.

Title: *Peanuts*
Producer: TVOntario/Films for the Humanities and Sciences
Series: Here's How
Year Released: 1991
Call Number: 635
Length: 10 minutes
Price: $49.00
Reviewed in: *Video Rating Guide for Libraries*
Grade Level: 1–3
Keywords: Carver, George Washington; Inventions; Peanuts; Technology

Kids observe the farming of peanuts, use shells in art projects, and learn about George Washington Carver's hundreds of uses for the peanut plant. Teacher's guide available for purchase.

Title: *Peeping Beauty*
Producer: Live Oak Media
Series: Not Applicable
Year Released: 1994
Call Number: Easy Fiction
Length: 9 minutes
Price: $38.00
Reviewed in: *School Library Journal*
Grade Level: PreK–2
Keywords: Ballet; Chickens; Literature

Based on the book by Mary Jane Auch, this video tells the story of Poulette the hen, who—starstruck by her dream of becoming a famous ballerina— is taken in by a slick talent scout (a fox) who offers her the lead in his production of *Peeping Beauty*. Poulette cleverly uses her ballet skills to avoid becoming a chicken dinner. Includes teacher's guide.

Title: *Pegasus*
Producer: Lightyear Entertainment
Series: Stories to Remember
Year Released: 1990
Call Number: Fiction
Length: 27 minutes
Price: $13.00
Reviewed in: *Video Rating Guide for Libraries*
Grade Level: K–6
Keywords: Literature; Mythology

The Greek myth of the winged horse is adapted by award-winning children's author, Doris Orgel. Parents' Choice Award.

Title: *People of the Desert*
Producer: Rainbow Educational Video
Series: Native Americans
Year Released: 1993
Call Number: 305.897
Length: 30 minutes
Price: $89.00
Reviewed in: *Booklist, Media and Methods, School Library Journal, Video Rating Guide for Libraries*
Grade Level: 4–6
Keywords: Indians of North America; Native Americans

This authentic recreation of an Anasazi cliff-dwelling village shows how these ancestors of the modern Hopi adapted to their environment. Their life style and cultural development are seen through the everyday experiences of an Indian family. Examples of their weapons, tools, pottery, and art are shown.

Title: *People of the Forest*
Producer: Peter Matulavich/Rainbow Educational Media
Series: Native Americans
Year Released: 1994
Call Number: 973
Length: 25 minutes
Price: $99.00
Reviewed in: *Booklist, Video Rating Guide for Libraries*

Grade Level: 3–5
Keywords: Indians of North America; Native Americans

Dense forests, streams, mirror lakes, and waterfalls were home to the Iroquois, the Cherokee, the Chippewa, and others. The typical life of these Eastern Woodland Indians is seen through a Chippewa family. The men and women had their separate chores to perform. In the video, Little Flower is a young girl who experiences the frustration of being allowed to do "only" women's work—cooking, sewing, basket making—but she really wants to hunt, fish, and trap. Includes teacher's guide.

Title: *People of the Northwest Coast*
Producer: Peter Matulavich/Rainbow Educational Media
Series: Native Americans
Year Released: 1994
Call Number: 305.897
Length: 25 minutes
Price: $99.00
Reviewed in: *Booklist, School Library Journal, Video Rating Guide for Libraries*
Grade Level: 4–6
Keywords: Indians of North America; Social Studies

Native American peoples of the Northwest have many names— Tlinget, Haida, Salish, Tsimshian. Despite different names and different languages, they share a common background of survival along the rugged coastlines and dense forests. They fished the rivers and streams, hunted and trapped in the forest, built long houses from cedar, and carved many intricate items such as totem poles and masks. This video provides a portrait of these people in their day-to-day lives. Includes teacher's guide.

Title: *People of the Rainforest*
Producer: Schlessinger Video Productions/Library Video Company
Series: Rainforest for Children
Year Released: 1996
Call Number: 574
Length: 25 minutes
Price: $29.95

Reviewed in: *School Library Journal*
Grade Level: 3–6
Keywords: Rain Forests; Science—Life

Filmed in the rain forest of Costa Rica, this video offers information on the people of the rain forest. The four layers of the rain forest are defined along with the interdepartment relationships of the ecosystem.

Title: *Perfect the Pig*
Producer: WNED-TV/Vestron Video
Series: Reading Rainbow
Year Released: 1989
Call Number: Easy Fiction
Length: 30 minutes
Price: $44.00
Reviewed in: *Video Rating Guide for Libraries*
Grade Level: K–4
Keywords: Animals; Literature; Pigs

James Coco narrates the high-flying adventures of a special pig with wings in this program featuring a book by Susan Jeschke. LeVar Burton has an adventure of his own when he discovers Kermit the Frog at the library and they have a discussion about life, happiness, and the pursuit of Kermit's "special friend," Miss Piggy. Real pigs are also featured in a visit to a hog farm in rural Oahu in Hawaii.

Title: *Picture Book of Martin Luther King, Jr., A*
Producer: Live Oak Media
Series: Not Applicable
Year Released: 1990
Call Number: Biography
Length: 9 minutes
Price: $38.00
Reviewed in: *Elementary School Library Collection, School Library Journal*
Grade Level: 1–4
Keywords: African Americans; Biographies; King, Martin Luther, Jr.; Literature

From the book by David A. Adler, with illustrations by Robert Casilla, the text joins with illustrations to capture the life and times of Dr. King and give the viewer an appreciation and understanding of his efforts to secure equal rights for all people. Includes teacher's guide.

Title: *Pigs* (2d ed.)
Producer: Churchill Video Ventures/Churchill Media
Series: Not Applicable
Year Released: 1995
Call Number: 636.5
Length: 9 minutes
Price: $50.00
Reviewed in: *School Library Journal*
Grade Level: K–5
Keywords: Animals; Pigs; Science—Life

It is dawn on a farm. A timid sparrow discovers bulky shapes and sounds of heavy breathing. Blimplike shapes arise—pigs. Faces, tails, and personalities are highlighted.

Title: *Pilgrims at Plymouth*
Producer: Video Dialog
Series: Not Applicable
Year Released: 1991
Call Number: 973.2
Length: 23 minutes
Price: $100.00
Reviewed in: *School Library Journal, Video Rating Guide for Libraries*
Grade Level: 4–6
Keywords: Colonial America; Pilgrims; Social Studies

With this program, students see, hear, and become a part of the Plymouth Plantation during the first winter; observe the building of the Pilgrims' houses; and witness the planting of crops. They see the Wampanoag tribe help the Pilgrims survive their first year in America by showing them how to plant Indian corn and by trading skins, furs, and corn with the Pilgrims for English tools. The program explores the Pilgrims' reasons for coming to America and relates their settlement in New England to the growth of Colonial America. Includes teacher's guide.

Title: *Plants: Green, Growing, Giving Life*
Producer: Cochran Communications/Rainbow Educational Video
Series: Not Applicable
Year Released: 1991
Call Number: 581.1
Length: 22 minutes
Price: $89.00
Reviewed in: *School Library Journal, Video Rating Guide for Libraries*
Grade Level: 4–6
Keywords: Plants; Science—Life

> This program gives examples of the diversity of plants. It shows how plants, like other living things, require food for energy and growth. Plants are also different from other living things in that, through photosynthesis, they can manufacture their own food. This video also shows how plants are made up of different parts like roots, stems, leaves, etc. Includes teacher's guide.

Title: *Plants of the Rainforest*
Producer: Schlessinger Video Productions/Library Video Company
Series: Rainforest for Children
Year Released: 1996
Call Number: 574
Length: 25 minutes
Price: $29.95
Reviewed in: *School Library Journal*
Grade Level: 3–6
Keywords: Rain Forests; Science—Life

> Like *People of the Rainforest*, this video was filmed in the rain forest of Costa Rica. Information on the plants of the rain forest is presented in the context of the four layers of the rain forest and the interdependent relationships of the ecosystem.

Title: *Polymers: Stretching and Bouncing Back*
Producer: Louisiana Public Broadcasting/GPN
Series: Dr. Dad's Ph3
Year Released: 1994
Call Number: 540
Length: 15 minutes
Price: $30.00

Reviewed in: *Booklist, School Library Journal*
Grade Level: 3–6
Keywords: Chemistry; Polymers; Science—Physical

Dr. Dad and the kids explore some of the properties of polymers, including their strength and flexibility. Using an old family recipe, they "whip up" a glue-based polymer right in the garage. Chemist Joyce Morningstar shares some facts about polymers and shows how these amazing materials are made and refined. Teacher's guide available for purchase.

Title: *Pony Express, The*
Producer: SelectVideo Publishing
Series: American Traditions
Year Released: 1994
Call Number: 973
Length: 50 minutes
Price: $25.00
Reviewed in: *Booklist, School Library Journal*
Grade Level: 5–6
Keywords: Pony Express; Postal Service; Social Studies

It only lasted for a year and a half in 1860 and '61, but in that time Americans from coast to coast thrilled at the exploits of an elite band of daring young horsemen who sped across the frontier carrying the mail from Missouri and California.

Title: *Positively Native*
Producer: TVOntario/Journal Films
Series: Many Voices
Year Released: 1992
Call Number: 305.8
Length: 15 minutes
Price: $49.00
Reviewed in: *Video Rating Guide for Libraries*
Grade Level: 4–6
Keywords: Multicultural; Stereotypes

Martin makes a video about his native way of life, hoping to dispel some of the stereotypes he faces daily. He is pleased with the response to the finished video, but wonders if he can keep on trying to make changes. Teacher's guide available for purchase.

Title: *Power Up? Energy in Our Environment*
Producer: Cochran Communications/Rainbow Educational Video
Series: Not Applicable
Year Released: 1992
Call Number: 333.79
Length: 22 minutes
Price: $89.00
Reviewed in: *Book Report, Library Talk, Video Rating Guide for Libraries*
Grade Level: 4–6
Keywords: Energy; Environmental Concerns; Science—Physical

This video focuses on various issues relating to energy in the environment. Students see how we use and rely on energy in our daily lives, sources of energy, what fossil fuels are, and how burning fossil fuels contribute to air pollution, smog, acid rain, and the greenhouse effect. Students also see how they personally can help solve environmental problems related to energy through conservation. Includes teacher's guide.

Title: *Praying Mantis*
Producer: Digital Nutshell/Lucerne Media
Series: Science in Your Own Backyard
Year Released: 1995
Call Number: 595.7
Length: 10 minutes
Price: $145.00
Reviewed in: *School Library Journal*
Grade Level: 5–6
Keywords: Insects; Praying Mantis; Science—Life

The praying mantis, so called because it folds its forelegs as if praying, is part of the family mantidae. Its fragile, sticklike appearance belies its surprising proficiency as a hunter. Close-ups reveal each stage in the life cycle of this unusual insect.

Title: *Prince and the Pauper, The*
Producer: Golden Films/Sony Wonder
Series: Enchanted Tales
Year Released: 1995
Call Number: Fiction
Length: 48 minutes

Price: $15.00
Reviewed in: *School Library Journal*
Grade Level: 1–6
Keywords: Literature; Princes

This is a fully animated retelling of the classic tale of a young ragamuffin mistaken for a prince.

Title: *Professor Parrot Speaks Spanish*
Producer: Sound Beginnings
Series: Not Applicable
Year Released: 1997
Call Number: 468.3
Length: 30 minutes
Price: $29.95
Reviewed in: *Booklist, School Library Journal*
Grade Level: PreK–2
Keywords: Early Childhood; Spanish Language

Join Professor Parrot on an adventure of making friends while learning over 150 words and phrases in Spanish. Songs, games, dances, and puppets are used to teach students the Spanish language. Teacher's guide and audiocassette tape are included with video.

Title: *Protecting Our Endangered Species*
Producer: New Castle Communications
Series: Not Applicable
Year Released: 1996
Call Number: 574.529
Length: 30 minutes
Price: $99.00
Reviewed in: *Booklist*
Grade Level: 4–6
Keywords: Ecology; Endangered Species; Environmental Concerns

This video discusses how endangering animals and plants threatens the existence of the rest of the world. It shows success stories of recovering endangered animals, and children discuss what they have done and want to do to save plants and animals from extinction. Includes teacher's guide.

Title: *Protecting the Web*
Producer: Pyramid Film and Video
Series: Not Applicable
Year Released: 1989
Call Number: 333.91
Length: 15 minutes
Price: $225.00
Reviewed in: *Video Rating Guide for Libraries*
Grade Level: 4–6
Keywords: Animals; Ecosystem; Pets; Science—Life

Using the metaphor of a spider's web, this film helps viewers understand that all living things are part of the earth's ecosystem, and that the choices they make in everyday life can help or hurt other living creatures. It encourages students to become more aware of the animals in their own lives, to appreciate wildlife, and to be responsible pet owners.

Title: *Pueblo, The*
Producer: Schlessinger Video Productions
Series: Indians of North America Video Collection 2
Year Released: 1994
Call Number: 979.1
Length: 30 minutes
Price: $40.00
Reviewed in: *Booklist, School Library Journal*
Grade Level: 4–6
Keywords: Indians of North America; Native Americans; Pueblo Indians

Leading Native American scholars discuss the history of the Pueblo, including myths and stereotypes. There are interviews combined with archival photographs and film footage, tribal music, crafts, and ceremonies to help students examine the spiritual relationship with nature, the role of women in Indian society, and the role of the U.S. government in Indian affairs.

Title: *Puerto Ricans*
Producer: Schlessinger Video Productions
Series: Multicultural Peoples of North America
Year Released: 1993

Call Number: 305.8
Length: 30 minutes
Price: $40.00
Reviewed in: *Booklist, School Library Journal, Video Rating Guide for Libraries*
Grade Level: 4–6
Keywords: Multicultural; Puerto Ricans

This program examines Puerto Ricans by meeting a variety of Puerto Rican families, learning their traditions, exploring their culture, and understanding their history.

Title: *Push and Pull: Simple Machines at Work*
Producer: Rainbow Educational Media
Series: Not Applicable
Year Released: 1990
Call Number: 621.8
Length: 20 minutes
Price: $89.00
Reviewed in: *Booklist, School Library Journal, Science Books and Films, Video Rating Guide for Libraries*
Grade Level: 3–5
Keywords: Science—Physical; Simple Machines

Machines help dig, lift, and move. Every day we use things that we don't even think of as machines—a door knob, a knife, roller skates, a light bulb. All machines, no matter how complicated they look, are made up of combinations of simple machines. This program examines and explains the six types of simple machines: the lever, the wheel and axle, the pulley, the inclined plane, the screw, and the wedge. Visuals and graphics further demonstrate how each is used. Includes teacher's guide.

Title: *Quilt*
Producer: National Film Board of Canada
Series:
Year Released: 1997
Call Number: 791.43
Length: 6 minutes 40 seconds
Price: $139.00
Reviewed in: *Booklist, School Library Journal*

Grade Level: K–6
Keywords: Art; Computers; Quilt

This abstract animated film uses computer technology and experimental techniques to choreograph quilt motifs and designs to music.

Title: *Radio and Television*
Producer: TVOntario/Films for the Humanities and Sciences
Series: Here's How
Year Released: 1991
Call Number: 791.4023
Length: 10 minutes
Price: $49.00
Reviewed in: *Video Rating Guide for Libraries*
Grade Level: 1–3
Keywords: Radios; Technology; Television

After visits to a radio station and a television studio and control room, children make a TV studio out of a cardboard box and put on a radio show. Teacher's guide available for purchase.

Title: *Railroaders*
Producer: Big Kids Productions
Series: What Do You Want to Be When You Grow Up?
Year Released: 1994
Call Number: 385
Length: 35 minutes
Price: $15.00
Reviewed in: *Booklist*, *School Library Journal*
Grade Level: PreK–2
Keywords: Careers; Railroads

This video introduces children to the world of railroads. From freight trains to passenger trains, children learn about conductors, engineers, brakemen, switchmen, and others who work on the railroads.

Title: *Ralph S. Mouse*
Producer: Churchill Media
Series: Not Applicable
Year Released: 1990

Call Number: Fiction
Length: 40 minutes
Price: $60.00
Reviewed in: *Video Rating Guide for Libraries*
Grade Level: K–6
Keywords: Literature; Mice

In this, Ralph's third outing, he must leave the Mountain View Inn. If he stays, his friend Matt the bellman might lose his job to an overabundance of mice on the premises. Ralph persuades his friend Ryan to take him to school, where the fun—and the danger—begin. Includes teacher's guide.

Title: *Reading the Best: Introducing the Newbery Winners*
Producer: Words, Inc./Cheshire Book Companions
Series: Not Applicable
Year Released: 1991
Call Number: 808
Length: 64 minutes
Price: $135.00
Reviewed in: *Video Rating Guide for Libraries*
Grade Level: 4–6
Keywords: Literature; Newbery Medal

From "A Wrinkle in Time" to "Summer of the Swans," this four-part series highlights dozens of classics. Each book is introduced and summarized to stimulate reading interest. Kids are encouraged to read for fun and seek out Newbery winners and Honor Books to make sure they're reading the best. Includes teacher's guide.

Title: *Red Riding Hood and the Well-Fed Wolf* (Revised)
Producer: Churchill Media
Series: Not Applicable
Year Released: 1990
Call Number: 398.2
Length: 15 minutes
Price: $100.00
Reviewed in: *Booklist, Video Rating Guide for Libraries*
Grade Level: 3–6
Keywords: Food; Health; Nutrition

The traditional Little Red Riding Hood story with a delicious twist. Here's the ugly wolf, all dressed up in Grandma's clothes and looking forward to a dinner of succulent Red Riding Hood. But Red, and her walking, talking foods, have a different idea of what constitutes a good meal. This revision uses the Food Guide Pyramid introduced by the USDA. Includes teacher's guide.

Title: *Reducing, Reusing, and Recycling: Environmental Concerns*
Producer: Rainbow Educational Media
Series: Not Applicable
Year Released: 1990
Call Number: 363.7
Length: 20 minutes
Price: $89.00
Reviewed in: *Booklist, Media and Methods, School Library Journal, Science Books and Films, Video Rating Guide for Libraries*
Grade Level: 4–6
Keywords: Ecology; Recycling

Solid waste is almost anything a person throws away, including trash and garbage. This program focuses on the problems created by solid waste and offers ways to help alleviate these problems. Students demonstrate the "Three Rs" approach, and we see that we are indeed responsible for our environment and for the future of our planet. Includes teacher's guide.

Title: *Reproductive Systems*
Producer: National Geographic Society Educational Services
Series: Your Body Series
Year Released: 1994
Call Number: 612
Length: 16 minutes
Price: $79.00
Reviewed in: *School Library Journal*
Grade Level: 4–6
Keywords: Human Body; Science—Life

Learn about the female and male reproductive systems. Animation and medical photography show fertilization and the union of the male and female sex cells, and follow a developing new life. Watch the fertilized egg, the zygote, divide over and over, then see it travel to the uterus, where it grows for nine months. See the developments at six and a half weeks, when the embryo's heart begins to beat and its hands and feet start to grow. Includes teacher's guide.

Title: *Reptile*
Producer: BBC Wildvision, BBC Lionheart TV, Dorling Kindersley
 Vision in association with Oregon Public Broadcasting/Dorling
 Kindersley/Houghton Mifflin
Series: Eyewitness Video
Year Released: 1995
Call Number: 597.9
Length: 35 minutes
Price: $13.00
Reviewed in: *School Library Journal*
Grade Level: PreK–6
Keywords: Animals; Reptiles

Viewers will journey into a three-dimensional "virtual museum"
where live-action, wildlife photography creates the sensation of being there. The program presents a view of the marvels and mysteries of the natural world. Also included is behind-the-scenes, "making
of the series" footage. Narrated by Martin Sheen.

Title: *Respect Yourself and Others, Too*
Producer: Sunburst Communications
Series: Not Applicable
Year Released: 1994
Call Number: 177
Length: 18 minutes
Price: $99.00
Reviewed in: *Booklist, School Library Journal*
Grade Level: 2–4
Keywords: Behavior; Friendship; Self-esteem

This program teaches social sensitivity as a key step in promoting
respect and understanding among students. It emphasizes the importance of respecting the rights and needs of others, and illustrates
the problems that result from put-downs, fighting, or ignoring others' feelings. It helps students develop empathy and discover that
when they show respect for others, they increase their own self-
respect. Includes teacher's guide, worksheets.

Title: *Robins and How They Live*
Producer: AIMS Media
Series: Animals and How They Live
Year Released: 1994

Call Number: 598
Length: 18 minutes
Price: $100.00
Reviewed in: *School Library Journal*
Grade Level: 4–6
Keywords: Birds; Robins

Close-up photography captures the sights and sounds of the American robin as it illustrates the life cycle of a family of robins in their natural habitat. The program shows their migratory patterns, their nesting and mating habits, and their locating and defending territory. Also shown is the complete hatching process of a new chick from start to finish. Includes teacher's guide.

Title: *Rock Ptarmigan*
Producer: TVOntario
Series: Nature Watch
Year Released: 1989
Call Number: 598
Length: 25 minutes
Price: $49.00
Reviewed in: *Video Rating Guide for Libraries*
Grade Level: 2–6
Keywords: Adaptation; Birds

Rock ptarmigans live in some of the most hostile environments on earth, so they must adapt every aspect of their lives to the elements. Viewers follow a family through their short reproductive cycle, from courting to teaching survival skills to the young. Teacher's guide available for purchase.

Title: *Rocks and Minerals*
Producer: Creative Adventure/United Learning
Series: Junior Geologist
Year Released: 1993
Call Number: 552
Length: 8 minutes
Price: $55.00
Reviewed in: *Video Rating Guide for Libraries*
Grade Level: 2–4
Keywords: Geology; Rocks; Science—Earth

Students are introduced to basic explanations of minerals, the rock cycle, fossils, and rock identification. Segments addressed include: What are rocks made of? What is a mineral? What is the rock cycle? and How do geologists identify rocks? Includes teacher's guide, blackline masters.

Title: *Roman City*
Producer: Larry Klein for Unicorn Projects/PBS Video
Series: Not Applicable
Year Released: 1994
Call Number: 937
Length: 60 minutes
Price: $50.00
Reviewed in: *Booklist, School Library Journal*
Grade Level: 5–6
Keywords: Roman Empire; Social Studies

Explore ancient Rome in this animated and live-action video that tells the story of life in a city in the frontier of Gaul at the height of the Roman Empire. Host David Macaulay visits sites of Roman architecture in Pompeii, Herculaneum, Ostia, Nimes, Southern France, and Rome. Includes teacher's guide. Animated, thirty-minute version available.

Title: *Rumpelstiltskin*
Producer: Hanna-Barbera Home Video
Series: Timeless Tales from Hallmark
Year Released: 1990
Call Number: 398.2
Length: 30 minutes
Price: $95.00
Reviewed in: *Video Rating Guide for Libraries*
Grade Level: K–6
Keywords: Fairy Tales; Literature

Because of the boasting of a proud father, a young maiden is forced to turn straw into gold at the king's castle. There she meets an evil little man who first comes to her rescue but later tries to claim her firstborn child when she becomes queen. Through her own resourcefulness, the queen outsmarts the little man and guesses his name. The live-action production is enhanced by original music.

Title: *Sammy: And Other Songs from Getting to Know Myself*
Producer: Educational Activities
Series: Not Applicable
Year Released: 1993
Call Number: 782.42
Length: 30 minutes
Price: $20.00
Reviewed in: *Ladies Home Journal, Video Rating Guide for Libraries*
Grade Level: PreK–1
Keywords: Early Childhood; Movement

This movement-participation video features a rainbow of children stretching, jumping, and discovering the joy of movement.

Title: *Santa Fe Trail, The*
Producer: Delphi Productions/United Learning
Series: Not Applicable
Year Released: 1991
Call Number: 979.003
Length: 22 minutes
Price: $95.00
Reviewed in: *School Library Journal, Video Rating Guide for Libraries*
Grade Level: 5–6
Keywords: Pioneers; Social Studies; U.S. History

This video traces the history of the Santa Fe Trail and its contribution to the development of the American West. It is divided into the following segments: the Coronado expedition, the first glimpse of riches to be had, the early traders, dangers on the Trail, the journey itself, frontier forts along the Trail, and the end of the Trail with the completion of the railway. Includes teacher's guide, blackline masters.

Title: *Satellites*
Producer: TVOntario
Series: Look Up
Year Released: 1990
Call Number: 629.44
Length: 115 minutes
Price: $49.00

Reviewed in: *Video Rating Guide for Libraries*
Grade Level: 3–6
Keywords: Radios; Satellites; Science—Space

Students learn about satellites: what they are, how they work, how they are launched and remain in orbit, and how they are used. Related activities include pretending to be a satellite in orbit, studying radio signals, and examining spinning toys. Includes guide.

Title: *Savior Is Born*
Producer: Rabbit Ears Productions
Series: Not Applicable
Year Released: 1992
Call Number: 232.92
Length: 30 minutes
Price: $10.00
Reviewed in: *School Library Journal*
Grade Level: K–5
Keywords: Christmas; Holidays; Religion

This video tells the story of the first Christmas: Jesus Christ's birth, according to the gospels of Luke and Matthew. Narrated by Morgan Freeman.

Title: *Say No and Keep Your Friends*
Producer: Sunburst Communications
Series: Not Applicable
Year Released: 1995
Call Number: 158.1
Length: 25 minutes
Price: $169.00
Reviewed in: *School Library Journal*
Grade Level: 5–6
Keywords: Behavior; Peer Pressure

Middle schoolers often find that saying no to a friend can mean the end of the friendship. Using pressure-filled situations typical of middle-school experience, this program demonstrates techniques that will help students stand up for themselves and still retain valued friendships. Includes teacher's guide.

Title: *School's Cool*
Producer: Region IV E.S.C./Film Ideas
Series: Not Applicable
Year Released: 1995
Call Number: 371.4
Length: 14 minutes
Price: $135.00
Reviewed in: *School Library Journal*
Grade Level: 3–6
Keywords: Behavior; Truancy

An ethnically diverse video that focuses on young children who give viewers their reasons why staying in school is important. A peer-to-peer video that demonstrates the importance of staying in school.

Title: *Science and the Seas*
Producer: California Academy of Sciences/Video Project
Series: Kids from CAOS
Year Released: 1995
Call Number: 513.2
Length: 30 minutes
Price: $60.00
Reviewed in: *Booklist, School Library Journal*
Grade Level: 6
Keywords: Endangered Species; Oceans; Science—Life

A three-part, inside look at an aquarium and its work to learn more about a variety of endangered aquatic species. "Sharks!" shows how scientists study the habits of these feared creatures and have discovered their critical role in the marine ecosystem. "Penguins" visits the aquarium's penguin-breeding colony, where the habits of these unusual birds are observed. "Swimming with Dolphins" dives into the dolphin tank to teach about these gentle, intelligent creatures. Includes teacher's guide.

Title: *Sculpture*
Producer: NBT Enterprises/Rainbow Educational Media
Series: Art Start
Year Released: 1995
Call Number: 731
Length: 20 minutes
Price: $79.00

Reviewed in: *School Library Journal*
Grade Level: 4–6
Keywords: Art; Sculpture

Learn the possibilities and limitations of clay by molding, rolling, squeezing, and stretching it. Children are shown how to create a sculpture of an imaginary creature.

Title: *Seals and How They Live*
Producer: AIMS Media
Series: Animals and How They Live
Year Released: 1994
Call Number: 599.74
Length: 19 minutes
Price: $195.00
Reviewed in: *School Library Journal*
Grade Level: 4–6
Keywords: Science—Life; Seals

Underwater photography provides an up-close view of seals living in their natural habitats. The program identifies distinguishing characteristics between families of true seals and fur seals, using as examples harbor seals, gray seals, and sea lions. Includes teacher's guide.

Title: *Seeing Numbers*
Producer: Human Relations Media
Series: Not Applicable
Year Released: 1995
Call Number: 513.2
Length: 25 minutes
Price: $175.00
Reviewed in: *School Library Journal*
Grade Level: 5–6
Keywords: Mathematics

This program provides visual images that establish a context in which students can explore number sense. Using an investigative reporting format, the video takes viewers into various areas where numbers are used and number sense is important. Posters and activities are provided in the kit.

Title: *Self Confidence: Step by Step*
Producer: Sunburst Communications
Series: Not Applicable
Year Released: 1994
Call Number: 158.1
Length: 23 minutes
Price: $149.00
Reviewed in: *Booklist, School Library Journal*
Grade Level: 5–6
Keywords: Behavior; Self-esteem

This program shows middle schoolers how self-confidence is built through small successes, with one success leading to another. It makes it clear that a good self-image is not tied to the clothes one wears or how one looks, but instead must be earned and internalized through taking constructive risks and developing individual competency. Practical steps for achieving the successes that build self-confidence are given. Includes teacher's guide.

Title: *Sesame Street Celebrates Around the World*
Producer: Children's Television Workshop/Random House Inc.
Series: My Sesame Street
Year Released: 1994
Call Number: 394.2
Length: 60 minutes
Price: $30.00
Reviewed in: *Booklist, School Library Journal*
Grade Level: PreK–3
Keywords: Holidays; New Year's Eve

Sesame Street characters celebrate New Year's Eve at locations around the world via a television broadcast on the Monster News Network.

Title: *Shark, Shark, Shark*
Producer: Bennett Marine Video/Childrens Television International
Series: *Blue Frontier, The*
Year Released: 1990
Call Number: 597
Length: 15 minutes
Price: $40.00
Reviewed in: *Video Rating Guide for Libraries*

Grade Level: 1–6
Keywords: Oceans; Science—Life; Sharks

A close look at one of the most feared and least understood of all animal species, the shark. Included is a sequence where a member of the Blue Frontier team hitches a ride on the dorsal fin of a whale shark. Teacher's guide available for purchase.

Title: *Sharks: Predators or Prey?*
Producer: Lucerne Media
Series: Preserving Our World
Year Released: 1994
Call Number: 597
Length: 23 minutes
Price: $245.00
Reviewed in: *School Library Journal*
Grade Level: 6
Keywords: Oceans; Science—Life; Sharks

Misconceptions about sharks have led to a public image of them as voracious man-eaters. Sharks have existed in oceans since the age of dinosaurs, but today commercial overfishing is threatening several species with extinction. This program dispels common myths and shows sharks as complex creatures that play an integral role in maintaining balance in the marine ecology.

Title: *Sheena Azak of Canada*
Producer: Colman Communications/Rainbow Eduational Media
Series: Children of Other Lands
Year Released: 1995
Call Number: 971
Length: 12 minutes
Price: $80.00
Reviewed in: *Booklist, School Library Journal, Video Rating Guide for Libraries*
Grade Level: 1–4
Keywords: Canada; Social Studies

Nine-year-old Sheena Azak lives with her family in Canyon City, a small isolated village in British Columbia. This program shows how Sheena's life has been affected by people and technologies far from her small village. An overview of life in Canada today is shown. Includes guide.

Title: *Show Time*
Producer: TVOntario/Films for the Humanities and Sciences
Series: Art's Place
Year Released: 1990
Call Number: 702
Length: 15 minutes
Price: $49.00
Reviewed in: *Video Rating Guide for Libraries*
Grade Level: K–3
Keywords: Art; Cooperation; Language Arts; Theater

Everyone pools artistic talent to put on a show about a lonely witch. Emma and Leo create masks; Jessie and Emma paint a backdrop; and everyone acts as Mirror narrates. Includes guide.

Title: *Sketching*
Producer: NBT Enterprises/Rainbow Educational Media
Series: Art Start
Year Released: 1995
Call Number: 741.2
Length: 20 minutes
Price: $79.00
Reviewed in: *School Library Journal*
Grade Level: 4–6
Keywords: Art; Drawing

This program emphasizes awareness and interpretation of body language, as well as speed of observation and rendering based on ideas dating back to the Renaissance.

Title: *Sky's the Limit*
Producer: Armstrong Moving Pictures/Pyramid Film and Video
Series: Not Applicable
Year Released: 1993
Call Number: 362.29
Length: 22 minutes
Price: $295.00
Reviewed in: *School Library Journal, Video Rating Guide for Libraries*
Grade Level: 1–6
Keywords: Drugs; Health

Elementary-aged children are given strategies to overcome peer pressure and avoid alcohol and other drugs. Two young children, pressured by their friends to experiment with alcohol, gain the self-esteem they need to say "no" with the help of a young, world champion, in-line skater. This story explains the harmful effects of alcohol and other drugs, helps children understand codependency, and demonstrates that although it takes courage, they can stand up to peer pressure and still feel good about themselves.

Title: *Slurps, Burps, and Spills!*
Producer: Swenson Green Productions
Series: Amazing Advantage for Kids
Year Released: 1994
Call Number: 395.54
Length: 20 minutes
Price: $15.00
Reviewed in: *Booklist*
Grade Level: 1–6
Keywords: Behavior; Manners

This video teaches children important lessons in manners and etiquette to help them feel confident and at ease in social situations. Explains proper table manners.

Title: *Snowballs and Sandcastles*
Producer: National Film Board of Canada/Bullfrog Films
Series: Look Again, Vol. 1
Year Released: 1990
Call Number: 525
Length: 8 minutes
Price: $150.00
Reviewed in: *Video Rating Guide for Libraries*
Grade Level: PreK–6
Keywords: Science—Life; Seasons

The seasonal opposites of winter and summer create very different worlds to be explored and enjoyed by people of all ages. This film provides opportunities for students to examine their assumptions about winter and summer and to discuss the effects that changing seasons have on our everyday lives. Includes teacher's guide.

Title: *Sojourner Truth*
Producer: Schlessinger Video Productions
Series: Black Americans of Achievement Video Collection 1
Year Released: 1992
Call Number: Biography
Length: 30 minutes
Price: $40.00
Reviewed in: *School Library Journal, Video Librarian, Video Rating Guide for Libraries*
Grade Level: 4–6
Keywords: African Americans; Biographies; Truth, Sojourner

This video biography contains interviews with leading authorities on the subject's life, accompanied by archival footage, photographs, and period music. Topics include basic biographical information, the inspirational and motivational factors in her life, her message, and the significance of Sojourner Truth in society today.

Title: *Solids in Our World*
Producer: TVOntario/GPN
Series: Riddle of Wizard's Oak
Year Released: 1990
Call Number: 510
Length: 15 minutes
Price: $49.00
Reviewed in: *Video Rating Guide for Libraries*
Grade Level: 4–6
Keywords: Mathematics; Solids

Kim, Paul, and Denis meet Walter the Wizard, who transports Denis to the Land of Shapes, Kim to the Land of Place, and Paul to the Land of Small, where they find clues to understanding the third dimension. Math skills include characteristics of solids and spatial visualization. Teacher's guide available for purchase.

Title: *Solids, Liquids, and Gases*
Producer: Cochran Communications/Rainbow Educational Media
Series: Not Applicable
Year Released: 1994
Call Number: 530.4
Length: 22 minutes
Price: $89.00

Reviewed in: *Booklist, School Library Journal*
Grade Level: 4–6
Keywords: Matter; Science—Physical

These three forms of matter exist all around us in our environment. This video explains the properties of solids, liquids, and gases, and gives examples of experiments demonstrated by students. Graphics and animation clarify the molecular differences between the three states of matter. Includes teacher's guide.

Title: *Songbird Story*
Producer: Framline Films/Bullfrog Films
Series: Not Applicable
Year Released: 1994
Call Number: 598
Length: 13 minutes
Price: $195.00
Reviewed in: *Booklist, School Library Journal*
Grade Level: K–6
Keywords: Endangered Species; Science—Life

In the backyards of North America, the songbirds' nesting habitats are being lost to development of the land. The decline of migratory songbirds is a complex problem with no simple solutions. But, to save the birds from extinction, the children learn that there is no time to waste. Includes teacher's guide.

Title: *Sound the Alarm: Firefighters at Work*
Producer: Video Dialog/Rainbow Educational Media
Series: Community Helpers
Year Released: 1994
Call Number: 352.3
Length: 15 minutes
Price: $89.00
Reviewed in: *Booklist, School Library Journal*
Grade Level: K–3
Keywords: Community; Fire Fighters; Social Studies

A community is a place where people live. Fire fighters are community helpers who stay busy all the time. They visit schools to teach fire safety; they keep their trucks and equipment clean and safe; they risk their lives protecting people and their property from fires.

Title: *Sound/Radio Broadcasting*
Producer: GPN
Series: Dr. Dad's Ph3
Year Released: 1994
Call Number: 791.4023
Length: 15 minutes
Price: $30.00
Reviewed in: *Booklist*
Grade Level: 3–6
Keywords: Radios; Science—Physical; Sound; Technology

Dr. Dad and the neighborhood kids explore the basics of radio communication and discover how mechanical sound energy can be converted into electromagnetic waves and back again. Teacher's guide available for purchase.

Title: *Source of Life? Water in Our Environment*
Producer: Cochran Communications/Rainbow Educational Video
Series: Not Applicable
Year Released: 1992
Call Number: 333.91
Length: 22 minutes
Price: $89.00
Reviewed in: *School Library Journal, Video Rating Guide for Libraries*
Grade Level: 4–6
Keywords: Environmental Concerns; Pollution; Water Cycle

Living things need water to survive. This full-motion video explains where water is found and how it's used in homes, industry, and agriculture. The major causes of water pollution are examined along with ways that society can address these problems, including the necessity for water conservation. Includes teacher's guide.

Title: *Speak Up for Yourself*
Producer: Health Education Systems/Lucerne Media
Series: Safe Child Program 1–3
Year Released: 1989
Call Number: 614.8
Length: 45 minutes
Price: $395.00
Reviewed in: *Video Rating Guide for Libraries*

Grade Level: 1
Keywords: Personal Safety; Safety

Divided into five segments of four to twenty minutes each, this video teaches children personal skills for prevention of abuse. Curriculum guide available.

Title: *Spiders*
Producer: Digital Nutshell/Lucerne Media
Series: Science in Your Own Backyard
Year Released: 1995
Call Number: 595.44
Length: 10 minutes
Price: $145.00
Reviewed in: *School Library Journal*
Grade Level: 5–6
Keywords: Science—Life; Spiders

The program introduces students to various spiders that have evolved in different shapes and colors suited to their habitat. They see how the spiders spin webs and trap prey, and observe the mating ritual, egg production and behavior of these small (and often useful to humans) animals.

Title: *Start with a Story: Baby Rattlesnake*
Producer: MacLean Media/Film Ideas
Series: Not Applicable
Year Released: 1993
Call Number: 398.24
Length: 20 minutes
Price: $150.00
Reviewed in: *School Library Journal*
Grade Level: PreK–3
Keywords: Families; Folk Tales; Native Americans; Snakes

Lynn Moroney shares her adaptation of the Native American teaching tale, originally told to her by Chickasaw storyteller Te Ata. This story of family love and forgiveness tells what happens when a baby rattlesnake begs to have a rattle before he is old enough. Includes teacher's guide.

Title: *Starting with Stars*
Producer: Pyramid Film and Video
Series: Not Applicable
Year Released: 1992
Call Number: 523
Length: 14 minutes
Price: $225.00
Reviewed in: *Video Rating Guide for Libraries*
Grade Level: 3–6
Keywords: Astronomy; Space

"How many stars are in the sky?" That question, posed by a young boy to his father on a camping trip, is the beginning of a journey into outer space.

Title: *Stepping Out with Hap Palmer*
Producer: Educational Activities
Series: Not Applicable
Year Released: 1994
Call Number: 782.42
Length: 30 minutes
Price: $20.00
Reviewed in: *Booklist*
Grade Level: 4–6
Keywords: Early Childhood; Movement

Hap Palmer and team use music and movement to teach basic skills and use of imagination. Includes "Stepping Out on the Town," "Flick a Fly," "Wiggy Wiggy Wiggles," "Everything Has a Shape," "Sally the Swinging Snake," "All the Ways of Jumping Up and Down," "Weekly Rap," "Percival the Parrot," and "Rubber Band Man."

Title: *Story of Read-Alee-Deed-Alee, The: Program 13*
Producer: Society for Visual Education
Series: Story of Read-Alee-Deed-Alee, Set 7
Year Released: 1995
Call Number: 372.4
Length: 20 minutes
Price: $59.00
Reviewed in: *School Library Journal*
Grade Level: K–1
Keywords: Alphabet Skills; Language Arts

This early reading program combines the whole language approach with basic phonics. "Program 13: The Cold Gold" covers shapes, the letter "s," and patterns of "old/ole."

Title: *Story of Read-Alee-Deed-Alee, The: Program 14*
Producer: Society for Visual Education
Series: Story of Read-Alee-Deed-Alee, Set 7
Year Released: 1995
Call Number: 372.4
Length: 20 minutes
Price: $59.00
Reviewed in: *School Library Journal*
Grade Level: K–1
Keywords: Alphabet Skills; Language Arts

This early reading program combines the whole language approach with basic phonics. "Program 14: Dirt on My Shirt" covers the alphabet, the letter "c," and patterns of "irt/art."

Title: *Strangers Aren't Bad, They're Just Strangers*
Producer: Health Education Systems/Lucerne Media
Series: Safe Child Program 1–3
Year Released: 1989
Call Number: 614.8
Length: 27 minutes
Price: $395.00
Reviewed in: *Video Rating Guide for Libraries*
Grade Level: K
Keywords: Personal Safety; Safety

Divided into five segments of four to seven minutes each, this video teaches children personal skills for the prevention of abuse. Curriculum guide available.

Title: *Struggling to Survive: Tropical Rain Forests*
Producer: Cochran Communications/Rainbow Educational Media
Series: Not Applicable
Year Released: 1996
Call Number: 524.5
Length: 27 minutes

Price: $89.00
Reviewed in: *School Library Journal*
Grade Level: 4–6
Keywords: Rain Forests; Science—Earth

This program explores the different layers of the forests, which contain the most complex communities of life on Earth. It shows the many useful products we get from rain forests, including foods and medicines. The program examines how some countries are trying to find ways to use the resources of the forests without destroying them, and how students themselves can help save these treasures of biodiversity. Includes teacher's guide.

Title: *Sun, Earth, Moon*
Producer: National Geographic Society Educational Services
Series: Not Applicable
Year Released: 1995
Call Number: 500
Length: 20 minutes
Price: $79.00
Reviewed in: *School Library Journal*
Grade Level: 4–6
Keywords: Science—Space; Space

Learn how the Sun and Moon produce changing seasons, rising and falling tides, and spectacular eclipses. Students demonstrate the concepts of gravity and the effects of the Earth's rotation on its axis. Join astronomers to witness a total solar eclipse. Includes teacher's guide.

Title: *Symbols*
Producer: NBT Enterprises/Rainbow Educational Media
Series: Art Start
Year Released: 1995
Call Number: 702
Length: 20 minutes
Price: $79.00
Reviewed in: *School Library Journal*
Grade Level: 4–6
Keywords: Art; Symbols

Students use felt-tip pens to create an instantly recognizable symbol describing a facet of their school day. Emphasis is on simplicity.

Title: *Take a Chance: Exploring Probability*
Producer: Children's Television Workshop/PBS Video
Series: Math Talk
Year Released: 1995
Call Number: 519.2
Length: 15 minutes
Price: $40.00
Reviewed in: *School Library Journal*
Grade Level: 4–6
Keywords: Mathematics; Probability

Cartoon characters, music videos, quiz shows, carnival games, and soap operas all work together to teach mathematics. Includes teacher's guide.

Title: *Taking Chances: Teens at Risk*
Producer: Sunburst Communications
Series: Not Applicable
Year Released: 1994
Call Number: 152.4
Length: 27 minutes
Price: $169.00
Reviewed in: *Booklist, School Library Journal*
Grade Level: 4–6
Keywords: Behavior; Risk Taking; Safety

From the youngster who skateboards recklessly to the one who cheats on a test to the "good" kid who joins peers in shoplifting, risky behavior is all too common in the volatile pre- and early teen years. This program helps middle schoolers look at risk critically and understand its sources. It demonstrates that risk can be positive as well as negative and teaches students a technique for deciding in advance whether a risk is worth taking. Includes teacher's guide.

Title: *Tessa on Her Own*
Producer: Great Plains Television/MarshMedia
Series: Key Concepts in Personal Development
Year Released: 1994
Call Number: Easy Fiction
Length: 14 minutes
Price: $80.00

Reviewed in: *School Library Journal*
Grade Level: K–4
Keywords: Foxes; Literature; Responsibility

Instead of learning how to hunt for herself, Tessa relies on her brother Rex to share his meals with her. But when Tessa strikes out on her own, she learns the importance of work. The coastal mountains and the Ojai Valley of Southern California are featured. Includes teacher's guide.

Title: *Thanksgiving Day*
Producer: Live Oak Media
Series: Not Applicable
Year Released: 1993
Call Number: 394.2
Length: 6 minutes
Price: $38.00
Reviewed in: *Video Rating Guide for Libraries*
Grade Level: K–4
Keywords: Holidays; Literature; Thanksgiving

Based on a book by Gail Gibbons, illustrations and text introduce and explain the history, traditions, and customs surrounding the celebration of Thanksgiving Day. Includes teacher's guide.

Title: *Theories of Personalities*
Producer: Lucerne Media
Series: Science and Technology—Today and Tomorrow
Year Released: 1994
Call Number: 152.4
Length: 20 minutes
Price: $195.00
Reviewed in: *Booklist*
Grade Level: 6
Keywords: Behavior; Personalities; Science

Current theories of personalities including trait, psychoanalytic, humanistic, social learning, and cognitive are discussed. Critical issues are examined. Includes teacher's guide.

Title: *There Goes a Bulldozer*
Producer: KidVision
Series: Not Applicable
Year Released: 1994
Call Number: 629.2
Length: 39 minutes
Price: $11.00
Reviewed in: *Booklist*
Grade Level: PreK–2
Keywords: Construction; Transportation

Construction foreman Dave takes children exploring into the world of heavy construction from jackhammers to bulldozers.

Title: *There Goes a Police Car*
Producer: KidVision
Series: Not Applicable
Year Released: 1994
Call Number: 363.2
Length: 35 minutes
Price: $11.00
Reviewed in: *Booklist*
Grade Level: PreK–2
Keywords: Community; Police; Transportation

Officers Becky and Dave take kids into the world of law enforcement as they meet police officers in squad cars and helicopters and on horses, bikes, and motorcycles.

Title: *Three-Legged Cat, The*
Producer: Weston Woods Studios
Series: Not Applicable
Year Released: 1995
Call Number: Easy Fiction
Length: 9 minutes
Price: $60.00
Reviewed in: *Booklist*
Grade Level: K–3
Keywords: Cats; Literature

Adapted from the book by Margaret Mahy, Mrs. Gimble's peg-leg cat, Tom, is taken for a hat and goes for a ride atop her rascally, roving brother's bald head.

Title: *Thumbs Up for Kids! AIDS Education*
Producer: Media Express/AIMS Media
Series: Not Applicable
Year Released: 1990
Call Number: 616.97
Length: 23 minutes
Price: $80.00
Reviewed in: *Video Rating Guide for Libraries*
Grade Level: K–3
Keywords: AIDS; Health

Ruby Petersen-Unger defines what germs are and how they are spread. Song, dance, rap tunes, and visual effects help convey the message that AIDS is hard to get and that it's safe to play, share toys, and attend class with someone who has AIDS.

***

Title: *Thurgood Marshall*
Producer: Schlessinger Video Productions
Series: Black Americans of Achievement Video Collection 1
Year Released: 1992
Call Number: Biography
Length: 30 minutes
Price: $40.00
Reviewed in: *School Library Journal, Video Librarian, Video Rating Guide for Libraries*
Grade Level: 4–6
Keywords: African Americans; Biographies; Marshall, Thurgood

This video biography contains interviews with leading authorities on the subject's life, accompanied by archival footage, photographs, and period music. Topics include basic biographical information, the inspirational and motivational factors in his life, his message, and the significance of Thurgood Marshall in society today.

***

Title: *Timberrr! From Logs to Lumber*
Producer: Bulldog Entertainment/Instructional Video
Series: Not Applicable
Year Released: 1995
Call Number: 331.7
Length: 30 minutes
Price: $20.00
Reviewed in: *School Library Journal*

Grade Level: PreK–3
Keywords: Careers; Lumberjacks

Join the fun as Mac discovers what it's like to be a real lumberjack. Watch as giant machines harvest trees. One mammoth machine does it all: cuts, delimbs, and stacks the logs. See all the heavy machinery in action—skidders, loaders, forklifts, and heavy trucks.

Title: *Time*
Producer: Crystalroe Productions/DK Publishing
Series: Hullaballoo
Year Released: 1995
Call Number: 529
Length: 30 minutes
Price: $10.00
Reviewed in: *School Library Journal*
Grade Level: PreK–1
Keywords: Early Childhood; Time

This program combines animation, puppetry, games, and songs to teach children about time.

Title: *Time for Horatio, A*
Producer: MarshMedia
Series: Key Concepts in Self-Esteem
Year Released: 1990
Call Number: Easy Fiction
Length: 19 minutes
Price: $80.00
Reviewed in: *Video Rating Guide for Libraries*
Grade Level: K–4
Keywords: Behavior; London; Time

A kitten travels to the Greenwich Royal Observatory and discovers that the world is running on "mean" time. He returns to London determined to set the world straight. The story promotes harmony among people, investigates our system for telling time, and explores the sights of London. Includes teacher's guide, hardcover book.

Title: *Time, Money, and Measurement*
Producer: Bennett Marine Video
Series: Tell Me Why, Vol. 23
Year Released: 1991
Call Number: 525
Length: 30 minutes
Price: $15.00
Reviewed in: *Video Rating Guide for Libraries*
Grade Level: 3–6
Keywords: Mathematics; Measurement; Money; Time

This video encyclopedia answers questions about time, money, and measurement.

Title: *Timid Dinosaurs*
Producer: TVOntario/GPN
Series: Magic Library
Year Released: 1990
Call Number: Easy Fiction
Length: 15 minutes
Price: $49.00
Reviewed in: *Video Rating Guide for Libraries*
Grade Level: 2–3
Keywords: Language Arts; Literature; Similes

In the Magic Library, Zazi, Norbert, and Leon, three eager young mice, are treated to a story from the storyreader, an eccentric rabbit. Their reading skills are honed as they enjoy "Long Neck and Thunder Foot" by Helen Piers. Guide available for purchase.

Title: *To Jew Is Not a Verb*
Producer: TVOntario/Journal Films
Series: Many Voices
Year Released: 1992
Call Number: 305.8
Length: 15 minutes
Price: $49.00
Reviewed in: *Video Rating Guide for Libraries*
Grade Level: 4–6
Keywords: Jewish Culture; Multicultural; Stereotypes

David learns about the pervasiveness of stereotyping when trading baseball cards, and gets important lessons about his Jewish faith during Passover celebrations with his family. He is compelled to reassess his priorities. Teacher's guide available for purchase.

Title: *To Save a Whale*
Producer: Bennett Marine Video/Children's Television International
Series: Blue Frontier
Year Released: 1990
Call Number: 599.74
Length: 15 minutes
Price: $40.00
Reviewed in: *Video Rating Guide for Libraries*
Grade Level: 1–6
Keywords: Science—Life; Whales

Humpback whales are known for the haunting and eerie songs they sing during the courtship ritual. They are the slowest of the great whales and were nearly wiped out by the whalers. This story is about the methods used to rescue the gentle giants from total extinction. Teacher's guide available for purchase.

Title: *Tom Thumb*
Producer: Lucerne Media
Series: Tell Me a Story
Year Released: 1994
Call Number: Easy Ficiton
Length: 30 minutes
Price: $99.00
Reviewed in: *School Library Journal*
Grade Level: 1–3
Keywords: Fairy Tales; Literature

This animated recreation of the traditional story of a thumb-sized boy is narrated by Geoffrey Matthews.

Title: *Too Many Pumpkins*
Producer: Live Oak Media
Series:
Year Released: 1997
Call Number: Easy Fiction
Length: 13 minutes

Price: $37.95
Reviewed in: *School Library Journal*
Grade Level: PreK–3
Keywords: Imagination; Literature; Pumpkins

Based on the book by Linda White, this video is about Rebecca Estelle, who ate too many pumpkins as a child and now hates the orange vegetable. When a huge pumpkin rolls off a truck and smashes in her yard, she pretends it is not there. Then spring comes and a pumpkin vine grows and soon there are pumpkins everywhere. Rebecca Estelle must use her imagination to get rid of the pumpkins.

Title: *Topsy-Turvy*
Producer: National Film Board of Canada/Bullfrog Films
Series: Look Again, Vol. 2
Year Released: 1990
Call Number: 537
Length: 9 minutes
Price: $150.00
Reviewed in: *Video Rating Guide for Libraries*
Grade Level: K–6
Keywords: Electricity; Science—Physical

In a young boy's dream world anything can happen—even magic. What magic is there in everyday things such as electricity and magnetism? Students discuss their own "magic tricks" and make hypotheses about why some events cannot really happen. Includes teacher's guide.

Title: *Tortoise and the Hare, The*
Producer: GPN/Vestron Video
Series: Reading Rainbow
Year Released: 1989
Call Number: 398.2
Length: 30 minutes
Price: $44.00
Reviewed in: *Video Rating Guide for Libraries*
Grade Level: K–4
Keywords: Competition; Literature

Gilda Radner narrates this program's feature book, which is illustrated by Janet Stevens. LeVar Burton faces a big challenge when he gets ready to compete against some of Hawaii's top bicyclists in the First Annual Rainbow Mini-Classic Bicycle Race.

Title: *Totally Tropical Rain Forest*
Producer: National Geographic Society Educational Services
Series: Really Wild Animals
Year Released: 1994
Call Number: 574.5
Length: 45 minutes
Price: $15.00
Reviewed in: *Booklist*
Grade Level: K–5
Keywords: Animals; Rain Forest

Dudley Moore narrates this children's video that explores the tropical rain forests with Spin and teaches students about the three-toed sloth and poison-arrow frog. Includes teacher's guide.

Title: *Train Adventures for Kids: The Magical World of Trains*
Producer: Iron Valley Production/Goldhill Home Media International
Series: Not Applicable
Year Released: 1994
Call Number: 629
Length: 31 minutes
Price: $25.00
Reviewed in: *Booklist*
Grade Level: PreK–2
Keywords: Railroads; Transportation

From powerful train locomotives to the smallest caboose, children learn about trains. It features passenger, freight, real and model trains, all set to an original music score.

Title: *Trash Troll, The*
Producer: Mitch Braff/Bullfrog Films
Series: Not Applicable
Year Released: 1994
Call Number: 363.73
Length: 13 minutes

Price: $195.00
Reviewed in: *Booklist*
Grade Level: K–4
Keywords: Ecology; Pollution; Trash

A gruff, environmentally conscious gnome admonishes three children for carelessly littering his beach with a plastic six-pack ring. He suggests they visit a nearby marine hospital to see for themselves the dangers that garbage can pose to ocean inhabitants. The hospital director shows birds, fish, and marine mammals all suffering from the effects of human pollution. Includes teacher's guide.

Title: *Traveling with Ooga-Booga on Trains, Trucks, and Airplanes*
Producer: ALA Video/Library Video Network
Series: Not Applicable
Year Released: 1992
Call Number: 629.004
Length: 45 minutes
Price: $20.00
Reviewed in: *Children's Video Review Newsletter, Video Librarian*
Grade Level: PreK–3
Keywords: Transportation

Friendly aliens from the planet Quirky Corky take the viewer on transportation-packed adventures. Each fifteen-minute segment features video travel on planes, trains, or trucks. Each segment has a teacher's guide.

Title: *Trees for Life*
Producer: National Geographic Society Educational Services
Series: On Nature's Trail
Year Released: 1995
Call Number: 574.5
Length: 23 minutes
Price: $99.00
Reviewed in: *Booklist*
Grade Level: 1–3
Keywords: Ecology; Forests; Science—Life; Trees

When a tree is cut down, the young adventurers set out to find a songbird that once lived in it. Their flights of fancy take them to several forests: tropical, old growth, and underwater! The kids discover the profusion of life that lives in a tree and how trees are important to life on Earth. Includes teacher's guide.

Title: *Trouble with Tobacco, The*
Producer: Colman Communications/Rainbow Educational Media
Series: Not Applicable
Year Released: 1996
Call Number: 362.29
Length: 12 minutes
Price: $80.00
Reviewed in: *School Library Journal*
Grade Level: 4–6
Keywords: Drugs; Health; Tobacco

This video shows what smoking is really about. It discusses how unappealing cigarette odor is to many people, and demonstrates how smoking reduces a person's athletic abilities. Major diseases caused by tobacco use, including cancer, emphysema, heart disease, and stroke, are covered. Includes teacher's guide.

Title: *Truck Song*
Producer: AIMS Media
Series: Not Applicable
Year Released: 1989
Call Number: Easy Fiction
Length: 13 minutes
Price: $50.00
Reviewed in: *Video Rating Guide for Libraries*
Grade Level: K–3
Keywords: Literature; Transportation; Trucks

In this video based on the book by Diane Siebert, the author celebrates trucks and the life of truckers with a rhymed text evoking the driving rhythm of a transcontinental truck's journey across country.

Title: *Tuesday*
Producer: American School Publishers
Series: Children's Literature
Year Released: 1992
Call Number: Easy Fiction
Length: 5 minutes
Price: $37.00

Reviewed in: *Video Rating Guide for Libraries*
Grade Level: K–5
Keywords: Frogs; Literature

From the book by Caldecott Medalist David Wiesner, it's Tuesday evening, around eight o'clock in a small town, and something odd is happening. Hundreds of frogs on flying lily pads are rising into the sky. Students see the amphibians startle the dogs, turn drying bedsheets into flying carpets, invade homes, and perplex the local police.

Title: *Turkey: Between Europe and Asia*
Producer: Camera Q
Series: Not Applicable
Year Released: 1990
Call Number: 956.1
Length: 19 minutes
Price: $90.00
Reviewed in: *School Library Journal, Video Rating Guide for Libraries,*
Grade Level: 4–6
Keywords: Europe; Social Studies; Turkey

Explore the factors that shaped Turkey's past, such as its geography, history, and religion, and the forces that will shape Turkey's future, such as Mediterranean tourists' spots, industry, agriculture, and the Turkish people themselves. Life styles of the rural peasants of the countryside, the residents of Istanbul (Turkey's largest city), and the city dwellers of Ankara (Turkey's capital) are shown. Includes teacher's guide.

Title: *Two Faces of Ozone, The*
Producer: United Learning
Series: Not Applicable
Year Released: 1992
Call Number: 363.72
Length: 15 minutes
Price: $90.00
Reviewed in: *Video Rating Guide for Libraries*
Grade Level: 5–6
Keywords: Environmental Concerns; Ozone; Pollution; Science—Earth

Close to the earth's surface, ozone, a major component of smog, is a serious pollutant. This video explains the causes of today's critical ozone questions and the depletion of the earth's ozone shield. Includes teacher's guide, blackline masters.

Title: *Ty's One Man Band*
Producer: GPN
Series: Reading Rainbow
Year Released: 1989
Call Number: Easy Fiction
Length: 30 minutes
Price: $44.00
Reviewed in: *Video Rating Guide for Libraries*
Grade Level: 3–6
Keywords: Bands; Music

Lou Rawls narrates the story of a mysterious stranger who created a one-man band out of odds and ends. LeVar Burton discovers lots of different music—a rap band, do-wop group, jazz, and salsa. Ben Vereen dances. Teacher's guide available.

Title: *Uncle Nick and the Magic Forest, Vol. 3: Lost in the Forest*
Producer: Magic Forest/H and F Dance/Victory Audio Video Services
Series: Not Applicable
Year Released: 1995
Call Number: 782.42
Length: 30 minutes
Price: $15.00
Reviewed in: *School Library Journal*
Grade Level: PreK–2
Keywords: Forests; Music

Kids can sing along with the flowers and dance with the animals that live in an enchanted forest.

Title: *Understanding and Resolving Conflicts*
Producer: United Learning
Series: Not Applicable
Year Released: 1994
Call Number: 152.4

Length: 23 minutes
Price: $95.00
Reviewed in: *Booklist*
Grade Level: 5–6
Keywords: Behavior; Conflict Resolution

This video program is designed to help students solve interpersonal and intergroup strife. By dramatizing conflicts, this video explores what causes conflict and suggests to students ways in which to resolve it without resorting to violence. Includes teacher's guide, blackline masters.

Title: *Unforgettable Pen Pal, The—A Story about Prejudice and Discrimination*
Producer: InnerVisions Productions/Kids' Media Group
Series: Human Race Club
Year Released: 1990
Call Number: 303.3
Length: 28 minutes
Price: $30.00
Reviewed in: *Video Rating Guide for Libraries*
Grade Level: K–4
Keywords: Behavior; Prejudice

A.J. and the club members learn lessons about prejudice and discrimination. This video helps kids understand the negative effects prejudice causes and the importance of forming their own opinions about others intelligently. Includes guide.

Title: *United States History Video Collection*
Producer: Schlessinger Video Productions/Library Video Company
Series: United States History
Year Released: 1996
Call Number: 973
Length: 20 videos, 30 minutes each
Price: $799.00
Reviewed in: *Booklist*
Grade Level: 5–6
Keywords: Social Studies; U.S. History

Important events and historical figures are shown through dramatic readings and performances. Documents, dates, and facts are presented in context. Women, minorities, and other groups are covered. Video coverage starts with the arrival of humans in North America and ends with rock and roll.

Title: *Using Manipulatives: Patterning/Classifying*
Producer: Educational Activities
Series: Math Problem Solving Strategies
Year Released: 1993
Call Number: 513
Length: 25 minutes
Price: $49.00
Reviewed in: *Booklist, Video Rating Guide for Libraries*
Grade Level: K–2
Keywords: Manipulatives; Mathematics

The first part shows students using counters and pattern blocks to solve problems by recognizing, completing, and recording patterns based on color and shape. In the second part, students use pattern blocks to solve problems by sorting and classifying. Includes teacher's guide.

Title: *Using Manipulatives: Using a Model/Estimating and Checking*
Producer: Educational Activities
Series: Math Problem Solving Strategies
Year Released: 1993
Call Number: 513
Length: 25 minutes
Price: $49.00
Reviewed in: *Video Rating Guide for Libraries*
Grade Level: K–2
Keywords: Manipulatives; Mathematics

In the first program, students use pattern blocks to investigate and predict the results of combining, subdividing, and changing shapes, and to understand the importance of geometry in the real world. In part two, play money and a calculator help teach estimation strategies, determining reasonableness, and estimating quantities. Includes teacher's guide.

Title: *Victor*
Producer: Milestone Productions/Barr Films
Series: Not Applicable
Year Released: 1989
Call Number: 305.8
Length: 27 minutes
Price: $75.00
Reviewed in: *Video Rating Guide for Libraries*
Grade Level: K–6
Keywords: Immigration; Mexican Americans; Multicultural

Through the experiences of Victor, a young Mexican boy, students will begin to see how difficult it is to emigrate from another country to the United States. A surprising climax helps students develop empathy and understanding for people of other cultures and languages. Includes teacher's guide.

Title: *Vietnam*
Producer: White Mountain Entertainment
Series: Cultures of the World
Year Released: 1994
Call Number: 959.7
Length: 20 minutes
Price: $79.00
Reviewed in: *School Library Journal*
Grade Level: 4–6
Keywords: Asia; Social Studies; Vietnam

Students see the differences between the north and south parts of Vietnam, two countries which are now one. The people of Hanoi in the North still rely primarily on human power for transportation, while transportation in the southern city of Ho Chi Minh (Saigon) is highly motorized. Includes teacher's guide.

Title: *Violence: Dealing with Anger in the Formative Years*
Producer: Centre Communication
Series: Not Applicable
Year Released: 1994
Call Number: 303.6
Length: 24 minutes
Price: $99.00

Reviewed in: *School Library Journal, Video Rating Guide for Libraries*
Grade Level: 4–6
Keywords: Behavior; Self-Control; Violence

Violence is a learned behavior, and this video teaches children alternative skills to use before violent reactions become habitual. Educator, martial artist, and conflict resolution expert Thomas Crum uses his B.L.T.—Breathe, Learn, Talk—methods and examples like Michael Jordan to show that true power springs from being centered and calm. Includes teacher's guide.

Title: *Volcanoes: Mountains of Fire*
Producer: Rainbow Educational Media
Series: Not Applicable
Year Released: 1995
Call Number: 551.2
Length: 24 minutes
Price: $99.00
Reviewed in: *Booklist, School Library Journal*
Grade Level: 5–6
Keywords: Science—Earth; Volcanoes

Ring of fire, lava lakes, hot spots—these are just a few of the items covered in this program. Students will see the three types of volcanoes and how they are formed. The program further explains how volcanoes are responsible for the continuing regeneration of our planet.

Title: *Voyage of the Loggerhead*
Producer: National Geographic Society Educational Services
Series: Not Applicable
Year Released: 1995
Call Number: 597
Length: 25 minutes
Price: $99.00
Reviewed in: *School Library Journal*
Grade Level: 4–6
Keywords: Oceans; Turtles

Follow Caretta, a baby loggerhead sea turtle, during the first eighteen months of her life. From her hatching on a Florida beach to her early adventures in the ocean, Caretta experiences many of the wonders and dangers of marine life. Through her story, learn about animal migration and navigation, ocean ecosystems, predator/prey relationships, and pollution's threat to marine life. Includes teacher's guide.

Title: *Voyage to the Moon*
Producer: Duncan Group/United Learning
Series: Junior Space Scientists
Year Released: 1995
Call Number: 523.3
Length: 10 minutes
Price: $55.00
Reviewed in: *School Library Journal*
Grade Level: 1–4
Keywords: Astronomy; Science—Space; Space

Through this story-line video, students get a close-up look at the moon through the eyes of the astronauts who first explored Earth's closest neighbor in space. Concepts such as the phases of the moon and gravity are explored. A historical review, beginning with President Kennedy's historic speech and ending with the astronauts exploring the lunar surface, is included. Includes teacher's guide, blackline masters.

Title: *Watch Out for the Tetrahedron!*
Producer: TVOntario/GPN
Series: Riddle of Wizard's Oak
Year Released: 1990
Call Number: 513.2
Length: 15 minutes
Price: $49.00
Reviewed in: *Video Rating Guide for Libraries*
Grade Level: 4–6
Keywords: Egypt; Mathematics; Pyramids

In ancient Egypt, Denis learns about pyramids; and from high in the night sky, Kim learns about cubes. A clue in the crystal garden helps them discover a four-sided solid with a strange name. Skills covered include the investigation of pyramids and the identification of a tetrahedron and its properties. Teacher's guide available for purchase.

Title: *We're No Dummies! We Don't Take Drugs*
Producer: Geffner Productions, Inc.
Series: Not Applicable
Year Released: 1993
Call Number: 362.29
Length: 33 minutes
Price: $30.00
Reviewed in: *Booklist*
Grade Level: K–3
Keywords: Drugs; Health

This educational video teaches kids about the dangers of drugs and how to stay away from them.

Title: *Westward Expansion: The Pioneer Challenge*
Producer: Rainbow Educational Media
Series: Not Applicable
Year Released: 1992
Call Number: 973.8
Length: 17 minutes
Price: $89.00
Reviewed in: *School Library Journal, Video Rating Guide for Libraries*
Grade Level: 4–6
Keywords: Pioneers; Social Studies; U.S. History

The westward expansion of the United States and how the pioneers met the challenges presented by geography are examined in this program. Students see the important role geography has played and will continue to play in America's future. Live-action footage is accompanied by historical stills and art photography. Includes teacher's guide.

Title: *What Do You Tell a Phone?*
Producer: Swenson Green Productions
Series: Amazing Advantage for Kids
Year Released: 1994
Call Number: 395.59
Length: 20 minutes
Price: $15.00

Reviewed in: *Booklist*
Grade Level: 1–6
Keywords: Behavior; Manners

This video teaches children lessons in manners and etiquette to help them feel confident and at ease in social situations. Explains proper telephone and doorway manners.

Title: *What Is an American?*
Producer: New Castle Communications
Series: My America: Building a Democracy
Year Released: 1994
Call Number: 332.673
Length: 26 minutes
Price: $79.00
Reviewed in: *School Library Journal*
Grade Level: K–6
Keywords: American Citizenship; Social Studies

The intangible rewards of U.S. citizenship provided by the Constitution and the Bill of Rights are covered. Students see how voting rights for the few become voting rights for the many. They learn how to prepare themselves to become effective, active, and productive citizens in a multiethnic, open society. Includes teacher's guide, activity masters.

Title: *What Is Life?*
Producer: United Learning
Series: Basic Biology
Year Released: 1992
Call Number: 574
Length: 11 minutes
Price: $80.00
Reviewed in: *Booklist, Video Rating Guide for Libraries*
Grade Level: 5–6
Keywords: Biology; Science—Life

Viewers see and hear about the characteristics of all living things and how they contrast to the characteristics of nonliving things. Students learn that all living organisms are made up of cells, the units of life. Includes teacher's guide, blackline masters.

Title: *What Now? Deciding What's Right*
Producer: January Productions
Series: Not Applicable
Year Released: 1990
Call Number: 170.44
Length: 25 minutes
Price: $60.00
Reviewed in: *Media and Methods*
Grade Level: 3–6
Keywords: Behavior; Values

This video encourages children to look at the alternatives and to weigh the possible consequences of their actions before reaching a decision or taking an action. This program will help students develop positive attitudes and behaviors and prepare them to make decisions in situations where value judgments are required.

Title: *What's inside the Earth?: An Introduction to the Earth's Interior, Crust, and Mineral Resources*
Producer: Peter Matulavich Productions/Rainbow Educational Media
Series: Not Applicable
Year Released: 1995
Call Number: 551
Length: 26 minutes
Price: $99.00
Reviewed in: *School Library Journal*
Grade Level: 5–6
Keywords: Earth; Science—Earth

Students will see how the earth's interior consists of several different layers; how the outer shell is broken into more than a dozen moving plates, the crust criss-crossed by cracks called faults. The end results of plate movements are shown. Earth resources are also explored. Includes teacher's guide.

Title: *What's the Earth Made of?*
Producer: National Geographic Society Educational Services
Series: Not Applicable
Year Released: 1995
Call Number: 550
Length: 20 minutes

Price: $99.00
Reviewed in: *School Library Journal*
Grade Level: 4–6
Keywords: Geology; Science—Earth

Students join host Mike Dun as he visits active volcanoes and dangles from cliffs in a quest to learn about our planet's workings. Mike talks with experts who let him in on the latest findings—including recent action at the Mid-Ocean Ridge. Includes teacher's guide.

Title: *When Anger Turns to Rage*
Producer: Sunburst Communications
Series: Not Applicable
Year Released: 1995
Call Number: 152.4
Length: 28 minutes
Price: $189.00
Reviewed in: *School Library Journal*
Grade Level: 5–6
Keywords: Anger; Behavior

Anger often gives rise to a fury that middle schoolers can neither understand nor control. This program helps preteens understand this natural but troubling emotion and demonstrates ways to deal with angry feelings. Students are shown the anger-management skills that can lead to better relationships between students and a more peaceful learning environment. Includes teacher's guide.

Title: *When Food Is an Obsession: Overcoming Eating Disorders*
Producer: Human Relations Media
Series: Not Applicable
Year Released: 1994
Call Number: 616.2
Length: 28 minutes
Price: $189.00
Reviewed in: *Booklist, Video Rating Guide for Libraries*
Grade Level: 5–6
Keywords: Eating Disorders; Food; Health; Self-esteem

A seventeen-year-old girl speaks about the barrage of conflicting messages she has received from society since childhood: food equals pleasure, but beauty equals thinness. The program ends with pre-ventative techniques to help teens accept their bodies despite societal messages, and recovery strategies for those who may now suffer from eating disorders.

Title: *When I Feel Alone*
Producer: New Leaf Media/Film Ideas
Series: What Do I Do?
Year Released: 1995
Call Number: 152.4
Length: 15 minutes
Price: $150.00
Reviewed in: *School Library Journal*
Grade Level: 3–6
Keywords: Behavior; Feelings; Self-esteem

Most of us feel alone at some time or another, but we can also feel alone when things happen that are out of our control—like when parents are divorcing, or being left out when friends get together. This video shows ways to cope with the feelings.

Title: *When I Feel Different*
Producer: New Leaf Media/Film Ideas
Series: What Do I Do?
Year Released: 1995
Call Number: 305.8
Length: 14 minutes
Price: $150.00
Reviewed in: *School Library Journal*
Grade Level: 3–6
Keywords: Behavior; Diversity; Feelings; Self-esteem

It always seems important to be just like everyone else, but feeling different can sometimes allow us to feel special. The differences explored are socioeconomic, physical, and ethnic.

Title: *When Mom and Dad Divorce*
Producer: Colman Communications/Rainbow Educational Media
Series: Not Applicable
Year Released: 1994
Call Number: 306.89
Length: 15 minutes
Price: $80.00

Reviewed in: *Booklist, School Library Journal*
Grade Level: 4–6
Keywords: Behavior; Divorce; Families

Anger, depression, denial, guilt, loneliness, fear, shame, and sadness are discussed and shown as normal reactions to divorce and separation. The video encourages young people to express their feelings with a sympathetic adult. Includes teacher's guide.

Title: *When Should You Tell? Dealing with Abuse*
Producer: Sunburst Communications
Series: Not Applicable
Year Released: 1995
Call Number: 614.8
Length: 15 minutes
Price: $99.00
Reviewed in: *Booklist, School Library Journal*
Grade Level: 2–4
Keywords: Molestation; Personal Safety; Safety

Getting young victims of sexual abuse to tell someone can be a key step in preventing further abuse. Using one child's experience to demonstrate that no girl or boy ever needs to keep scary secrets, this program helps abused children recognize that what they are experiencing is not the norm, and that they can be helped by telling an adult they can trust. Includes teacher's guide.

Title: *Where Do Animals Go in Winter?*
Producer: National Geographic Society Educational Services
Series: Not Applicable
Year Released: 1995
Call Number: 591.51
Length: 15 minutes
Price: $79.00
Reviewed in: *School Library Journal*
Grade Level: K–3
Keywords: Animals; Science—Life; Winter

Students learn how animals adjust to the cold temperatures and scarcity of food during winter. Animals change behavior, diet, shelter, and appearance. See what squirrels, honeybees, bears, snakes, deer mice, fish, birds, elk, turkeys, and bison do to survive. Includes teacher's guide.

Title: *Whitewash*
Producer: Churchill Media
Series: Not Applicable
Year Released: 1994
Call Number: 305.38
Length: 25 minutes
Price: $100.00
Reviewed in: *Booklist, TV Guide*
Grade Level: K–6
Keywords: African Americans; Behavior; Prejudice

This tells the story of Helen Angel, a young African American girl whose life takes a traumatic turn when her face is spray-painted by a racist gang. It features the voices of Ruby Dee as the grandmother and Linda Lavin as the teacher. Includes teacher's guide.

Title: *Witches and Mice*
Producer: TVOntario/GPN
Series: Magic Library
Year Released: 1990
Call Number: Easy Fiction
Length: 15 minutes
Price: $49.00
Reviewed in: *Video Rating Guide for Libraries*
Grade Level: 2–3
Keywords: Literature; Mice; Witches

A crazy witch appears in the Magic Library, where Zazi and Norbert are waiting for story time. She tells them a story about witches and mice: "The Witch in the Ditch." Literature points covered include folk tales, recall of information, drawing conclusions, and understanding characters. Teacher's guide available for purchase.

Title: *Women in Rural America*
Producer: United Learning
Series: Not Applicable
Year Released: 1995
Call Number: 331.4
Length: 23 minutes
Price: $95.00
Reviewed in: *School Library Journal*

Grade Level: 5–6
Keywords: Farms; Social Studies; U.S. History; Women

This program provides a look at the daily lives of farm women in our nation's heartland during the first half of the twentieth century. Historic changes in social, political and material culture are highlighted as the work done by the women is shown. Includes teacher's guide, blackline masters.

Title: *Women Space Pioneers*
Producer: Global Science Productions/Churchill Media
Series: Not Applicable
Year Released: 1995
Call Number: 629.45
Length: 25 minutes
Price: $150.00
Reviewed in: *Booklist, School Library Journal*
Grade Level: 4–6
Keywords: Astronauts; Science—Space; Women

A tribute to the first women astronauts, this documentary features archival footage and interviews with the men and women who shaped the future of space travel. Host Nichelle Nichols, *Star Trek's* Lt. Uhuru, was instrumental in helping recruit the first women for NASA.

Title: *World of Circles*
Producer: Allied Video
Series: Assistant Professor
Year Released: 1992
Call Number: 515.15
Length: 24 minutes
Price: $30.00
Reviewed in: *Video Librarian*
Grade Level: 4–6
Keywords: Circles; Geometry; Mathematics

A circle and its parts are defined. The program illustrates and explains radius, diameter, circumference, and area. Special attention is given to the concept of pi.

Title: *Writing on the Wall, The*
Producer: Little Eagle Productions/Churchill Media
Series: Not Applicable
Year Released: 1995
Call Number: 305.8
Length: 45 minutes
Price: $150.00
Reviewed in: *Booklist*
Grade Level: K–6
Keywords: Jewish Americans; Multicultural; Prejudice; Social Studies

This CBS Schoolbreak Special, inspired by an actual event, tells the story of a rabbi who teaches three teenage boys about tolerance after their "innocent" anti-Semitic prank outrages the community. A story of ignorance, forgiveness, and personal growth, and a video to expose prejudice and promote understanding.

Title: *Yankton Sioux, The*
Producer: Schlessinger Video Productions
Series: Indians of North America Video Collection 1
Year Released: 1993
Call Number: 970.0004
Length: 30 minutes
Price: $40.00
Reviewed in: *Booklist, School Library Journal*
Grade Level: 4–6
Keywords: Indians of North America; Native Americans; Sioux Indians

Leading Native American scholars discuss the history of the Sioux, including myths and stereotypes. There are interviews combined with archival photographs and film footage, tribal music, crafts, and ceremonies to help students examine the spiritual relationship with nature, the role of women in Indian society, and the role of the U.S. government in Indian affairs.

Title: *Yertle the Turtle and Other Stories*
Producer: Green Light Media/Random House Home Video
Series: Dr. Seuss Video Classics
Year Released: 1992
Call Number: Easy Fiction

Length: 30 minutes
Price: $10.00
Reviewed in: *Video Rating Guide for Libraries*
Grade Level: K–3
Keywords: Literature; Turtles

Compilation of three stories by Dr. Seuss narrated by John Lithgow. Also includes "Gertrude McFuzz" and "The Big Brag."

Title: *You and Your Hospital*
Producer: Rainbow Educational Media
Series: Community Helpers
Year Released: 1995
Call Number: 362
Length: 19 minutes
Price: $89.00
Reviewed in: *Booklist, School Library Journal*
Grade Level: 1–3
Keywords: Community; Hospitals; Social Studies

Angela breaks her arm and is taken to the local hospital by her parents. This visit introduces students to a community hospital and the medical people that are there to help.

Title: *Zoo Crew: Do the Zoo*
Producer: Big Kids Productions
Series: What Do You Want to Be When You Grow Up?
Year Released: 1995
Call Number: 636
Length: 30 minutes
Price: $15.00
Reviewed in: Publishers Weekly, *School Library Journal*
Grade Level: PreK–6
Keywords: Careers; Occupations; Zoos

Explores the world of zoo workers. Original songs and footage of zoo animals and workers are shown.

Title: *Zoofari: A Real Life Adventure into the Wilds of the Zoo*
Producer: White Tree Pictures
Series: Not Applicable
Year Released: 1994
Call Number: 590.74
Length: 32 minutes
Price: $15.00
Reviewed in: *School Library Journal*
Grade Level: PreK–2
Keywords: Animals; Zoos

This video takes kids on a tour of the zoo, where they see all kinds of different animals, from flamingos to polar bears.

SECTION III

RECOMMENDED VIDEOS ARRANGED BY SUBJECT

The keywords from the entries in the previous section also comprise the subject used to organize Part III.

Use this list to find videos that support various curricular topics.

You can use the margins to list additional videos on the same topic found in your own—or other—libraries.

ADAPTATION

Rock Ptarmigan

AFRICA

Anansi and the Moss-Covered Rock
Galimoto
Giraffes and How They Live
Great Snake
Jomo and Mata

AFRICAN AMERICANS

Alice Walker
Amistad Revolt, The: All We Want Is Make Us Free
Bigmama's
Black Is My Color: The African American Experience
Booker T. Washington
Colin Powell
George Washington Carver
Harriet Tubman
Heritage of the Black West
Holiday Facts and Fun: Kwanzaa
Holiday Facts and Fun: Martin Luther King Day
Jackie Robinson
Jesse Owens
Langston Hughes
Making It Happen: Masters of Invention
Mary McLeod Bethune
Mildred D. Taylor
Picture Book of Martin Luther King, Jr., A
Sojourner Truth
Thurgood Marshall
Whitewash

AIDS

AIDS: A Different Kind of Germ
Thumbs Up for Kids! AIDS Education

AIRPLANES

Big Plane Trip, The
Come Fly with Us

ALCOTT, LOUISA MAY

Louisa May Alcott

ALMANACS

Animated Almanac, The

ALPHABET SKILLS

Do the Alphabet
Dr. Seuss's ABC
Story of Read-Alee-Deed-Alee, The: Program 13
Story of Read-Alee-Deed-Alee, The: Program 14

AMERICAN CITIZENSHIP

What Is an American?

AMPHIBIANS

Amphibian
Fish, Amphibians, and Reptiles

ANATOMY, HUMAN

Just the Facts (for Boys)
Just the Facts (for Girls)

ANGER

Angry John
I Get So Mad!
When Anger Turns to Rage

ANIMALS

Amazing North America
Amphibian
Animals of the Amazon River Basin
Antarctic Adventure
At the Zoo
Babies and Their Parents
Baby Animals
Bear Cubs, Baby Ducks, and Kooky Kookaburras
Bears!
Big Cats of the World
Bird
Born to Be Wild
Cat
Cool Cats, Raindrops, and Things that Live in Holes
Coot Club
Cougar: King of the Mountain
Creepy Creatures and Slimy Stuff

Critter Songs: A Celebration of Children and Wildlife
Cubs and Kittens
Dog
Everything Grows
Ferret Husbandry
Fish, Amphibians, and Reptiles
Flying, Trying, and Honking Around
Horses . . . Close Up and Very Personal
Horton Hatches the Egg
How Animals Survive
KangaZoo Club 1: Baboons-Sea Lions-Tigers
KangaZoo Club 2: Monkeys-Crocodiles-Lions
KangaZoo Club 3: Gorillas-Dolphins-Cheetahs
Komodo Dragon: The Largest Lizard
Let's Explore . . . Furry, Fishy, Feathery Friends
Nature Friends!
Perfect the Pig
Pigs (2d ed.)
Protecting the Web
Reptile
Totally Tropical Rain Forest
Where Do Animals Go in Winter?
Zoofari: A Real Life Adventure into the Wilds of the Zoo

ANTARCTIC

Antarctic Adventure

APACHE INDIANS

Apache, The

ARGENTINA

Argentina

ART

Barry's Scrapbook: A Window into Art
Collage
Drawing
Fiber
Let's Create for Halloween
Let's See
Made for Art
Maya Art and Architecture
Painting
Pastels
Quilt
Sculpture
Sketching
Symbols

ARTHUR, KING

Merlin and the Dragons

ARTISTS

Girl's World, A
Let's See

ASIA

Australia
Cambodia
Indonesia
Kuwait
Laos
Malaysia
Vietnam

ASIAN AMERICANS

From East to West: The Asian-American Experience

ASTRONAUTS

Living in Space
Women Space Pioneers

ASTRONOMY

Astronomy 101: A Family Adventure and Beginner's Guide to the
  Night
Starting with Stars
Voyage to the Moon

ATLAS

Animated Atlas, The

AUSTRALIA

Australia

AUTHORS

Getting to Know William Steig
Henry Wadsworth Longfellow
Langston Hughes

Louisa May Alcott
Marc Brown
Meet Jack Prelutsky
Meet Leo Lionni
Mildred D. Taylor

AUTOMOBILES

*Built for Speed: A High Speed Live Action Adventure at the
    Racetrack*
How a Car Is Built

AZTEC INDIANS

Aztec, The

BABIES

Baby Animals
Bear Cubs, Baby Ducks, and Kooky Kookaburras
Cubs and Kittens

BALLET

Miss Christy's Dancin' Ballet
Peeping Beauty

BALTIC STATES

Baltic States, The: Facing Independence

BANDS

Ty's One Man Band

BEARS

Bears!
Berenstain Bears Forget Their Manners
Berenstain Bears Get Stage Fright/Go Bonkers
Born to Be Wild

BEHAVIOR

Angry John
Being a Friend: What Does It Mean?
Berenstain Bears Forget Their Manners
Berenstain Bears Get Stage Fright/Go Bonkers
Breaking Out of the Under Achievement Trap
Casey's Revenge
Clarissa
Focus on Friendship
Focus on Honesty
Focus on Responsibility
Gangs: Decisions and Options
How Do You Do Your How Do You Dos?
Hurtful Words
I Can Make Good Choices
I Get So Mad!
I Hate My Brother Harry
Kid's Guide to Divorce, A
Kid's Guide to Feeling Good about Yourself, A
Kid's Guide to Friendship, A
Kid's Guide to Manners, A
Kid's Guide to Personal Behavior 1: Tattling, Disobeying, and Fibbing
Kid's Guide to Personal Behavior 2: Rudeness, Whining, and Bickering
Knight School

Lean Mean Machine, The—A Story about Handling Emotions
Let's Be Friends
Let's Create for Halloween
Molly's Magic
More than Manners
My Body, My Buddy: Caring and Sharing
My Body, My Buddy: Teasing and Bullying
My Body, My Buddy: Winning and Losing
No More Teasing!
Oops! I Messed Up!
Respect Yourself and Others, Too
Say No and Keep Your Friends
School's Cool
Self Confidence: Step by Step
Slurps, Burps, and Spills!
Taking Chances: Teens at Risk
Theories of Personalities
Time for Horatio, A
Understanding and Resolving Conflicts
Unforgettable Pen Pal, The—A Story about Prejudice and Discrimination
Violence: Dealing with Anger in the Formative Years
What Do You Tell a Phone?
What Now? Deciding What's Right
When Anger Turns to Rage
When I Feel Alone
When I Feel Different
When Mom and Dad Divorce
Whitewash

BETHUNE, MARY MCLEOD

Mary McLeod Bethune

BIOGRAPHIES

Alice Walker
Booker T. Washington
Colin Powell

George Washington Carver
Getting to Know William Steig
Harriet Tubman
Henry Wadsworth Longfellow
Holiday Facts and Fun: Martin Luther King Day
Jackie Robinson
Jesse Owens
Langston Hughes
Louisa May Alcott
Marc Brown
Mary McLeod Bethune
Meet Jack Prelutsky
Meet Leo Lionni
Mildred D. Taylor
Picture Book of Martin Luther King, Jr., A
Sojourner Truth
Thurgood Marshall

BIOLOGY

Introducing the Cell
What Is Life?

BIRDS

Bird
First Look at Birds, A
Hummingbirds and How They Live
Robins and How They Live
Rock Ptarmigan

BIRTHDAYS

Made for Art

BLUEBONNETS

Legend of the Bluebonnet

BOATS

All about Boats

BREAD

Bread: From Farm to Table

BRIDGES

Big Cable Bridges

BROTHERS AND SISTERS

Casey's Revenge
I Hate My Brother Harry
I'll Fix Anthony
Jomo and Mata

BROWN, MARC

Marc Brown

BUILDINGS

Building Skyscrapers

BULLIES

My Body, My Buddy: Teasing and Bullying
No More Teasing!

CAMBODIA

Cambodia

CAMOUFLAGE

How Animals Survive
Insect Disguises

CANADA

Sheena Azak of Canada

CAREERS

Careers in Math: From Architects to Astronauts
Girl's World, A
Grandpa Worked on the Railroad
Job of a TV Meteorologist
Lenny the Lumberjack

Milk and Cookies
Math . . . Who Needs It?
Railroaders
Timberrr! From Logs to Lumber
Zoo Crew: Do the Zoo

CARVER, GEORGE WASHINGTON

George Washington Carver
Peanuts

CATS

Big Cats of the World
Cat
Cat in the Hat Comes Back, The
Cougar: King of the Mountain
Cougars and How They Live
Koko's Kitten
Three-Legged Cat, The

CELLS

Cell
Introducing the Cell

CHEMISTRY

It's Chemical: Phase Changes
Polymers: Stretching and Bouncing Back

CHEROKEE INDIANS

Cherokee, The

CHICKENS

Peeping Beauty

CHRISTMAS

Country Mouse and the City Mouse, The: A Christmas Tale
Multi-Cultural Christmas, A
Savior Is Born

CICADAS

Cicadas: The 17-Year Invasion

CIRCULATORY SYSTEMS

Circulatory and Respiratory Systems

CLOCKS

Clocks and Watches

COLONIAL AMERICA

Johnny Tremain
Pilgrims at Plymouth

COLLAGE

Collage

COLORS

Colors
Pastels

COMANCHE INDIANS

Comanche, The
Legend of the Bluebonnet

COMMUNITY

Away We Go: All about Transportation
All about Neighborhoods
Cops Are Tops: Our Police at Work
Information Please! Your Library in Action
Keeping Your Community Clean
Moving the Mail: Postal Employees at Work
Sound the Alarm: Firefighters at Work
There Goes a Police Car
You and Your Hospital

COMPETITION

Kiki and the Cuckoo
My Body, My Buddy: Winning and Losing
Tortoise and the Hare, The

COMPUTERS

Computers: Where They Come From and How They Work
Digital Environment, The

CONCRETE

Concrete Trucking

CONFLICT RESOLUTION

Understanding and Resolving Conflicts

CONSTRUCTION

Big Cable Bridges
Building Skyscrapers
Concrete Trucking
I Can Build!
There Goes a Bulldozer

COOPERATION

Show Time

COUGARS

Cougar: King of the Mountain
Cougars and How They Live

COUNTING

Count with Me!
*Celebrate 100 Kit: Everything Your Class Needs to Count Up to
   the 100th Day of School*

COWS

Clarissa
Cows!
Dairy Farm
Milk Cow, Eat Cheese

CREATION

Christianity
Creation

CREATIVE THINKING

Molly's Magic

CREEK INDIANS

Creek, The

CRISIS

Dingles, The

CULTURE

Hair Scare

CUSTOMS

Creating Cultural Diversity

DAIRY FARMS

Clarissa
Dairy Farm
Let's Go to the Farm with Mac Parker
Milk and Cookies
Milk Cow, Eat Cheese

DANCE

Cinderella . . . Frozen in Time: Ice Capades
Hip-Hop Kidz: Learn to Hip-Hop Dance
Miss Christy's Dancin' Ballet
Miss Christy's Dancin' Jazz

DECIMALS

Decimals to Be Exact, Part One

DICTIONARIES

Animated Dictionary, The

DINOSAURS

Dinosaurs: Lessons from Bones
Land of Dinosaurs

DISEASES

Body's Defenses against Disease, The
Our Internal Defender

DIVERSITY

When I Feel Different

DIVORCE

Kid's Guide to Divorce, A
When Mom and Dad Divorce

DOGS

Dog
Harry and the Lady Next Door
Harry, the Dirty Dog
Henry and Mudge in Puddle Trouble
My Way Sally
Officer Buckle and Gloria

DRAGONFLY

Dragonfly

DRAWING

Drawing
Sketching

DRUGS

Sky's the Limit
Trouble with Tobacco, The
We're No Dummies! We Don't Take Drugs

DWELLINGS

Cool Cats, Raindrops, and Things that Live in Holes

EARLY CHILDHOOD

All about Shapes
Big Bird Gets Lost
Colors
Count with Me!
Do the Alphabet
Dr. Seuss's ABC
Everything Grows
Kids Make Music
Let's Play Games
Marc Brown Does Play Rhymes
Me and My Family
Monkey Moves
Move like the Animals
Professor Parrot Speaks Spanish
Sammy: And Other Songs from Getting to Know Myself
Stepping Out with Hap Palmer
Time

EARTH

What's inside the Earth?:An Introduction to the Earth's Interior

EARTHQUAKES

Earthquakes: Our Restless Planet

EASTER

Easter Egg Farm, The

EATING DISORDERS

When Food Is an Obsession: Overcoming Eating Disorders

ECOLOGY

Backyard Wilderness
Between the Walls
Communities of Living Things
Eco-Rap: Voices from the Hood
Garbage Day!
Great Kapok Tree, The
Journey of the Blob
Kylie's Concert
Making a Difference
Murky Water Caper, The
Oil Spills
Protecting Our Endangered Species
Reducing, Reusing and Recycling: Environmental Concerns
Trash Troll, The
Trees for Life

ECOSYSTEM

Protecting the Web

EGYPT

Watch Out for the Tetrahedron!

ELECTIONS

Electing a President: The Process

ELECTRICITY

Electricity and Electrical Safety
Topsy-Turvy

ELEPHANTS

Horton Hatches the Egg
Jomo and Mata

ENCYCLOPEDIA

Animated Encyclopedia, The

ENDANGERED SPECIES

Arkelope
Bollo Caper, The
Kylie's Concert
Protecting Our Endangered Species
Science and the Seas
Songbird Story

ENERGY

Heat, Temperature, and Energy
Power Up? Energy in Our Environment

ENGLAND

My Way Sally

ENVIRONMENTAL CONCERNS

Backyard Wilderness
Connections
Eco-Rap: Voices from the Hood
Frosty Returns
Journey of the Blob
Making a Difference
Murky Water Caper, The
Oil Spills Over a Barrel
Power Up? Energy in Our Environment
Protecting Our Endangered Species
Source of Life? Water in Our Environment
Two Faces of Ozone, The

ESTIMATING

Help Wanted

ETIQUETTE

How Do You Do Your How Do You Dos?
More than Manners

EUROPE

European Folktales, Vol. 10
Hungary: Between East and West
Turkey: Between Europe and Asia

EXERCISE

Monkey Moves
Move like the Animals
My Body, My Buddy: Healthy Food
My Body, My Buddy: Healthy Fun

EXPERIMENTS

Dr. Zed's Brilliant Science Activities
My First Science Video

EXPLORERS

Being an Explorer

EXTINCTION

Arkelope

FABLES

Aesop's Fables
Great Snake

FAIRY TALES

Emperor's New Clothes, The
Fisherman and His Wife, The
Gingerbread Man, The
Many Moons
Rumpelstiltskin
Tom Thumb

FALL

Fall Brings Changes

FAMILIES

Babies and Their Parents
Bigmama's
Birthday Basket for Tia, A
Casey's Revenge
Children of Other Lands: Andres Orozoco of Mexico
Cougars and How They Live
Cubs and Kittens
I Hate My Brother Harry
Irish Americans
Italian Americans
Japanese Americans
Kid's Guide to Divorce, A
Korean Americans
Me and My Family
Papa Piccolo
Start with a Story: Baby Rattlesnake
When Mom and Dad Divorce

FARMS

Baby Animals
Dairy Farm
Women in Rural America

FEAR

Otherwise Known as Sheila the Great

FEELINGS

Lean Mean Machine, The—A Story About Handling Emotions
My Body, My Buddy: Caring and Sharing
When I Feel Alone
When I Feel Different

FERRETS

Ferret Husbandry

FIBER

Fiber

FINGER-PLAY

Marc Brown Does Play Rhymes

FIRE

Fire and Rescue
Fire in the Forest
Fire Safety: Hall of Flame

FIRE FIGHTERS

Big Red
Fire and Rescue
Mose the Fireman
Sound the Alarm: Firefighters at Work

FIRST LADIES

First Ladies

FISH

Fish
Fish, Amphibians, and Reptiles

FLAGS

Old Glory

FLIGHT

Flight
Flying, Trying, and Honking Around

FOLK TALES

Anansi and the Moss-Covered Rock
Durwin's World
European Folktales, Vol. 10
Fool of the World and the Flying Ship, The
Start with a Story: Baby Rattlesnake

FOOD

Bread: From Farm to Table
Food
Meal Planning: The Food Pyramid in Action
Milk and Cookies
Red Riding Hood and the Well-Fed Wolf
When Food Is an Obsession: Overcoming Eating Disorders

FOOD CHAIN

Food Chain (AIMS)
Food Chain (NGS)

FORESTS

Fire in the Forest
Lenny the Lumberjack
Trees for Life
Uncle Nick and the Magic Forest, Vol. 3: Lost in the Forest

FOSSILS

I Dig Fossils: A Real Life Adventure for Children of All Ages
Land of Dinosaurs

FOXES

Tessa on Her Own

FRACTIONS

Fractions and All Their Parts, 1
Fractions and All Their Parts, 2
Fractions and All Their Parts, 3

FRIENDSHIP

Being a Friend: What Does It Mean?
Eureeka's Castle: Sing Along with Eureeka
Gullah Gullah Island: Sing Along with Binyah Binyah
Focus on Friendship
Kid's Guide to Friendship, A
Koko's Kitten
Let's Be Friends
Respect Yourself and Others, Too

FROGS

Tuesday

GAMES

Let's See

GANGS

Gangs: Decisions and Options

GARBAGE

Garbage Day!
Keeping Your Community Clean

GEOGRAPHY

Challenging Geography: Explorers Discover America

GEOLOGY

Continents Adrift: An Introduction to Continental Drift and Plate Tectonics
Formation of Continents and Mountains
Glaciers: Nature's Conveyor Belt
How Does the Land Build Up?
How Does the Land Wear Down?
Our Changing Earth
Our Planet Earth
Rocks and Minerals
What's the Earth Made of?

GEOMETRY

All about Angles
Help Wanted
King Comes Calling, The
Manor House Mystery, The: Problem-Solving in Geometry
World of Circles

GERMAN AMERICANS

German Americans

GERMS

Germs

GHOSTS

Are You Afraid of the Dark? Ghostly Tales

GIRAFFES

Giraffes and How They Live

GLACIERS

Glaciers: Nature's Conveyor Belt

GLOBES

Finding Your Way: Using Maps and Globes

GORILLAS

Koko's Kitten

GOVERNMENT

Our Federal Government: The Legislative Branch
Our Federal Government: The Presidency
Our Federal Government: The Supreme Court

GUM

Chewing Gum

GUN SAFETY

Big Shot

GROWTH

Everything Grows

HABITATS

Communities of Living Things

HALLOWEEN

By the Light of the Halloween Moon
Holiday Facts and Fun: Halloween
Let's Create for Halloween
McGruff on Halloween

HANDS

I Am Joe's Hand

HANUKKAH

In the Month of Kislev

HAZARDOUS WASTE

Journey of the Blob

HEALTH

AIDS: A Different Kind of Germ
Body's Defenses against Disease, The
Bread: From Farm to Table
Food
Germs
Growing Up! For Boys
Growing Up! For Girls
I Am Joe's Hand
Just the Facts (for Boys)
Just the Facts (for Girls)
Kid's Guide to Personal Hygiene, A

Libre Quiero Ser (I Want to Be Free)
Me and My Body
Meal Planning: The Food Pyramid in Action
My Body, My Buddy: Healthy Food
Our Internal Defender
Red Riding Hood and the Well-Fed Wolf
Sky's the Limit
Thumbs Up for Kids! AIDS Education
Trouble with Tobacco, The
We're No Dummies! We Don't Take Drugs
When Food Is an Obsession: Overcoming Eating Disorders

HELICOPTERS

Heli-Kids: A Helicopter Adventure for Kids

HISPANIC AMERICANS

One World, Many Worlds: Hispanic Diversity in the United States

HOLIDAYS

Country Mouse and the City Mouse, The: A Christmas Tale
Creating Cultural Diversity
Easter Egg Farm, The
Food for Thought
Holiday Facts and Fun: Halloween
Holiday Facts and Fun: Kwanzaa
Holiday Facts and Fun: Martin Luther King Day
Holiday Facts and Fun: Valentine's Day
In the Month of Kislev
McGruff on Halloween
Multi-Cultural Christmas, A
Savior Is Born
Sesame Street Celebrates Around the World
Thanksgiving Day

HONESTY

Focus on Honesty

HORROR

Are You Afraid of the Dark? Ghostly Tales

HORSES

Colt Called Lucky, A
Horses . . . Close Up and Very Personal

HOSPITALS

You and Your Hospital

HUGHES, LANGSTON

Langston Hughes

HUMAN BODY

Body's Defenses against Disease, The
Circulatory and Respiratory Systems
Growing Up! For Boys
Growing Up! For Girls
I Am Joe's Hand
Just the Facts (for Boys)

Just the Facts (for Girls)
Me and My Body
Our Internal Defender
Reproductive Systems

HUMAN RELATIONS

Let's Be Friends
No More Teasing

HUMMINGBIRDS

Hummingbirds and How They Live

HUNGARY

Hungary: Between East and West

ICE CREAM

Ice Cream and Popsicles

ICE SKATING

Cinderella . . . Frozen in Time: Ice Capades

IMAGINATION

Arthur Writes a Story
Dog and His Boy, A
Too Many Pumpkins

IMMIGRATION

Victor

INDIANS OF NORTH AMERICA

Apache, The
Aztec, The
Cherokee, The
Creek, The
Comanche, The
Dancing with the Indians
Iroquois, The
Native American Life
Navajo, The
People of the Desert
People of the Forest
People of the Northwest Coast
Pueblo, The
Yankton Sioux, The

INDONESIA

Indonesia

INSECTS

Cicadas: The 17-Year Invasion
Creepy Creatures and Slimy Stuff Insects
Insect Disguises
Insects and Spiders: The Private World of Jean Henri Fabre
Mosquito, The
Praying Mantis

INVENTIONS/INVENTORS

Chewing Gum
Clocks and Watches
Ice Cream and Popsicles
Inventors and Inventions
Making It Happen: Masters of Invention
Peanuts

IRELAND

Molly's Magic

IRISH AMERICANS

Irish Americans

IROQUOIS INDIANS

Iroquois, The

ISLAMIC RELIGION

Food for Thought

ITALIAN AMERICANS

Italian Americans

ITALY

Papa Piccolo

JAPANESE AMERICANS

Japanese Americans

JAZZ

Miss Christy's Dancin' Jazz
Journey through Jazz, Parts 1 and 2

JEWISH AMERICANS

In the Month of Kislev
To Jew Is Not a Verb
Writing on the Wall, The

JUMPROPE

How to Chinese Jumprope

KING, MARTIN LUTHER JR.

Holiday Facts and Fun: Martin Luther King Day
Picture Book of Martin Luther King, Jr., A

KITTENS

Koko's Kitten

KNIGHTS

Knight School
Knight-Time Tale, A

KOALAS

Kylie's Concert

KOREAN AMERICANS

Korean Americans

KUWAIT

Kuwait

KWANZAA

Holiday Facts and Fun: Kwanzaa

LANGUAGE ARTS

Dog and His Boy, A
Ghost Story
Good Thing about Spots, A
Harry the Dirty Dog
Jungle for Joey, A
Knight-Time Tale, A
Made for Art
Mice in the Library
Nina's Strange Adventure
Papa Piccolo
Pattern Patrol
Over a Barrel
Show Time
Story of Read-Alee-Deed-Alee, The: Program 13
Story of Read-Alee-Deed-Alee, The: Program 14
Timid Dinosaurs

LAOS

Laos

LASERS

Lasers: The Special Light

LEOPARDS

Bollo Caper, The
Good Thing about Spots, A

LIBRARY SKILLS

Animated Almanac, The
Animated Atlas, The
Animated Dictionary, The
Animated Encyclopedia, The
Beyond the Stacks: Finding Fun in the Library
Finding It Fast in the Library
Information Please! Your Library in Action
Mysteries Revealed—Basic Research Skills

LIFE CYCLE

Dragonfly

LIONNI, LEO

Meet Leo Lionni

LITERATURE

Abuelita's Paradise
Aesop's Fables
Alexander and the Terrible, Horrible, No Good, Very Bad Day
Alexander, Who Used to Be Rich Last Sunday
All the Colors of the Earth
Amazing Grace

Anansi and the Moss-Covered Rock
Anatole
Are You Afraid of the Dark? Ghostly Tales
Arthur Writes a Story
Ashok by Any Other Name
Bigmama's
Bollo Caper, The
By the Light of the Halloween Moon
Cat in the Hat Comes Back, The
Coot Club
Dingles, The
Durwin's World
Easter Egg Farm, The
Emperor's New Clothes, The
European Folktales, Vol. 10
Fisherman and His Wife, The
Fool of the World and the Flying Ship, The
Galimoto
Gingerbread Man, The
Goblin Mischief
Great Snake
Growing Pains
Hailstones and Halibut Bones
Harry and the Lady Next Door
Henry and Mudge in Puddle Trouble
Hiawatha
Hill of Fire
Horton Hatches the Egg
I Hate My Brother Harry
I'll Fix Anthony
In the Month of Kislev
Jomo and Mata
Knight-Time Tale, A
Koko's Kitten
Kiki and the Cuckoo
Legend of the Bluebonnet
Many Moons
Merlin and the Dragons
Mice in the Library
Officer Buckle and Gloria
Otherwise Known as Sheila the Great
Peeping Beauty
Pegasus
Perfect the Pig
Picture Book of Martin Luther King, Jr., A

Prince and the Pauper, The
Ralph S. Mouse
Reading the Best: Introducing the Newbery Winners
Rumpelstiltskin
Tessa on Her Own
Thanksgiving Day
Three-Legged Cat, The
Timid Dinosaurs
Tom Thumb
Too Many Pumpkins
Tortoise and the Hare, The
Truck Song
Tuesday
Witches and Mice
Yertle the Turtle and Other Stories

LIZARDS

Komodo Dragon: The Largest Lizard

LONDON

Time for Horatio, A

LONGFELLOW, HENRY WADSWORTH

Henry Wadsworth Longfellow

LUMBERJACKS

Timberrr! From Logs to Lumber

MACHINES

I Love Big Machines

MAGIC

My First Magic Video

MALAYSIA

Malaysia

MAMMALS

First Look at Mammals, A

MANIPULATIVES

Using Manipulatives: Patterning/Classifying
Using Manipulatives: Using a Model/Estimating and Checking

MANNERS

Berenstain Bears Forget Their Manners
How Do You Do Your How Do You Dos?
Kid's Guide to Manners, A
More Than Manners
Slurps, Burps, and Spills!
What Do You Tell a Phone?

MAPS

Finding Your Way: Using Maps and Globes

MARS

Mars, the Red Planet

MARSHALL, THURGOOD

Thurgood Marshall

MATHEMATICS

All about Angles
Careers in Math: From Architects to Astronauts
Celebrate 100 Kit: Everything Your Class Needs to Count Up to the 100th Day of School
Count with Me!
Decimals to Be Exact, Part One
Evening Things Out: Understanding Averages
Fractions and All Their Parts, 1
Fractions and All Their Parts, 2
Fractions and All Their Parts, 3
Fractions: Multiplication and Division
Help Wanted
King Comes Calling, The
Manor House Mystery, The: Problem-Solving in Geometry
Math . . . Who Needs It?
Metric System
Seeing Numbers
Take a Chance: Exploring Probability
Time, Money, and Measurement
Using Manipulatives: Patterning/Classifying
Using Manipulatives: Using a Model/Estimating and Checking
Watch Out for the Tetrahedron!
World of Circles

MATTER

It's Chemical: Phase Changes
Matter
Solids in Our World
Solids, Liquids, and Gases

MAYANS

Maya Art and Architecture

MEASUREMENTS

Metric System
Time, Money, and Measurement

MERLIN

Merlin and the Dragons

METEOROLOGIST

Job of a TV Meteorologist

METRIC SYSTEM

Metric System

MEXICAN AMERICANS

Birthday Basket for Tia, A
Victor

MEXICO

Children of Other Lands: Andres Orozoco of Mexico

MICE

Anatole
Between the Walls
Country Mouse and the City Mouse, The: A Christmas Tale
Goblin Mischief
Ralph S. Mouse
Witches and Mice

MICROSCOPES

How to Use a Microscope

MINERALS

Every Stone Has a Story

MOLESTATION

Kid's Guide to Self-Protection, A
When Should You Tell? Dealing with Abuse

MONEY

Alexander, Who Used to Be Rich Last Sunday
Time, Money, and Measurement

MOONS

Many Moons

MOSES

Moses in Egypt
Moses the Lawgiver

MOSQUITOES

Mosquito, The

MOVEMENT

Sammy: And Other Songs from Getting to Know Myself
Stepping Out with Hap Palmer

MULTICULTURAL

Abuelita's Paradise
Apache, The
Ashok by Any Other Name
Aztec, The

Birthday Basket for Tia, A
Black Is My Color: The African American Experience
Children of Other Lands: Andres Orozoco of Mexico
Come Join Our Multicultural Band, Vol.1
Creating Cultural Diversity
Food for Thought
From East to West: The Asian-American Experience
Galimoto
German Americans
Hair Scare
How We're Different and Alike
Irish Americans
Italian Americans
Japanese Americans
Korean Americans
Multi-Cultural Christmas, A
One World, Many Worlds: Hispanic Diversity in the United States
Positively Native
Puerto Ricans
To Jew Is Not a Verb
Victor
Writing on the Wall, The

MULTIPLICATION

Fractions: Multiplication and Division

MUSEUMS

Barry's Scrapbook: A Window into Art
Fire Safety: Hall of Flame

MUSIC

At the Zoo
Come Join Our Multicultural Band, Vol.1

Critter Songs: A Celebration of Children and Wildlife
Eureeka's Castle: Sing Along with Eureeka
Gullah Gullah Island: Sing Along with Binyah Binyah
Journey through Jazz, Parts 1 and 2
Kids Make Music
Marc Brown Does Play Rhymes
Let's Play Games
Ty's One Man Band
Uncle Nick and the Magic Forest, Vol. 3: Lost in the Forest

MYSTERY

Ghost Story
Mice in the Library
Over a Barrel

MYTHOLOGY

Pegasus

NAMES

Ashok by Any Other Name

NATIVE AMERICANS

Apache, The
Aztec, The
Cherokee, The
Comanche, The
Creek, The
Dancing with the Indians
Hiawatha

Iroquois, The
Legend of the Bluebonnet
Native American Life
Navajo, The
People of the Desert
People of the Forest
Pueblo, The
Start with a Story: Baby Rattlesnake
Yankton Sioux, The

NATURE

Nature Friends!

NAVAJO INDIANS

Navajo, The

NEW YEAR'S EVE

Sesame Street Celebrates Around the World

NEWBERY MEDAL

Reading the Best: Introducing the Newbery Winners

NIGHT

Night

NUMBERS

Count with Me!
Evening Things Out: Understanding Averages

NUTRITION

Food
Meal Planning: The Food Pyramid in Action
My Body, My Buddy: Healthy Food
Red Riding Hood and the Well-Fed Wolf

OCCUPATIONS

Careers in Math: From Architects to Astronauts
Lenny the Lumberjack
Zoo Crew: Do the Zoo

OCEANS

Animal Life in a Tidepool
Aquaspace Adventure
Oceans: Earth's Last Frontier
Science and the Seas
Shark, Shark, Shark
Sharks: Predators or Prey?
Voyage of the Loggerhead

OIL PRODUCTION

Field Trip to the Oil Refinery
Oil Spills

OTTERS

Nina's Strange Adventure

OWENS, JESSE

Jesse Owens

OZONE

Two Faces of Ozone, The

PAINTING

Painting

PATTERNS

Pattern Patrol

PEANUTS

Peanuts

PEER PRESSURE

Say No and Keep Your Friends

PENGUINS

Antarctic Adventure

PERSONAL HYGIENE

Kid's Guide to Personal Hygiene, A

PERSONAL SAFETY

It's Your Body
McGruff and the Dangerous Stranger
McGruff's Self-Care Alert
Speak Up for Yourself
Strangers Aren't Bad, They're Just Strangers
When Should You Tell? Dealing with Abuse

PERSONALITIES

Theories of Personalities

PETROLEUM

Field Trip to the Oil Refinery

PETS

Ferret Husbandry
Let's Explore . . . Furry, Fishy, Feathery Friends
Protecting the Web

PHYSICAL EDUCATION

Cinderella . . . Frozen in Time: Ice Capades
Hip-Hop Kidz: Learn to Hip-Hop Dance
How to Chinese Jumprope
Miss Christy's Dancin' Ballet
Miss Christy's Dancin' Jazz
Monkey Moves
Move like the Animals
My Body, My Buddy: Healthy Fun

PIGS

Perfect the Pig
Pigs

PILGRIMS

Early Settlers
Pilgrims at Plymouth

PILOTS

Girl's World, A

PIONEERS

Santa Fe Trail, The
Westward Expansion: The Pioneer Challenge

PLANETS

Mercury, Venus, and Mars
Our Solar System: The Inner Planets
Patrick Stewart Narrates the Planets

PLANTS

Plants: Green, Growing, Giving Life

POETRY

Hailstones and Halibut Bones
Hiawatha

POLICE

Cops Are Tops: Our Police at Work
There Goes a Police Car

POLLUTION

Murky Water Caper, The
Source of Life? Water in Our Environment

Trash Troll, The
Two Faces of Ozone, The

POLYMERS

Polymers: Stretching and Bouncing Back

PONY EXPRESS

Pony Express, The

POSTAL SERVICE

Moving the Mail: Postal Employees at Work
Pony Express, The

POWELL, COLIN

Colin Powell

PRAYING MANTIS

Praying Mantis

PREJUDICE

All the Colors of the Earth

How We're Different and Alike
Unforgettable Pen Pal, The—A Story About Prejudice
Whitewash
Writing on the Wall, The

PRELUTSKY, JACK

Meet Jack Prelutsky

PRESIDENTS

Electing a President: The Process
Our Federal Government: The Presidency

PRIMATES

Born to Be Wild
Jungle for Joey, A

PRINCES

Prince and the Pauper, The

PRINCESSES

Many Moons

PROBABILITY

Take a Chance: Exploring Probability

PROBLEM-SOLVING

King Comes Calling, The
Manor House Mystery, The: Problem-Solving in Geometry

PUBERTY

Growing Up! For Boys
Growing Up! For Girls

PUEBLO INDIANS

Pueblo, The

PUERTO RICANS

Abuelita's Paradise
Puerto Ricans

PUMPKINS

Too Many Pumpkins

PYRAMIDS

Watch Out for the Tetrahedron!

QUILTS

Quilt

RACE CARS

Built for Speed: A High Speed Live Action Adventure

RADIOS

Radio and Television
Satellites
Sound/Radio Broadcasting

RAILROADS

Grandpa Worked on the Railroad
Railroaders
Train Adventures for Kids: The Magical World of Trains

RAIN FORESTS

Animals of the Amazon River Basin
Animals of the Rainforest
Great Kapok Tree, The

People of the Rainforest
Plants of the Rainforest
Rainforest for Children Video Series
Struggling to Survive: Tropical Rain Forests
Totally Tropical Rain Forest

READING

Beyond the Stacks: Finding Fun in the Library
Growing Pains
Jungle for Joey, A

RECYCLING

Reducing, Reusing, and Recycling: Environmental Concerns

RELIGION

Christianity
Creation
Moses in Egypt
Moses the Lawgiver
Savior Is Born

REPTILES

Cool Creatures: Reptiles
Fish, Amphibians, and Reptiles
Komodo Dragon: The Largest Lizard
Reptile

RESEARCH SKILLS

Mysteries Revealed—Basic Research Skills

RESPIRATORY SYSTEMS

Circulatory and Respiratory Systems

RESPONSIBILITY

Focus on Responsibility
Kid's Guide to Personal Behavior 1: Tattling, Disobeying, and Fibbing
Kid's Guide to Personal Behavior 2: Rudeness, Whining, and Bickering
Tessa on Her Own

REVENGE

Casey's Revenge

RISK-TAKING

Taking Chances: Teens at Risk

RIVERS

Connections

ROBINS

Robins and How They Live

ROBINSON, JACKIE

Jackie Robinson

ROCKS

Every Stone Has a Story
Rocks and Minerals

ROMAN EMPIRE

Roman City

RUSSIA

Baltic States, The: Facing Independence
Fool of the World and the Flying Ship, The

SAFETY

Big Bird Gets Lost
Big Red
Big Shot
Dingles, The
Fire and Rescue
Fire in the Forest

Fire Safety: Hall of Flame
It's Your Body
Kid's Guide to School Safety
Kid's Guide to Self-Protection, A
Last Hit, The: Children and Violence
McGruff and the Dangerous Stranger
McGruff on Halloween
McGruff's Self-Care Alert
Mose the Fireman
My Body, My Buddy: Healthy Fun
Office Buckle and Gloria
Speak Up for Yourself
Strangers Aren't Bad, They're Just Strangers
Taking Chances: Teens at Risk
When Should You Tell? Dealing with Abuse

SATELLITES

Satellites

SCHOOL

Celebrate 100 Kit: Everything Your Class Needs to Count Up to the 100th Day of School

SCHOOL SAFETY

Kid's Guide to School Safety

SCIENCE

Connections
Dr. Zed's Brilliant Science Activities

Hurricanes, Tornados, and Thunderstorms
My First Science Video
Theories of Personalities

SCIENCE—EARTH

Circle of Water
Continents Adrift: An Introduction to Continental Drift and Plate Tectonics
Dinosaurs: Lessons from Bones
Earthquakes: Our Restless Planet
Every Stone Has a Story
Formation of Continents and Mountains
Hill of Fire
How Does the Land Build Up?
How Does the Land Wear Down?
I Dig Fossils: A Real Life Adventure for Children of All Ages
Land of Dinosaurs
Night
Our Changing Earth
Our Planet Earth
Rocks and Minerals
Struggling to Survive: Tropical Rain Forests
Two Faces of Ozone, The
Volcanoes: Mountains of Fire
What's inside the Earth?: An Introduction to the Earth
What's the Earth Made Of?

SCIENCE—LIFE

Animals of the Rainforest
Aquaspace Adventure
Arkelope
Babies and Their Parents
Cell Division
Cicadas: The 17-Year Invasion
Circulatory and Respiratory Systems
Communities of Living Things
Cool Creatures: Reptiles

Cows!
Creepy Creatures and Slimy Stuff
Dinosaur!
Dragonfly
First Look at Birds, A
First Look at Mammals, A
Fish
Food Chain (AIMS)
Food Chain (NGS)
How Animals Survive
Hummingbirds and How They Live
Insect Disguises
Insects
Insects and Spiders: The Private World of Jean Henri Fabre
Introducing the Cell
Mosquito, The
Nina's Strange Adventure
Oceans: Earth's Last Frontier
People of the Rainforest
Pigs
Plants: Green, Growing, Giving Life
Plants of the Rainforest
Praying Mantis
Protecting the Web
Science and the Seas
Reproductive Systems
Seals and How They Live
Shark, Shark, Shark
Sharks: Predators or Prey?
Snowballs and Sandcastles
Songbird Story
Spiders
To Save a Whale
Trees for Life
What Is Life?
Where Do Animals Go in Winter?

SCIENCE—PHYSICAL

Electricity and Electrical Safety
Heat, Temperature, and Energy
How Things Work

It's Chemical: Phase Changes
Lasers: The Special Light
Matter
Polymers: Stretching and Bouncing Back
Power Up? Energy in Our Environment
Push and Pull: Simple Machines at Work
Solids, Liquids, and Gases
Sound/Radio Broadcasting
Topsy-Turvy

SCIENCE—SPACE

Astronomy 101: A Family Adventure and Beginner's Guide
Exploring Our Solar System
Living in Space
Mars, the Red Planet
Mercury, Venus, and Mars
Our Solar System: The Inner Planets
Patrick Stewart Narrates the Planets
Satellites
Sun, Earth, Moon
Voyage to the Moon
Women Space Pioneers

SCULPTURE

Sculpture

SEALS

Daisy Discovers the World
Seals and How They Live

SEASONS

Fall Brings Changes
Snowballs and Sandcastles

SELF-CONTROL

Violence: Dealing with Anger in the Formative Years

SELF-ESTEEM

Amazing Grace
Being a Friend: What Does It Mean?
Clarissa
I Can Make Good Choices
I'll Fix Anthony
Kid's Guide to Feeling Good about Yourself, A
My Body, My Buddy: Teasing and Bullying
My Way Sally
Oops! I Messed Up!
Respect Yourself and Others, Too
Self Confidence: Step by Step
When Food Is an Obsession
When I Feel Alone
When I Feel Different

SELF-PROTECTION

Kid's Guide to Self-Protection, A

SEMINOLE INDIANS

Dancing with the Indians

SEQUENCING

Goblin Mischief
I Can Build!

SHAPES

All about Shapes
World of Circles

SHARING

My Body, My Buddy: Caring and Sharing

SHARKS

Shark, Shark, Shark
Sharks: Predators or Prey?

SIKH CULTURE

Hair Scare

SIMILES

Timid Dinosaurs

SIMPLE MACHINES

Push and Pull: Simple Machines at Work

SIOUX INDIANS

Yankton Sioux, The

SNAKES

Creepy Creatures and Slimy Stuff
Start with a Story: Baby Rattlesnake

SNOW

Frosty Returns

SOCIAL STUDIES

All about Neighborhoods
American Independence
America's State Capitals, Vols. 1–4
Amistad Revolt, The: All We Want Is Make Us Free
Argentina
Baltic States, The: Facing Independence
Cambodia
Challenging Geography: Explorers Discover America
Cops Are Tops: Our Police at Work
Early Settlers
Electing a President: The Process
Field Trip to the Oil Refinery
Finding Your Way: Using Maps and Globes
First Ladies
Hungary: Between East and West
Information Please! Your Library in Action
Johnny Tremain
Keeping Your Community Clean
Kuwait
Laos

Let's Go to the Farm with Mac Parker
Milk Cow, Eat Cheese
Moving the Mail: Postal Employees at Work
Old Glory
Our Federal Government: The Legislative Branch
Our Federal Government: The Presidency
Our Federal Government: The Supreme Court
People of the Northwest Coast
Pilgrims at Plymouth
Pony Express, The
Roman City
Santa Fe Trail, The
Sheena Azak of Canada
Sound the Alarm: Firefighters at Work
Turkey: Between Europe and Asia
United States History Video Collection
Vietnam
Westward Expansion: The Pioneer Challenge
What Is an American?
Women in Rural America
Writing on the Wall, The
You and Your Hospital

SOLAR SYSTEM

Exploring Our Solar System
Our Solar System: The Inner Planets

SOLIDS

Solids in Our World

SORTING

King Comes Calling, The

SOUND

Sound/Radio Broadcasting

SOUTH AMERICA

Animals of the Amazon River Basin
Argentina
Great Kapok Tree, The

SOVIET UNION

Baltic States, The: Facing Independence

SPACE

Exploring Our Solar System
Living in Space
Mars, the Red Planet
Starting with Stars
Sun, Earth, Moon
Voyage to the Moon

SPIDERS

Anansi and the Moss-Covered Rock
Spiders

STATE CAPITALS

America's State Capitals, Vols. 1–4

STEIG, WILLIAM

Getting to Know William Steig

STEREOTYPES

Positively Native
To Jew Is Not a Verb

STOCK CARS

Built for Speed: A High Speed Live Action Adventure at the Racetrack

STORIES IN RHYME

All the Colors of the Earth
Cat in the Hat Comes Back, The

STORMS

Dingles, The

SUBMARINES

Aquaspace Adventure

SUPREME COURT

Our Federal Government: The Supreme Court

SYMBOLS

Symbols

TALL TALES

Mose the Fireman

TAYLOR, MILDRED D.

Mildred D. Taylor

TECHNOLOGY

Big Cable Bridges
Building Skyscrapers
Chewing Gum
Clocks and Watches
Computers: Where They Come From and How They Work
Concrete Trucking
Digital Environment, The

Finding It Fast in the Library
Flight
How Things Work
How to Make Your Own Great Video with Just a Camcorder
How to Use a Microscope
I Can Build!
Ice Cream and Popsicles
Inventors and Inventions
Lasers: The Special Light
Making It Happen: Masters of Invention
My First Magic Video
Peanuts
Radio and Television
Sound/Radio Broadcasting

TELESCOPES

Astronomy 101: A Family Adventure and Beginner's Guide to the Night

TELEVISION

Radio and Television

THANKSGIVING

Thanksgiving Day

THEATER

Amazing Grace
Berenstain Bears Get Stage Fright/Go Bonkers
How to Make Your Own Great Video with Just a Camcorder
Show Time

TIDEPOOLS

Animal Life in a Tidepool

TIME

Time
Time for Horatio, A
Time, Money, and Measurement

TOBACCO

Libre Quiero Ser (I Want to Be Free)
Trouble with Tobacco, The

TOY-MAKING

Galimoto

TRANSPORTATION

All about Boats
Away We Go: All about Transportation
Big Plane Trip, The
Built for Speed: A High Speed Live Action Adventure at the
    Racetrack
Come Fly with Us
Heli-Kids: A Helicopter Adventure for Kids
How a Car Is Built
I Love Big Machines
There Goes a Bulldozer
There Goes a Police Car

Train Adventures for Kids: The Magical World of Trains
Traveling with Ooga-Booga on Trains, Trucks, and Airplanes
Truck Song

TRASH

Trash Troll, The

TREES

Great Kapok Tree, The
Trees for Life

TRUANCY

School's Cool

TRUCKS

Truck Song

TRUTH, SOJOURNER

Sojourner Truth

TUBMAN, HARRIET

Harriet Tubman

TURKEY

Turkey: Between Europe and Asia

TURTLES

Voyage of the Loggerhead
Yertle the Turtle and Other Stories

U.S. HISTORY

American Independence
Challenging Geography: Explorers Discover America
Heritage of the Black West
Old Glory
Santa Fe Trail, The
United States History Video Collection
Westward Expansion: The Pioneer Challenge
Women in Rural America

VALENTINE'S DAY

Holiday Facts and Fun: Valentine's Day

VALUES

Colt Called Lucky, A
Daisy Discovers the World
Emperor's New Clothes, The
Eureeka's Castle: Sing Along with Eureeka
Fisherman and His Wife, The
Focus on Honesty

Gullah Gullah Island: Sing Along with Binyah Binyah
Kid's Guide to Personal Behavior 1: Tattling, Disobeying
Kid's Guide to Personal Behavior 2: Rudeness, Whining
Jungle for Joey, A
Knight School
Nina's Strange Adventure
What Now? Deciding What's Right

VETERINARIANS

Girl's World, A

VIDEO PRODUCTION

How to Make Your Own Great Video with Just a Camcorder

VIETNAM

Vietnam

VIOLENCE

Last Hit, The: Children and Violence
Violence: Dealing with Anger in the Formative Years

VOLCANOES

Hill of Fire
Volcanoes: Mountains of Fire

WALKER, ALICE

Alice Walker

WASHINGTON, BOOKER T.

Booker T. Washington

WATCHES

Clocks and Watches

WATER

Murky Water Caper, The

WATER CYCLE

Circle of Water
Source of Life? Water in Our Environment

WEATHER

Hurricanes, Tornadoes, and Thunderstorms
Job of a TV Meteorologist

WHALES

To Save a Whale

WINTER

Where Do Animals Go in Winter?

WITCHES

Witches and Mice

WOMEN

Women in Rural America
Women Space Pioneers

YELLOWSTONE NATIONAL PARK

Fire in the Forest

ZOOS

Amazing North America
At the Zoo
KangaZoo Club 1: Baboons-Sea Lions-Tigers
KangaZoo Club 2: Monkeys-Crocodiles-Lions
KangaZoo Club 3: Gorillas-Dolphins-Cheetahs
Zoo Crew: Do the Zoo
Zoofari: A Real Life Adventure into the Wilds of the Zoo

APPENDIX A

DISTRIBUTORS AND PRODUCERS

100% Productions
P.O. Box 753
Orangevale, CA 95662
Phone: (800) 483–3383; (916) 987–0112
Fax: (916) 987–7936

411 Video Information
P.O. Box 1223
Pebble Beach, CA 93953
Phone: (408) 622-9441
Fax: (408) 622-9439
E-mail: 411video@Mbay.net
Web site: www.mtnds.com/411video

A & M Video Productions
2122 N. Maplewood Ave.
Chicago, IL 60647
Phone: (773) 342–8877

Access Network
3720 76th Ave.
Edmonton, Alberta, Canada T6B 2N9
Phone: (403) 440–7777
Fax: (403) 440–8899

Advantage Learning Systems, Inc.
2610 Industrial St.
Wisconsin Rapids, WI 54495–0036
Phone: (800) 338–4204
Fax: (715) 424–4242

Adventure Productions
3404 Terry Lake Rd.
Ft. Collins, CO 80524
Phone: (303) 493–8776

African American Images
1909 W. 95th St.
Chicago, IL 60643
Phone: (800) 552–1991; (312) 445–0322

AGC Educational Media
(Altshul Group Corporation)
1560 Sherman Ave.
Evanston, IL 60201

Phone: (800) 323–9084; (800) 323–5448
Fax: (847) 328–6706
E-mail: AGCMedia@starnetinc.com

AIMS Media
(AIMS Multimedia)
9710 DeSoto Ave.
Chatsworth, CA 91311–4409
Phone: (800) 367–2467; (818) 773–4300
Fax: (818) 341–6700
Web site: www.aims-multimedia.com

Alarion Press
P.O. Box 1882
Boulder, CO 80306–1882
Phone: (800) 523–9177
Fax: (303) 443–9098

Alcazar Productions
P.O. Box 429
Waterbury, VT 05676–0429
Phone: (800) 541–9904
Fax: (802) 244–6128

Alfred Higgins Productions, Inc.
6350 Laurel Canyon Blvd., Ste. 305
North Hollywood, CA 91606
Phone: (800) 766–5353; (818) 762–3300
Fax: (818) 762–8223

Allied Video Corp.
P.O. Box 702618
Tulsa, OK 74170
Phone: (800) 926–5892; (918) 744–5892
E-mail: allied@farpointer.net

Alpha Omega Publication/Bridgestone Multimedia
300 N. McKemy Ave.
Chandler, AZ 85226–2618
Phone: (800) 622–3070; (602) 438–2717
Fax: (602) 940–8924
E-mail: aop@netzone.com

Alphabet Factory
43 W. 85th St., Ste. 2A

New York, NY 11024
Phone: (212) 787–3459

Ambrose Video Publishing
28 W. 44th St., Ste. 2100
New York, NY 10036
Phone: (800) 526–4663

American Library Association Video/Library Video Network
320 York Rd.
Towson, MD 21204–5179
Phone: (800) 441–8273; (410) 887–2082
Fax: (410) 887–2091
E-mail: inlib@mail.bcpl.lib.md.us

American School Publishers
(division of) SRA/McGraw-Hill
200 Danieldale Rd.
DeSoto, TX 75115–9961
Phone: (800) 843–8855; (614) 860–1877

Archmedia Interactive Inc.
2828 Routh St., Ste. 695
Dallas, TX 75201
Phone: (214) 880–9090
Fax: (214) 720–9055

Baker and Taylor Video
501 S. Gladiolus
Momence, IL 60954
Phone: (800) 775–2600
Fax: (412) 787–0368
Web site: www.btent.com

Barr Media Group
12801 Schabarum Ave., Box 7878
Irwindale, CA 91706
Fax: (818) 814–2672

BBC Worldwide
Woodlands, 80 Wood La.
London W12 OTTUK
Phone: # 0 181 743 5588 or 0 181 576 2000

Beacon Films
(division of) Altschul Group Corp.
1560 Sherman Ave., Ste. 100
Evanston, IL 60201
Phone: (800) 323–9084; (847) 328–6700
Fax: (847) 328–6706
E-mail: AGCMedia@starnetinc.com

Benchmark Films
569 N. State Rd.
Briarcliff Manor, NY 10510
Phone: (800) 438–5564

Bennet Media Services
P.O. Box 1365, 625 Sunny Meadow
Durant, OK 74702
Phone: (800) 528–0912
Fax: (405) 924–4228

Berlet Films
1646 W. Kimmel Rd.
Jackson, MI 49201
Phone: (517) 784–6969

Better Books Co
Dept. 883, P.O. Box 9770
Ft. Worth, TX 76147–2770
Phone: (800) 335–1853
Fax: (817) 335–2300

Big Kids Productions
1606 Dywer Ave.
Austin, TX 78704
Phone: (800) 477–7811

BMG Video
1540 Broadway
New York, NY 10036
Phone: (212) 930–4000

Bogner Entertainment Inc.
P.O. Box 641428
Los Angeles, CA 90064
Phone: (310) 473–0139
Fax: (310) 473–6417

Bulldog Entertainment
N. 6480 Riverview Rd.
Porterfield, WI 54159
Phone: (800) 409-6229; (715) 854–3382
Fax: (715) 854–3382

Bullfrog Films
Box 149
Oley, PA 19547
Phone: (800) 543–3764; (610) 779–8226
Fax: (610) 370–1978
E-mail: bullfrog@igc.org
Web site: www.igc.apc.org/bullfrog/index.html

Cambridge Educational
P.O. Box 2153
Charleston, WV 25328–2153
Phone: (800) 468–4227

Capital Cities/ABC Video Publishing, Inc.
1200 High Ridge Rd.
Stamford, CT 06905–0815
Phone: (203) 968–9100
Fax: (203) 329–6464

Carolina Biological
2700 York Rd.
Burlington, NC 27215
Phone: (800) 334–5551; (910) 584–0381
Fax: (910) 584–3399

Carousel Film and Video
260 Fifth Ave.
New York, NY 10001
Phone: (800) 683–1660; (212) 683–1660
Fax: (212) 683–1662
E-mail: carousel@pipeline.com

Cathedral Film, Inc.
Box 4029
Westlake Village, CA 91359
Phone: (800) 338–3456
Fax: (818) 865–1327

Centre Communications
P.O. Box 1544
Oak Park, IL 60304
Phone: (800) 886–1166
Fax: (303) 444–1168

Champions on Film and Video
745 State Circle, P.O. Box 1941
Ann Arbor, MI 48106
Phone: (800) 521–2832
Fax: (313) 761–8711
Web site: www.school-tech.com

Charles Clark Co., Inc.
4540 Preslyn Dr.
Raleigh, NC 27616
Phone: (800) 247–7009; (919) 954–7550
Fax: (919) 954–7554

Cheshire Corp.
P.O. Box 61109
Denver, CO 80206
Phone: (303) 333–9729

Children's Television International
(division of) Glad Productions, Inc.
14512A Lee Rd.
Chantilly, VA 20151–1636
Phone: (800) 284–4523
Fax: (703) 502–3009

ChildVision Education Films
(division of) Big Kids Productions
1606 Dywer Ave.
Austin, TX 78704
Phone: (800) 488–1913
Web site: www.awardvids.com

Chip Taylor Communications
15 Spollett Dr.
Derry, NH 03038–5728
Phone: (800) 876–2447; (603) 434–9262
Fax: (603) 432–2723
E-mail: chip@chiptaylor.com
Web site: www.chiptaylor.com/index.htm

Churchill Media
(division of) Society for Visual Education (SVE)
6677 N. Northwest Hwy.
Chicago, IL 60631
Phone: (800) 829–1900; (773) 775–9550
Fax: (800) 624–1678; (773) 777–5691
Web site: www.svemedia.com

Cinema Guild
1697 Broadway
New York, NY 10019
Phone: (800) 723–5522; (212) 246–5522
Fax: (212) 246–5525
E-mail: TheCinemaG@aol.com
Web site: www.cinemaguild.com/cinemaguild

City Productions, Inc.
65 Union St., Ste. 360
6041 Mt. Moriah, Ste. 16
Memphis, TN 38115
Phone: (800) 947–2489; (901) 363–9200
Fax: (901) 362–1894

CLEARVUE/eav
6465 N. Avondale Ave.
Chicago, IL 60631–1996
Phone: (800) 253–2788; (312) 775–9433
Fax: (800) 444–9855

Comex Systems, Inc.
The Mill Cottage
Mendham, NJ 07945
Phone: (800) 543–6959; (201) 543–2862
Fax: (201) 543–9644

Coronet/MTI Film and Video
(division of) Simon & Schuster
108 Wilmot Rd.
Deerfield, IL 60015
Phone: (800) 621–2131; (708) 940–1260

Crocus Entertainment
630 Twelve Oaks Ctr.
Wayzata, MN 55391
Phone: (612) 473–9002

Crystal Productions
P.O. Box 2159
Glenview, IL 60025
Phone: (800) 255–8629; (847) 657–8144
Fax: (847) 657–8149
E-mail: crystalprod@aol.com

CTI/Glad Productions, Inc.
14512A Lee Rd.
Chantilly, VA 22021–2203
Phone: (800) 284–4523

Curriculum Associates, Inc.
P.O. Box 2001
North Billerica, MA 01862–0901
Phone: (800) 225–0248; (508) 667–8000
Fax: (800) 366–1158
E-mail: cainfo@curricassoc.com
Web site: www.curricassoc.com/cainfo/

Dallas Educational Enterprises
113 Point Royal Dr.
Rockwall, TX 75087
Phone: (214) 475–0782

Delphi Productions
3160 4th St.
Boulder, CO 90304
Phone: (800) 548–8200

Demco Media
Box 7488
Madison, WI 53707–7488
Phone: (800) 448–8939

Disney Educational Productions
105 Terry Dr., Ste. 120
Newtown, PA 18940
Phone: (800) 295–5010

Distribution Video and Audio
1610 N. Myrtle
Clearwater, FL 34615
Phone: (800) 683–4147
Fax: (813) 441–3069

E-mail: movies@dva.com
Web site:www.dva.com

DK Multimedia
(Dorling Kindersley)
95 Madison Ave.
New York, NY 10016
Phone: (800) 225–3362; (212) 213–4800
Fax: (212) 213–5240

Double Diamond
P.O. Box 1557
New Canaan, CT 06840
Phone: (800) 938–2737; (203) 972–9286
Fax: (203) 972–9341

Earful of Books
8120 Research Blvd., Ste. 115
Austin, TX 78758
Phone: (800) 532–7382
Fax: (512) 452–7832

Educational Activities, Inc.
P.O. Box 392
Freeport, NY 11520
Phone: (800) 645–3739
Fax: (516) 623–9282
E-mail: learn@edact.com

Educational Resources
1550 Executive Dr.
Elgin, IL 60123
Phone: (800) 624–2926
Fax: (847) 888–8689
Web site: www.edresources.com

Educational Video Network, Inc.
1492 19th St.
Huntsville, TX 77340
Phone: (800) 762–0060; (409) 295–5767
Fax: (409) 294–0233
E-mail: evn@edvidnet.com
Web site: www.edvidnet.com

Encyclopaedia Britannica Educational Corporation
310 South Michigan Ave.
Chicago, IL 60604
Phone: (800) 554–9862
Fax: (312) 347–7966
E-mail: info@ebec.com

Environmental Media
P.O. Box 1016
Chapel Hill, NC 27514
Phone: (800) 368–3382

Fase Productions
4801 Wilshire Blvd.
Los Angeles, CA 90010
Phone: (800) 888–0600; (213) 965–8794
Fax: (214) 937–7440

Fast Forward Productions
P.O. Box 3226
Santa Monica, CA 90405
Phone: (213) 450–4500

FFH Video *see* Films for the Humanities and Sciences

Film Ideas
3710 Commercial Ave., Ste. 13
Northbrook, IL 60062
Phone: (800) 475–3456; (708) 480–5760
Fax: (708) 480–7496

Filmic Archives
The Cinema Center
Botsford, CT 06404–0386
Phone: (800) 366–1920; (203) 261–1920
Fax: (203) 268–1796

Films for the Humanities and Sciences
P.O. Box 2053
Princeton, NJ 08534–2053
Phone: (800) 257–5126; (609) 275–1400
Fax: (609) 275–3767

Fire Dog Pictures
10 Hill St.

Mill Valley, CA 94941
Phone: (800) 815–1234

Frameline
346 9th St.
San Francisco, CA 94103
Phone: (415) 703–8654

FUBUTU Home and Educational Media
5302 Walker Court, P.O. Box 830472
Stone Mountain, GA 30083
Phone: (800) 798–9863; (770) 431–5927
Fax: (770) 779–3892
E-mail: fubutu@atl.mindspring.com
Web site: www.fubutu.com

Full Circle Communications
1131 South College Ave.
Tulsa, OK 74104–4120
Phone: (800) 940–8849; (918) 585–8849
Fax: (918) 585–3911
E-mail: fullcir@aol.com

Gateway Films/Vision Video
2030 Wentz Church Rd., P.O. Box 540
Worcester, PA 19490–0540
Phone: (800) 523–0226; (610) 584–3500
Fax: (610) 584–4610
E-mail: visionvid@aol.com

Geffner Productions
P.O. Box 620784
Little Neck, NY 11362
Phone: (718) 225–7562
Fax: (718) 279–8101

George F. Cram Co.
301 LaSalle St.
Indianapolis, IN 46201
Phone: (800) 227–4199
Fax: (317) 635–2720

Goldhil Home Media
137 E. Thousand Oaks Blvd., Ste. 207
Thousand Oaks, CA 91360

Phone: (805) 495–0735
Fax: (805) 373–1603

Goldsholl: Learning Videos
420 Frontage Rd.
Northfield, IL 60093
Phone: (708) 446–8300

GPN (Great Plains National)
P.O. Box 80669
Lincoln, NE 68501
Phone: (800) 228–4630; (402) 472–2007
Fax: (800) 306–2330
E-mail: gpn@unl.edu

Grace Products
1761 International Pkwy., Ste. 135
Richardson, TX 75801
Phone: (800) 527–4014

HRM Video (Human Relations Media)
175 Tompkins Ave.
Pleasantville, NY 10570–9973
Phone: (800) 431–2050; (914) 769–7496
Fax: (914) 747–1744

Ingram Library Services
1 Ingram Blvd.
La Vergne, TN 37086
Phone: (800) 937–5300

Injoy Video or Injoy Productions
3970 Broadway, Ste. B4
Boulder, CO 80304
Phone: (800) 326–2082; (303) 447–2082
Fax: (303) 449–8788

Instructional Media for Education
P.O. Box 6418
High Point, NC 27262
Phone: (800) 605–9275
Fax: (910) 869–9624

Instructional Video
727 O St.

Lincoln, NE 68508–1323
Phone: (800) 228–0164
Fax: (402) 475–6500

Janson Associates
Plaza West, 88 Semmens Rd.
Harrington Park, NJ 07640
Phone: (800) 952–6766; (201) 784–8488
Fax: (201) 784–3993

January Productions
210 6th Ave., P.O. Box 66
Hawthorne, NJ 07507–0066
Phone: (800) 451–7450; (201) 423–4666
Fax: (201) 423–5569

Journal Films
(division of) AGC (Altschul Group Corporation)
Educational Media
1560 Sherman Ave., Ste. 100
Evanston, IL 60201
Phone: (800) 323–9084; (847) 328–6700
Fax: (847) 328–6706
E-mail: AGCMedia@starnetinc.com

Kepco Enterprises
15210 Leafy La.
Dallas, TX 75248
Phone: (800) 888–8725

Kids' Media Group
5240 Oakland Ave.
St. Louis, MO 63110–1436

KidVision
75 Rockefeller Plaza
New York, NY 10019
Phone: (800) 354–3843

Knight and Hale Game Calls
Drawer 670–LSNS, 5732 Canton Rd.
Cadiz, KY 42211
Phone: (800) 500–9357; (502) 924–0755
Fax: (502) 924–1763

Knowledge Unlimited/Zeno Press Children's Books
P.O. Box 52
Madison, WI 53701–0052
Phone: (800) 356–2303; (608) 836–6660
Fax: (608) 831–1570
E-mail: newscurrents@KU.com

Landmark Media Inc.
3450 Slade Run Dr.
Falls Church, VA 22042
Phone: (800) 342–4336
Fax: (703) 536–9540

Laurie Hepburn Production
P.O. Box 556
Mamaroneck, NY 10543
Phone: (800) 275–9101

Learning Seed
330 Telser Rd.
Lake Zurich, IL 60047
Phone: (800) 634–4941; (847) 540–8855
Fax: (800) 998–0854
E-mail: learnseed@aol.com.

Learning Services
P.O. Box 10636
Eugene, OR 97440–2636
Phone: (800) 877–9378
Fax: (800) 877–3278

Learning Tree Publishing
P.O. Box 4116
Englewood, CO 80155

Let's Create, Inc.
50 Cherry Hill Rd.
Parsippany, NJ 07054
Phone: (800) 790–6655; (201) 299–0633

Library Video Company
P.O. Box 580
Wynnewood, PA 19006
Phone: (800) 843–3620; (610) 645–4000
Fax: (610) 645–4040

Lightyear Entertainment
350 Fifth Ave., Ste. 5101
New York, NY 10118
Phone: (800) 229–7867; (212) 536–4610
Fax: (212) 563–1932

Listening Library, Inc.
One Park Ave.
Old Greenwich, CT 06870–1727
Phone: (800) 243–4504

Little Mammoth Media
750 Ralph McGill Boulevard, N.E.
Atlanta, GA 30312
Phone: (800) 543–8433; (404) 221–0236
Fax: (404) 584–5247

Live Oak Media
P.O. Box 652
Pine Plains, NY 12567
Phone: (518) 398–1010
Fax: (518) 398–1070

Lucerne Media
37 Ground Pine Rd.
Morris Plains, NJ 07950
Phone: (800) 341–2293; (201) 538–1401
Fax: (201) 538–0855

MarshMedia
P.O. Box 8082
Shawnee Mission, KS 66208
Phone: (800) 821–3303; (816) 523–1059
Fax: (816) 333–7421
E-mail: order@marshmedia.com
Web site: www.marshmedia.com

Mazon Productions, Inc.
P.O. Box 2427
Northbrook, IL 60065
Phone: (800) 332–4344; (847) 272–2824

MBG Videos
(division of) Herb Halpern Productions
500 S. Ewing Ave., Ste. C

St. Louis, MO 63103
Phone: (314) 531–1100

Media Basics Video
Lighthouse Square, 705 Boston Post Rd.
Guilford, CT 06437
Phone: (800) 542–2505
Fax: (203) 458–9816

Media Guild
11722 Sorrento Valley Rd., Ste. E
San Diego, CA 92121
Phone: (800) 886–9191; (619) 755–9191
Fax: (619) 755–4931

Meridian Education Corporation
236 E. Front St., Dept E-96
Bloomington, IL 61701
Phone: (800) 727–5507; (309) 827–5455

Milestone Film and Video
275 W. 96th St., Ste. 28C
New York, NY 10025
Phone: (212) 865–7449
Fax: (212) 222–8952

Miramar Productions
200 Second Ave. W.
Seattle, WA 98119–4204
Phone: (800) 245–6472; (206) 284–4700
Fax: (206) 286–4433
E-mail: miramar@usa.net

Modern Curriculum
108 Wilmot Rd.
Deerfield, IL 60015
Phone: (800) 777–8100
Fax: (708) 940–3640

MPI Media Group
16101 S. 108th Ave.
Orland Park, IL 60462
Phone: (800) 777–2223; (708) 460–0555
Fax: (708) 460–0175

MVP, Inc.
9030 Eton Ave. #C
Connego Park, CA 91304
Phone: (800) 637–3555
Fax: (818) 709–7846
E-mail: mvphebt@aol.com

National Film Board of Canada
1251 Ave. of the Americas, 16th Fl.
New York, NY 10020–1173
Phone: (800) 542–2164; (212) 586–5131
Web site: www.nfb.ca/E/index.html

National Geographic Educational Services
P.O. Box 98019
Washington, DC 20036
Phone: (800) 368–2728
Fax: (301) 921–1575
E-mail: ngshotline@aol.com

New Castle Commications, Inc.
229 King St.
Chappaqua, NY 10514
Phone: (800) 723–1263; (914) 238–0600
Fax: (914) 238–8445
E-mail: ideas@newcastlecom.com

New Dimension Media
85803 Lorane Hwy.
Eugene, OR 97405
Phone: (800) 288–4456; (541) 484–7125
Fax: (541) 484–5267

New Video Group
126 5th Ave., 15th Fl.
New York, NY 10011
Phone: (800) 423–1212; (212) 206–8600
Fax: (212) 206–9001

Ninos
P.O. Box 1163
Ann Arbor, MI 48106–1163
Phone: (800) 634–3304
Fax: (313) 747–8526

NoodleHead Network
107 Intervale Ave.
Burlington, VT 05401
Phone: (800) 639–5680

Northern Lights Productions
276 Newbury St.
Boston, MA 02116
Phone: (800) 284–6521; (617) 267–0391
Fax: (617) 267–8957

Nystrom Co.
3333 Elston Ave.
Chicago, IL 60618–5898
Phone: (800) 621–8086
Fax: (312) 463–0515

Paragon Media
2115 Sixth Ave.
Seattle, WA 98121
Phone: (800) 424–7963

PBS Video
1320 Braddock Pl.
Alexandria, VA 22314–1698
Phone: (800) 344–3337; (800) 424–7963
Fax: (703) 739–5269
Web site: www.pbs.org

Penguin USA
120 Woodbine St.
Bergenfield, NJ 07621
Phone: (800) 331–4624

Penton Overseas, Inc.
2470 Impala Dr.
Carlsbad, CA 92008
Phone: (800) 748–5804; (619) 431–0060
Fax: (619) 431–8110
E-mail: Pentonosea@aol.com

Phoenix Films and Video
2349 Chaffee Dr.
St. Louis, MO 63146
Phone: (800) 221–1274; (314) 569–0211
Fax: (314) 569–2834

Physics Curriculum and Instruction
22585 Woodhill Dr.
Lakeville, MN 55044
Phone: (612) 461–3470
Fax: (612) 461–3467

PPI-Peter Pan Video
88 St. Francis St.
Newark, NJ 07105
Phone: (800) 272–4214

Professional Media Service
(Follett)
19122 South Vermont Ave.
Gardena, CA 90248
Phone: (800) 223–7672; (310) 532–9024
Fax: (800) 253–8853

Pyramid Media
P.O. Box 1048
Santa Monica, CA 90406–1048
Phone: (800) 421–2304; (310) 828–7577
Fax: (310) 453–9083
E-mail: info@pyramedia.com

Quality Books
1003 W. Pines Rd.
Oregon, IL 61061–9680
Phone: (800) 423–4203

Questar, Inc.
P.O. Box 11345
Chicago, IL 60611–0345
Phone: (800) 633–5633; (312) 266–9400
Fax: (312) 266–9523
E-mail: questarchi@aol.com
Web site: www.questar1.com

Rabbit Ears/
Simon & Schuster Children's Publishing
1230 Ave. of the Americas, 4th Fl.
New York, NY 10022
Phone: (800) 800–3277

Rainbow Educational Media
3043 Barrow Dr.
Raleigh, NC 27604
Phone: (800) 331–4047
Fax: (919) 954–7554

Random House Home Video
400 Hahn Rd.
Westminster, MD 21157
Phone: (800) 733–3000

Reading Adventures
2165 Sunnydale Blvd., Ste. E
Clearwater, FL 34625
Phone: (800) 284–4149; (831) 441–4149

Ready Reference Press
P.O. Box 5249
Santa Monica, CA 90409
Phone: (800) 424–5627
Fax: (310) 475–4895

Rick Levy Management
1881 S. Kirkman Rd., # 715
Orlando, FL 32811
Phone: (407) 521–6135
Fax: (407) 521–6153

RideSafe
P.O. Box 888, 30W260 Butterfield Rd., #212
Warrenville, IL 60555
Phone: (800) 285–7433

Rigby Interactive Library
P.O. Box 1650
Crystal Lake, IL 60039–1650
Phone: (800) 822–8661
Fax: (800) 427–4429

Rosewood Publications
2075 Pioneer Ct.
San Mateo, CA 94403
Phone: (800) 223–7899

Schlessinger Video Productions
(division of) Library Video Company
P.O. Box 580
Wynnewood, PA 19006
Phone: (800) 843–3620; (610) 645–4000
Fax: (610) 645–4040

Scholastic, Inc.
Distribution Center
2931 East McCarty St.
Jefferson City, MO 65102
Phone: (800) 724–6527
Web site: www.scholastic.com

School Media Associate
2700 N.E. Expressway C-800
Atlanta, GA 30345
Phone: (800) 451–5226

Schoolmasters Video
745 State Circle, Box 1941
Ann Arbor, MI 48106
Phone: (800) 521–2832; (313) 761–5072
Fax: (800) 654–4321
E-mail: kidvideos@AOL.COM

Science Research Associates (SRA)
1121 Eton Dr.
Richardson, Tx 75080
Phone: (800) 621–0664

Segments of Knowledge
424 N. Calhoun St.
Tallahassee, FL 32301
Phone: (800) 816–6463; (904) 224–7400
Fax: (904) 224–7414

SelectVideo Publishing
5475 Peoria St., Ste. 4C
Denver, CO 80249
Phone: (800) 742–1455

Sherry Nelson Productions
P.O. Box 1603
Atascadero, CA 93423
Phone: (805) 239–4113
Fax: (805) 239–4113

Shoe String Press
P.O. Box 657
2 Lindsley St.
North Haven, CT 06473
Phone: (203) 239–2702

Society for Visual Education (SVE)
6677 N. Northwest Hwy.
Chicago, IL 60631
Phone: (800) 829–1900; (713) 775–9550
Fax: (800) 624–1678; (713)-777–5691
Web site: www.svemedia.com

Sony Wonder
550 Madison Ave., Rm. 2341
New York, NY 10022
Phone: (212) 833–4548
Web site: www.sonywonder.com

Sound Beginnings
World Trade Center
P.O. Box 420726
Dallas, TX 75342
Phone: (800) 460–6802
E-mail: staff@soundbeginings.com
Web site: www.soundbeginnings.com/

Southwest Media Services, Inc.
P.O. Box 140
Wimberly, TX 78676
Phone: (512) 847–3539
Fax: (512) 847–3009

SpaceSmart, Inc.
P.O. Box 576
Windermere, FL 34786
Phone: (407) 876–5326
Fax: (407) 876–1554

SRA School Group
P.O. Box 543
Blacklick, OH 43004
Phone: (800) 468–5850

SRA/McGraw-Hill
220 Danieldale Rd.
DeSoto, TX 75115–9961
Phone: (888) 772–4543

St. Paul's Books and Media
50 St. Paul's Ave.
Boston, MA 02130
Phone: (800) 876–4463; (617) 522–8911
Fax: (617) 524–8035

Stage Fright Productions
P.O. Box 373
Geneva, IL 60134
Phone: (708) 208–9845

Sunburst Communications
101 Castleton St.
Pleasantville, NY 10570
Phone: (800) 431–1934
Fax: (914) 769–2109

SVE *see* Society for Visual Education

Tapeworm Video Distributors
27833 Hopkins Ave., Ste. 6
Valencia, CA 91355
Phone: (800) 367–8437; (805) 257–4904
Fax: (805) 257–4820
E-mail: tapewo01@interserve.com
Web site: www.tapeworm.com

Tim Podell Productions
P.O. Box 244
Scarborough, NY 10510
Phone: (800) 642–4181
Fax: (914) 944–8110

TM Book/Video
P.O. Box 279
New Buffalo, MI 49117
Phone: (800) 892–2822
Fax: (219) 879–7909

Tom Snyder Productions
80 Coolidge Rd.
Watertown, MA 02172–2817
Phone: (800) 342–0236
Fax: (617) 926–6222
Web site: www.teachtsp.com

Troll Associates
100 Corporate Dr.
Mahwah, NJ 07430
Phone: (800) 526–0275

Turner Multimedia
10 N. Main St.
Yardley, PA 19067–1422
Phone: (800) 742–1096
Fax: (215) 493–5320

TVOntario
1140 Kildaire Farm Rd., Ste. 308
Cary, NC 27511
Phone: (800) 331–9566
Fax: (919) 380–0961
E-mail: U.S.sales@tvo.org

Unique Books, Inc.
4230 Grove Ave.
Gurnee, IL 60031
Phone: (800) 533–5443
Fax: (708) 623–7238

United Learning, Inc.
6633 W. Howard St., P.O. Box 48718
Niles, IL 60714–0718
Phone: (800) 424–0362; (312) 647–0600
Fax: (708) 647–0918

V.I.E.W. Video
34 E. 23rd St.

New York, NY 10010
Phone: (800) 843–9843; (212) 674–5550
Fax: (212) 979–0266

Vermont Story Works
R.D. #1 Box 1863
Vergennes, VT 05491
Phone: (800) 206–8383

Vestron Video
c/o Live Home Video
15400 Sherman Way, P.O. Box 10124
Van Nuys, CA 91410–0124
Phone: (800) 367–7765; (818) 988–5060
Fax: (818) 778–3125

Victory Audio Video Services
222 N. Sepulveda Blvd.
El Segundo, CA 90245
Phone: (310) 416–9140

Video Information
P.O. Box 1223
Pebble Beach, CA 93953
Phone: (408) 622–9441
Fax: (408) 622–9439

Video Project
200 Estates Dr.
Ben Lomond, CA 95005
Phone: (800) 475–2638; (408) 336–0160
Fax: (408) 336–2168
E-mail: videoproject@videoproject.org
Web site: http//www.videoproject.org/videoproject/

Video Resources
11767 S. Dixie Hwy., Ste. 222
Miami, FL 33156
Phone: (800) 356–6284
Fax: (305) 256–0567

Vision Video
(division of) Gateway Films
2030 Wentz Church Rd., P.O. Box 540
Worcester, PA 19490–0540

Phone: (800) 523–0226; (610) 584–3500
Fax: (610) 584–4610
E-mail: visionvid@aol.com

Waterford Institute
1590 E. 9400 S.
Sandy, UT 84093
Phone: (800) 767–9976
Fax: (801) 572–1667

Weston Woods
389 Newtown Tpk.
Weston, CT 06883–1199
Phone: (800) 243–5020; (206) 226–3355
Fax: (203) 226–3818

Wombat Films
(division of) AGC (Altschul Group Corporation)
1560 Sherman Ave.
Evanston, IL 60201
Phone: (800) 323–9084; (800) 323–5448; (847) 328–6700
Fax: (847) 328–6706
E-mail: AGCMedia@starnetinc.com

Word, Inc.
P.O. Box 2518
Waco, TX 76702–2518
Phone: (800) 933–9673

Zenger Media
(division of) Social Studies School Service
10200 Jefferson Blvd., P.O. Box 802
Culver City, CA 90232–0802
Phone: (800) 421–4246; (310) 839–2436
Fax: (800) 944–5432
E-mail: access@zengermedia.com
Web site: zengermedia.com.zenger

APPENDIX B
READING RAINBOW, WISHBONE, GHOSTWRITER VIDEOS

Reading Rainbow, *Wishbone*, and *GhostWriter* videos are high quality video series airing on the Public Broadcasting Service. The programs in the *Reading Rainbow* series are based on quality children's literature books. *Wishbone* videos are adaptations of classic literature. *GhostWriter* is a mystery series emphasizing literacy and reading. Listed below are titles from each series.

READING RAINBOW

Abiyoyo
The Adventures of Taxi Dog
Alistair in Outer Space
Alistair's Time Machine
Amazing Grace
And Still the Turtle Watched
Animal Cafe
Applemando's Dreams
Arthur's Eyes
Barn Dance!
Bea and Mr. Jones
Berlioz the Bear
Best Friends
Bicycle Man, The
Bionic Bunny Show, The
Bored—Nothing to Do!
Borreguita and the Coyote
Bringing the Rain to Kapiti Plain
Brush
Bugs
Chair for My Mother, A
Chickens Aren't the Only Ones
Come a Tide
Day Jimmy's Boa Ate the Wash, The
Desert Giant: The World of the Saguaro Cactus
Digging Up Dinosaurs
Dinosaur Bob and His Adventures with the Family Lazardo
Dive to the Coral Reefs
Duncan and Dolores
Feeling Florence and Eric Take the Cake
Follow the Drinking Gourd
Fox on the Job
Furry News: How to Make a Newspaper, The
Galimoto
Germs Make Me Sick
Gift of the Sacred Dog, The
Gila Monsters Meet You at the Airport
Gregory, The Terrible Eater
Hail to Mail
Hill of Fire
Hot-Air Henry
Humphrey the Lost Whale: A True Story

If You Give a Mouse a Cookie
Imogene's Antlers
Is This a House for Hermit Crab?
Jack, the Seal, and the Sea
June 29, 1999
Kate Shelley and the Midnight Express
Keep the Lights Burning, Abbie
Knots on a Counting Rope
Lady with a Ship on Her Head, The
Legend of the Indian Paintbrush, The
Liang and the Paintbrush
Life Cycle of the Honeybee, The
Little Nino's Pizzeria
Lotus Seed, The
Louis the Fish
Ludlow Laughs
Magic School Bus inside the Earth, The
Mama Don't Allow
Meanwhile Back at the Ranch
Milk Makers, The
Miss Nelson Is Back
Mrs. Katz and Tush
Mufaro's Beautiful Daughters
Mummies Made in Egypt
My Little Island
My Shadow
Mystery on the Docks
Nosey Mrs. Rat
Once There Was a Tree
Opt—An Illusionary Tale
Ox-Cart Man
Paper Crane, The
Patchwork Quilt, The
Paul Bunyan
Perfect the Pig
The Piggly in the Puddle
Purple Coat, The
Raccoons and Ripe Corn
Rechenka's Eggs
Robbery at the Diamond Dog Diner, The
Rumpelstiltskin
Runaway Duck, The
Ruth Law Thrills a Nation
Salamander Room, The
Sam the Sea Cow

Seashore Surprises
Silent Lotus
Simon's Book
Snowy Day: Stories and Poems
Sophie and Lou
Space Case
Sports Pages
Stay Away from the Junkyard!
Stellaluna
Summer
Sunken Treasure
Tar Beach
Three by the Sea
Three Days on a River in a Red Canoe
Three Hat Day, A
Through Moon and Stars
Tight Times
Tooth-Gnasher Superflash
Tortoise and the Hare, The
Ty's One Man Band
Wall, The
Watch the Stars Come Out

WISHBONE

Bark That Bark
Bark to the Future
Bone of Arc
Canine Cure
The Count's Account
Cyranose
Dances with Dogs
Digging Up the Past
Dogged Expose, A
Entrepawneur, The
Fleabitten Bargain
Frankenbone
Furst Impressions
Golden Retriever
Hercules Unleashed
Homer Sweet Homer
Hot Diggety Dawg

Hunchdog of Notre Dame
Impawssible Dream, The
Little Big Dog
Mixed Breeds
Muttketeer!
One Thousand and One Tails
Pantin' at the Opera
Pawloined Paper, The
Paw Prints of Thieves
Picks of the Litter
Prince and the Pooch, The
Rosie, Oh, Rosie, Oh!
Rushin' to the Bone
Salty Dog
Shakespaw
Slobbery Hound, The
Sniffing the Gauntlet
Tail in Twain, A
Tale of Two Sitters, A
Terrified Terrier, The
Twisted Tail
Viva Wishbone!

GHOSTWRITER

Am I Blue?
Building Bridges
A Crime of Two Cities
Don't Stop the Music
Get the Message
Ghost Story
Into the Comics
Just in Time
Lost in Brooklyn
Over a Barrel
To Catch a Creep
To the Light
What's Up with Alex?
Who Burned Mr. Brinker's Store?
Who Is Max Mouse?
Who's Who

APPENDIX C
CABLE IN THE CLASSROOM PROGRAMMERS

Cable in the Classroom is provided as a public service to schools by the cable television industry. It consists of free, basic cable service with hundreds of hours of commercial-free programs. Cable in the Classroom can be reached at (800) 743–5355 or www.ciconline.com. index.html.

Following are the programmers whose shows are seen over Cable in the Classroom.

A&E Network. Original biographies, mysteries, and specials. A&E Classroom, P.O. Box 1610, Grand Central Station, New York, NY 10163–1610; (212) 661–4500.
www.aetv.com

America's Talking. Twenty-four-hour news and information network. 2200 Fletcher Ave., Fort Lee, NJ 07024; (201) 585–6469.

Black Entertainment Television. Music, sports, news, and public-affairs programming. One BET Plaza, 1900 W. Place, NE, Washington, DC 20018; (800) 229–2388.
www.BETNetworks.com

Bravo. International films, music, and performing arts. Community Relations, 150 Crossways Park W., Woodbury, NY 11797; (516) 364–2222.
www.bravotv.com

C-SPAN. Live coverage of U.S. House of Representatives (U.S. Senate on C-SPAN 2) and public affairs. 400 N. Capitol Street, NW, Suite 650, Washington, DC 20001; (800) 523–7586.
www.c-span.org

CNBC. Financial and business news; interactive talk programming. 2200 Fletcher Ave., Fort Lee, NJ 07024; (201) 585–6469.
www.cnbc.com

Cable News Network. News and public affairs. Turner Educational Services, 1 CNN Ctr., Atlanta, GA 30348–5366; educators only: (800) 344–6219; others: (404) 827–1717.
www.cnn.com

Cartoon Network. Cartoon series and feature-length animation programming. Turner Educational Services, 1 CNN Ctr., Atlanta, GA 30348–5366; educators only: (800) 344–6219; others (404) 827–1717.
www.filmzone.com/SpaceGhost/cartoonnet.html

Courtroom Television Network. Live and taped coverage of courtroom trials with legal analysis and discussion. Cable in the Classroom Services Dept., 600 Third Ave., New York, NY 10016; (800) 333–7649.
www.courttv.com

Discovery Channel. Nonfiction nature, science and technology, history, and adventure programming. 7700 Wisconsin Ave., Bethesda, MD 20814–3522; (800) 3211–1838.
www.school.discovery.com

ESPN/ESPN2. Sports programming. Cable in the Classroom Dept., 935 Middle St., Bristol, CT 06010; (203) 585–2000.
www.espnnet.sportszone.com

Faith & Values Channel. Dramas, documentaries, and public affairs. Michelle Racik, 74 Trinity Pl., 9th Fl., New York, NY 10006; (212) 964–1663 ext. 126.

The Family Channel. Family-oriented movies, special, and original series; health and exercise programming. Kathleen Gordon, 2877 Guardian La., P.O. Box 2050, Virginia Beach, VA 23450–2050 (804) 459–6165
www.famfun.com

The History Channel. Historical documentaries, movies, and miniseries. 235 E. 45th St., 9th Fl., New York, NY 10017; (212) 661–4500.
www.historychannel.com

Home Box Office. Feature movies, specials, and sports programming. 1100 Avenue of the Americas, New York, NY 10036; (212) 512–1000.
www.homebox.com

The Learning Channel. Nonfiction science, history, and world-cultures programming; how-to shows; commercial-free entertainment for preschoolers. 7700 Wisconsin Ave., Bethesda, MD 20814–3522; (800) 321–1832.
school.discovery.com

Lifetime. Information and entertainment programming geared toward women. Worldwide Plaza, 309 W. 49th St., New York, NY 10019; (212) 424–7127.
www.lifetimetv.com

Mind Extension University. Distance education, interactive field trips, language programming, and teacher training. 9697 E. Mineral Ave., Englewood, CO 80112; (800) 777–MIND.
www.meu.edu

MTV. Music, entertainment, sports, style, news, and information for young adults. Community of the Future, 1515 Broadway, 25th Fl., New York, NY 10036; (800) 2468–MTV. www.mtv.com

Newstalk Television. Discussions on current national and local issues. Lee Tenebruso, Public Relations Dept., 303 W. 34th St., 12th Fl., New York, NY 10001; (212) 502–1545. www.newstalk.com

Nickelodeon. Entertainment and educational magazine shows for children ages 2–15. Affiliate Marketing Dept., 1515 Broadway, 39th Fl., New York, NY 10036; (212) 258–8000.

Public Broadcasting Service. Instructional, cultural, documentary, and news programming. Call your local PBS station, or write: PBS Learning Services, 1320 Braddock Pl., Alexandria, VA 22314; (703) 739–5000. www.pbs.org

SCI-FI Channel. Science-fiction movies and series; programming on science, technology, and space exploration. Carolyn Longo, 1230 Avenue of the Americas, New York, NY 10020; (212) 408–9168. www.scifi.com

Showtime. Feature movies, sports, and specials. 1633 Broadway, New York, NY 10019; (212) 708–1600. www.showtimeonline.com

Television Food Network. Entertaining and informative programming on cooking and nutrition. 1177 Avenue of the Americas, New York, NY 10036; (212) 398–8836.

USA Network. Movies, specials, sports, and series. Carolyn Longo, 1230 Ave. of the Americas, New York, NY 10020; (212) 408–9168. www.usanetwork.com

WAM! Educational programming on national sciences, social studies, literature, and teen issues for students ages 8–16. America's Youth Network, Encore, 5445 DTC Pkwy., Ste. 600, Englewood, CO 80111; (303) 771–7700.

The Weather Channel. Local, regional, and national weather; meteorological specials. Education Services, 2600 Cumberland Pkwy., Atlanta, GA 30339; (800) 471–5544.
www.weather.com

WGN/UVTV. Movies, series, specials, sports, children's shows, and original programming. 1 Technology Plaza, 7140 S. Lewis Ave., Tulsa, OK 74136–5422; (800) 331–4806.
www.uvtv.com

APPENDIX D
FORM FOR EVALUATING
INSTRUCTIONAL VIDEOS

EVALUATING VIDEOS FORM

CONTENT OF VIDEO

1. Audience: Who is its intended audience? _____
   Toward what age group is it aimed? _____
   Will it reach that audience effectively? _____

2. Authoritativeness: Who's involved in the production? _____
   How does it compare with other videos on the subject? _____
   _____

3. Organization: Is the story line easy to follow? _____
   Could the material have been organized differently? _____
   Is the script well-written? _____
   Is the treatment appropriate for the subject? _____
   Are there particular segments that would be useful for certain instructional needs? _____

4. Originality and Creativity: Is the material presented imaginatively? _____

5. Format: Is the video format effective? _____
   Would another medium be better for presenting the material? _____

6. Accompanying Materials: Are the teachers' guides or other printed material useful? _____
   _____

7. Narration and Acting: Are the narrators and actors appealing? _____
   Do they speak clearly? _____
   Are they believable? _____
   Are they condescending? _____

TECHNICAL ASPECTS

Consider the visual and sound quality of the production:

		good	fair	poor
1.	Composition of scenes	good	fair	poor
2.	Focus and exposure	good	fair	poor
3.	Color accuracy	good	fair	poor
4.	Animation quality (or claymation, picturemation, etc.)	good	fair	poor
5.	Legibility of titles, subtitles, etc.	good	fair	poor
6.	Effectiveness of special effects	good	fair	poor
7.	Audibility and fidelity of sound	good	fair	poor
8.	Music: appropriateness and appeal	good	fair	poor
9.	Editing: cuts, matching, continuity, pacing, etc.	good	fair	poor
10.	Multiple formats: live-action combined with stills	good	fair	poor

ABOUT THE AUTHORS

Barbara Stein is a university professor who teaches children and young adult materials courses. She also reviews children's videos for a newspaper.

Gary Treadway is a former classroom teacher who now works with T-Star (a technology initiative that delivers satellite programming to K-12 schools). He has also worked for many years with public educational television programming where he conducted numerous workshops on using video in the classroom.

Lauralee Ingram is an elementary school library media specialist who selects videos for her school and helps teachers incorporate them successfully into their instructional plans.